Martha Jane
& Me

Martha Jane & Me

A Girlhood in Wales

MAVIS
NICHOLSON

Chatto & Windus
LONDON

Published in 1991 by
Chatto & Windus Ltd
20 Vauxhall Bridge Road
London SW1V 2SA

A CIP catalogue record for this book is
available from the British Library.

ISBN 0 7011 3356 2

Designed by Humphrey Stone
Photoset by Rowland Phototypesetting Ltd,
Bury St Edmunds, Suffolk
Printed and bound in Great Britain by
Butler & Tanner Ltd, Frome and London

For my first family
MARTHA JANE AND POP
OLIVE IRENE AND DICK
SYLVIA AND GRAHAM
EILEEN

For my second family
GEOFF
STEVE AND JANE
LEWIS
HARRY AND JO

For my third family
BEN, TESS AND SAM

Acknowledgements

For their help over details and photos – love and thanks: To Vernon and Carrie Martin, next door. To my schoolfriends, Morfydd Davies, Norma D., Muriel Jones, Freda Poley, Gwyneth Ward. To the much-missed Eileen Sims, and to her sister, Elsie. To boyfriend Alan Thomas, and Steele, his brother. To Aunty Flo, Aunty Gladdy and Cousin Ruth. To Jon Hill, my nephew. To Les Blackman and Norman Coward. To Jacqueline Thomas in Neath Library and Gwyn Jenkins, Cimla Post Office. To Miss Jones, my first teacher. To Ishbel, Gerald Betts, Moira Davies, Margaret Lewis, Helen Tregarkes, Miss Charman, Zenith Kilnan, Michael Williams Betts, and to Briton Ferry's loyal chronicler, Cliff Morgan. And thanks to Sue Townsend for her timely note of encouragement, and to CC and AS without whom . . .

Contents

CONTENTS

5 Mansel Street, the Universe

Uncle Cyril with me on his motorbike

WHEN I TRY to picture myself as a little girl called Mavis Mainwaring I can see her appearance clearly. Straight black hair, solemn brown eyes, a dimple in her chin like Cary Grant's. She is dressed in her Sunday best, a marina green edge-to-edge swagger coat displaying a white crepe-de-Chine dress with large marina green spots. Black patent ankle-strap Shirley Temple shoes with white socks. White cotton gloves. Or later I can put her in thick black stockings and a short navy gymslip, barely covering navy knickers with a hanky in the pocket, and worn over a white, high-necked blouse with bishop sleeves. Not a neat picture this one. Dishevelled and a trifle wild-looking by now, this County school girl.

But then my memory holds her as though she is utterly still and silent. As if sealed in a capsule. Or, had it been around – this was the early thirties – as if on a television screen with the sound turned off.

She's a romantic, remote, detached, lonely child. Scared . . . surely, I couldn't have been. But this feeling persists. This slight, sad figure is watchful, and standing back. On the edge of things.

Yet she lived in a street full of children her own age. She was always out playing hop-scotch, whip-and-top, marbles, statues, film stars, kick-the-tin. Up the woods and up the trees. Collecting conkers, picking blackberries, pinching apples. Forcing herself with the other girls to go into the LADIES lavatories which smelt so offensively that you had to hold your nose and say, 'Touch your collar, never swallow, no scarlet fever in my house.'

But this memory of wariness keeps coming back. Was it really what I felt then? I think so. There was too much happening for my liking. I did not feel brave enough to take it all on. So, although I was very much part of the gang, even its leader, I felt withdrawn. The practical, bolder, jollier children seemed to take things more as they came.

Of course, it may be that I want to leave myself inside that capsule. Childhood is there for the recall, but frightening to probe into. So much of what we have become is rooted in it. And what we have failed to become. It's the start of all the things about ourselves that still embarrass us, and memory is bound to be bashful. But dive in. For that shy little girl longed for the limelight even when she funked it.

She had been asked at Sunday School to say a verse at the Harvest Thanksgiving service in the big chapel of Jerusalem English Baptist Church, Neath Road, Briton Ferry. It was the day when the pews would be packed with a kind and smiling grown-up congregation all sentimentally eager to see and hear the little ones make their Witness.

> 'Little drops of water, little grains of sand,
> Make a Mighty Ocean and a Pleasant Land'

was what she'd been asked to say. She knew the words off by heart. She had been taught them by her Sunday School teacher, who told her she had a very clear speaking voice. And, for good measure, she had been rehearsed at home by her mother.

There she was, sitting up in the gallery. She was wearing a new long-sleeved dress run up for her by Beryl, the dressmaker, who hadn't finished it until late Saturday night. The last fitting was Saturday morning in her front room, freezing cold. Beryl kept the pins for marking the seams in her mouth. Her scissors were cold and tickled as she shaped round the neck for the collar and round the tops of the arms for the sleeves, while this little girl stood utterly still in her old clodhopper shoes which didn't suit the delicate silky look of the new dress.

Time to stand up with the other five-year-olds each who had two lines to speak. 'Little drops of water . . .' she said, and then she couldn't speak. She burst into tears and ran out. Her mother was up out of her pew and was outside with open arms to meet her. Mavis Mainwaring told her mother she had felt sick, and tried hard to be really sick so that she could vindicate herself. But she didn't succeed, though it hardly seemed to matter to her mother who was assuring her that an attack of nerves was just like being ill.

Oh, but I'd let everyone down, especially Jesus. Mrs Powell, our Sunday School superintendent, had told us we were only doing our poems for Him. No need to feel nervous for we were safe in His arms. And we were doing it for His glory – not our own.

My first mistake then. I had said yes to doing it for the sake of a new frock. Because I had wanted to show off my clear speaking voice. And because I had hoped to impress everyone with the wisdom of the poem's words. Maybe bring a tear to somebody's eye with the touching simplicity of the message.

That somebody would not have been my grandmother. My grandmother had already told me that she thought the poem was daft. 'So what is it saying? Little drops of water, little grains of sand make a mighty ocean and a pleasant land? That every little one of us counts. Well, I've got news for you, my girl. You will find out they don't.'

It surprised me, young though I was, as it would have surprised anyone who knew my grandmother, that she should admit to being someone who didn't count. For you noticed Martha Jane. She would never get lost in a crowd. Martha Jane Davies was a person to be reckoned with. She was a person and a half who had fallen out even with God, a long time ago.

3

We lived in my grandmother's house: 5 Mansel Street, Briton Ferry. Or to give it its full title, as I used to do in the front of my copy books: 5 Mansel Street, Briton Ferry, Glamorgan, South Wales, Great Britain, Europe, Western Hemisphere, The World, The Universe. And it was my universe, peopled by my father Richard John Mainwaring, my mother Olive Irene, and her father and mother – my grandfather Joseph Morgan Davies and the one and only Martha Jane. Of the four adults, my grandfather, who was known to us all as Pop, was alone in having spoken Welsh from the cradle; so, as was usual in industrial South Wales at that time, I was brought up with Welsh as my accent but English as my language.

For a short time after my mother was married, the house was also home to her two brothers. There was Uncle Cyril, tall and fair, gentle and sweet-natured, whose full name was Evan Willy Cyril Rees Davies. He owned a motorbike even though he was still lame from an accident on his previous machine; the wheels had caught in tram lines and he had spun off. I was lifted onto the motorbike one day. She'll be scared, he was warned. She was not. He rode a little way down the lane with me sitting on the petrol tank in front of him. I don't know if I really remember that or if the image remains clear because of a tiny sepia photo of my Uncle and me on the bike in our back lane. He left when he married handsome Aunty Gladys Devereux. And Uncle Caradoc (known as Crad), short and dark and a terrific tease, left just before that to marry my County School-educated Aunty Florence Rowse. Five and a half years after I was born, my brother and sister arrived. The twins. Graham first and, fifteen minutes later, Sylvia.

Ours was a grey-stone house in a street of over sixty houses, all the same but for the colour of their front doors. Ours was tan with comb lines through the varnish which gave it a squiggly pattern. Like most of the terraces in the old town, Mansel Street was built in the 1870s to house the labour for the nearby iron and steel and tinplate works. And since nobody had the money to modernise, the houses remained much as they had been when they were first built.

At the top of our street was the main Cardiff–Swansea road (though we thought of it simply as *our* main road) and just beyond the houses on the far side of this were wooded hills. At the bottom of our street was Rockingham Terrace, its single row of houses facing the railway line and Briton Ferry station. We could see the trains pass from our front door.

We had three bedrooms. At first the front bedroom was where my grandfather and grandmother slept. Iron bedstead, feather mattress, tin bucket under the bed, dressing table, wardrobe, cold oilcloth on the floor, and a gas light. My two uncles had the smaller middle room which, with a squash, had just enough space for its double iron bedstead, chest of drawers and dressing table. Two hooks on the door for hanging any clothes that couldn't be folded in the drawers. Oilclothed floor again and no gas light. One candle in a tin holder. When they moved out, my grandmother moved in – away from her husband.

My mother and father and I slept in the back bedroom, which was the smallest. We also shared the front room, one of the three downstairs, where we were later joined by my brother and sister.

The middle room downstairs was where my grandmother kept her parlour furniture, and where she paid the club man when he called each week. Depending on how flush she was, she handed over anything up to half a crown; if she had nothing she sent someone else to the door to tell Mr Davies she'd see him next week. The club was the Refuge Friendly Society, a popular way of saving in our street, when only the Middle Classes used banks. My grandmother once told me, with a wink, she was putting money by for her burial. But I know she also drew out money for emergencies, which in her case included Christmas. That was the only other time when, with a rare fire in the grate, the middle room was regularly used. It was reserved for our Christmas and Boxing Day meals.

I loved the room because it was far more grandly furnished than ours. Beside the polished dining table with its velvet runner it contained a chaise-longue and two stiff armchairs in dark, almost black, leather. And shiny satin cushions which were nice to smooth. Two wall cupboards with spare glasses, table cloths, a box of apostle spoons and, in a paper bag, my grandmother's fox fur with a camphor ball. Along one wall, facing the big sash window, was a dresser with a cream-and-green dinner service and in its two tureens my grandmother kept odds and ends . . . Co-operative Stores dividend slips, the club cards, her spare hair nets, small gold safety pins, and a St John's Ambulance First Aid book. Jugs hung from hooks. Red glass with clear handles and a couple of old, badly-mended lustre jugs. In each you would find something interesting: a small roll of bandage, a coin, a hair clip, a bus ticket or a stub of a pencil with a rubber in its end along with a small ball of dust. And probably a piece of the jug that had yet to be fixed. A cut glass biscuit barrel was kept empty except on special occasions like Easter when it was filled with fancy biscuits.

At the back of the house was the kitchen with black-leaded hob and oven, and a coal fire right through the year. To one side of the kitchen a big wooden armchair with a coat over its back and in it my grandfather when he was at home. When he wasn't, the chair was left vacant. On the mantelpiece stood two china dogs, and two bronze horses with front legs raised and two near-naked men holding the reins alongside. There was a scrubbed top table with two wooden chairs, and two more matching chairs stood against the wall. A small coconut mat blackened by coal dust lay on the flagstone floor.

A glasshouse adjoined the kitchen. This held the gas boiler in which the weekly wash was done, and the puddings were boiled at Christmas. It also supplied buckets full of hot water for the bath, though smaller amounts for washing and washing up came from a kettle on the ancient gas cooker. Most of our meals were prepared on that too, but occasionally my grandmother cooked on a black iron bakestone over the kitchen fire.

Beyond the glasshouse, we had a small back garden, a white-washed outside lavatory with a cosy plank seat, and a black corrugated iron shed. Here we had the mangle where the washing was wrung, and my father kept the bike which, whatever the weather, he rode daily back and forth to the steelworks some six miles away. His tool box was there, too, and the iron lasts on which he mended our shoes.

In our house, as in every other house in the street, each day of the week was quite distinct from the others. On Monday the windows were all steamed up from the washing. And if it was a good drying day, the line in the garden was constantly heavy with billowing clothes. No cooking on that day, cold or warmed-up left-over's sufficed;.

Tuesday was set aside for ironing. This took place on the kitchen table which was covered with a blanket for padding. Early on we had black flat-irons heated on the open fire. You'd hear the constant thumping as a lot of elbow grease was used to flatten out the creases.

Wednesday was market day in the nearby town of Neath. If we didn't go there, it was a rush (half-day closing) to the Briton Ferry Co-op to pick up groceries and put in the order for the weekend. There they had an overhead wire track which sent the money rushing along in miniature cable-cars to the office – which then sent them hurtling back with our change. Or if we weren't paying cash they would send an up-dated bill for the goods we had on tick.

Thursday was the big baking day when the house smelt of fresh bread and cakes, tarts and pasties. Later there would be Welsh cakes sizzling on the bakestone when we came home from school, and we'd eat them warm with butter.

Friday was for cleaning the whole house out. This was also the day Mr Davies, the club man, called. He was the cleanest, mildest man you would ever meet. We didn't have a knocker on our door so he would rap on the door with his knuckles. At the same time he turned the knob and stepped inside, calling out, 'It's only me, Mrs Davies.'

Yet it was he, my grandmother told me, whose wife never let him see the colour of his own carpets. They were always covered in newspapers so that they wouldn't get marked. Since she also cleaned the bottom of his shoes the moment they arrived home – there was a damp cloth ready just inside the door – there was fat chance of any dirt getting on them anyway.

Once, Mr Davies disappeared for a few days and his neighbours set out to search for him. They discovered him in a cave in the woods, unshaven, unwashed, singing away to himself. They said he'd suffered a temporary loss of memory. Rubbish, declared my grandmother, he had just come to his senses and had taken the one and only holiday of his life.

She went along with the amnesia story only up to a point –

perhaps to save him from embarrassment and more to tease a little of the truth out of him.

'Are you suffering from headaches,' she asked him, 'after your touch of amnesia, Mr Davies?'

'Nice of you to ask me, Mrs Davies. Yes and no,' he answered.

'Well, it must be one or the other, mustn't it be, Mr Davies?' She wore the extra-concerned face she put on whenever she was hoping to get more out of people than they were expecting to reveal.

'When I am working my head is clear, thank the good Lord. But by the time I go home my head is thumping,' he explained.

'In that case you must ask that wife of yours to go easy on you. Not expect too much of you. Tell her you'll have to go up to the cave again if she doesn't have pity on you. Or better still, tell her you'll send her up for a couple of nights.'

'Oh come, come now, Mrs Davies, please. What are you suggesting?' He looked quite craftily at my grandmother.

'I'm suggesting a change is as good as a rest. And your loss of memory might have been fate giving you a bit of a chance to get out of earshot.'

Saturday was when the cockle woman called. A majestic figure with a basket on her head and one on either arm. It was the day we went up to the part-time newsagent at the top of the street (he sold his papers from the floor of his front room), and bought our comics or, when we were older, our *Girls' Crystal*. We visited the library to change our books. Went to the flicks in the afternoon. Or in the summer out to pick wimberries and, later in the season, blackberries for Sunday's tart.

And then Sunday . . . the strangest, most distinctive day of them all. I stayed in bed late and whatever I was doing I stopped and listened as the church bells started to ring. After dinner, Mr and Mrs Martin from next door would call and take me down to Sunday School where they taught. All of us in our best clothes.

When I was old enough, I went to chapel in the morning, Sunday School in the afternoon (calling at Cavalli's ice cream parlour on the way home, if I had any pocket money left over from Saturday, or if I avoided putting my collection in the plate), then back to chapel in the evening.

None of the grown-ups in our house went to chapel. But they were not unusual in that. In the whole street there were very few regular chapel-goers, whereas my mother remembered that when she was my age attendance at least once on Sunday was the general rule.

My father was made to go to church, not chapel, and except for the singing, which he enjoyed, he was bored stiff and, as he put it, played up rotten. He was reported to his father who thrashed him and said he could no longer sit with his pals. From then on, until he was old enough to rebel, he had to sit absolutely still in the pew next to his father and under the glare of the vicar. And he had not entered church or chapel since.

My mother said she couldn't be bothered to attend, she didn't know why. Perhaps she was too busy; anyway, she didn't feel the need to go any more: 'But you go, love, and make the most of it.' I did, especially after the evening service when there were walks with the boys.

But I'm anticipating. Briton Ferry as I knew it for ages did not stretch past one street to the right of Mansel Street, that was Vernon Street, and two to the left, Hoo Street and Osterley Street. They were the daring permimeters of a world that I could safely explore.

At the top of Osterley was the town park. It was an important day when a few of us were first allowed to pass by ourselves through the high iron gates with Jersey Park scrolled in their arch. We savoured the moment, for our mothers had taken a lot of persuading to let us go solo. Even when at last they said yes, one of them came to the belisha crossing to see us over the main road.

I remember it was an unstable, sunny day, a bit windy, and just as we passed a big fir tree the wind blew the sun in and everything went dark and cold. I shivered. I had so wanted to go to the park on my own – on my own, that is with my friends. But now that we were doing it, still holding hands like a group of unsteady invalids, I think we all felt a bit vulnerable. Not that any of us breathed a word of our timidity.

I seemed to be staring at a slightly menacing world. Empty, for one thing. The flower beds looked bare. There was no one around. No old men smoking pipes on park seats, nodding off while waiting for their daughter to collect them for dinner. No clutch of first-time mothers sitting rocking their prams, eking out the time until the baby's next feed. No park attendant strolling around with his pointed stick.

A man appeared suddenly round a corner from another path, whistling to himself, and I nearly jumped out of my skin.

I felt the world had emptied. What if this park were all that was left? Just us . . . Margaret, Glenys, Maureen, Muriel and me. And this old man who had made me jump. It was quieter than I had ever known it with the wind rustling the trees and bushes, twisting them into shapes, half-human, half-animal.

Our mothers had put us on our honour to go only as far as the circular flower bed in the middle of the first part of the park before the woods started. Walk around it once and then we were to go straight home.

We liked fussy signs from our mothers because it meant they loved us – as long as they also let us do what we wanted. After that first adventure, we regularly walked unaccompanied up to Jersey Park, which is how we got to know Fanny Bolitho.

Fanny lived in the house next to the park. She always kept an eye on us anyway. But she had a dog which barked as soon as it heard our footsteps. We pretended to be scared, and held onto each other as we rushed past. And as soon as we were past we'd call out it's name, teasing it to get it excited.

We thought Fanny Bolitho might be a witch, a good witch. She was the only woman we knew who wore gold hoop earrings through holes in her ears, and it didn't occur to us that she had had the holes pierced. We thought she had been born with them.

She often looked as though she were chuckling to herself about something. And as she walked round the park she whistled. We had been told that when she used to accompany silent films on the piano in the Public Hall, she composed the music she played. I liked her whistling but my grandmother said it was not ladylike. 'A whistling woman and a crowing hen, Is neither good for God nor men.' In other words my grandmother had never picked up the knack of whistling.

Fanny would wave to us when she met us in the park. With a

wink, she'd shout that she had better not find us pinching apples or running on the bank where it said: *Please Keep Off the Grass*. How did she know our plans, the magic woman? We had not told anybody what we were about to do.

I liked her because she wasn't like the other women I had met, and for a while I wanted to grow up free like Fanny. 'But wouldn't you want children?' Muriel asked me, when I told her that I was going to model myself on Fanny Bolitho. Neither of us thought it was possible to be a wild character and a mother.

The other place we were allowed to visit, as a sign of our increasing freedom, was B. C. Thomas's sweet shop on the same side of the main road as the park. B. C. also kept a shop opposite where he sold poultry food and which he advertised in the local cinema. '*Why does the chicken cross the road? To get to B. C. Thomas's, finest poultry food keeper.*'

Bryn Thomas looked like a pig, and I don't mean that rudely because it was an obvious truth. He was pink-skinned and fat and had a blond moustache which jutted out just like the top of a pig's snout. His eyelashes were long but scanty and he had very, very pale blue eyes. He also had two sisters Gladys and Sally and a brother Oliver whom I can't put a face to. Did he die young? Gladys was thin and Sally was plump and fair like Bryn.

Their sweet shop was dark and old-fashioned and always open late because it stood right next to the Public Hall. When a dance was on there, they did a good trade in pop and cigarettes. It wasn't very clean but they sold all the sweets we liked and they would let us have any mixture of sweets from the rows of glass jars. They also sold pop by the glass, or rather by the fish-paste pot if you only wanted a ha'pennyworth. This was fine if they had just opened the bottle, but if they had nearly reached the bottom the pop was completely flat.

But as much as anything we went into the shop to have a nose around. There were undercurrents. Sometimes they acted strangely. We had been tipped off by one of the older girls that they were squiffy more often than not. Squiffy was to do with being silly because you had drunk too much. And watch out for Sal, we'd been told; she showed it more. We hung around sitting on empty pop crates while Sally asked endlessly, 'How's your mother? I went to school with her. Now *she* was a scholar. Are you going to follow in her footsteps, good girl?' Gladys would chime in that she knew my mother when she was courting my father and what a smart dancer my father was. She hoped I was going to follow in his steps, good girl. They were kind and patient with us. But they were also soft, and we made fun of them. As we got older we would make up sad stories and tell them to Sal to see the tears come to her eyes. Gladys would keep a beady eye on us for we were always trying to get free sweets out of Sal. Or some chippings off the toffee tray. However squiffy they may have been, I can't remember getting a single extra sweet out of them.

We'd deliberately choose the pennyworth of sweets we were buying from the highest shelf so that we could watch one or other of the two sisters totter up on their rickety home-made wooden steps. 'I want just one hazel-nut toffee, Glad, from the second bottle on the left. Two nougats' (pronounced nuggets) 'from that fourth bottle along on the right,' we'd instruct. 'No, the fourth, Glad, not the third. Can't you count?' We spoke to them as we would never have dared address any other adult.

We never saw Gladys and Sal anywhere but in their sweet shop and never out of their overalls. And they were never without their cats. There were always several cats slinking about them like shadows or lying full-length in the dusty window hogging the single patch of sun which had faded the shop's one and only bit of display. It was a cardboard cut-out of a woman in a Jean Harlow hat and long-sleeved dress smoking a Craven 'A' cigarette.

No one was ever asked inside their house right next to the shop. We tried to wheedle our way in for we were told it was not possible to imagine the state it was in. They never did any housework. Pity, too, we were told, as they had some very nice pieces left them by their mother.

B. C. Thomas had quite a twang when he spoke. My father said he could forgive him his twang. So what if he did fancy himself as a bit la-de-da? He was no snob under it, and very kind if you only knew half of what he did for people.

When it was raining and we had nothing to do, B. C. Thomas let us stay talking to him for ages in his shop. And for all the time we spent there one of us might buy no more than a little budgie seed. He'd scoop it out of one of his sacks and charge a ha'penny or a penny. Sometimes he'd give it away just to get us out of his shop. That was after we had started getting familiar with him and moving round to his side of the counter, which offended him. That was his position only. 'Get moving. Out, all of you. Gercha . . . '

'Temper, temper,' we'd say, but scamper because he was going red from his neck upwards.

B. C. Thomas used to ride a bike – a racer which looked frail under his bulk. He rode it so slowly that we could easily keep up with him as we walked along the pavement. Sometimes we chose to walk a bit faster, just to rub it in, chatting to him although he couldn't answer for keeping his mind on steering.

We never talked to him when he was passing a stationary car. We felt we had to concentrate on his actions as much as he did. He'd attempt to put his arm out to indicate that he was going to move around the car, and the wobbling that went on, at the pace of a snail, was worth keeping silent for. We even came to admire his precarious sense of balance. It took a lot of skill, we agreed, to pedal so slowly and stay upright at the same time.

Thomas the Hall, as the sweet shop was called by the regulars, also stayed open late in the summer months, because next to the Public Hall was Briton Ferry's other special feature, its outdoor roller skating rink.

This didn't close, even during the war. We would have been about eight years of age when we first went to try out the hired roller skates. But soon we acquired our own, and became good enough to warrant special skaters' outfits. They were short, puffed-sleeved cotton dresses with a completely circular skirt which flared out as we did a corkscrew spin, showing our matching knickers.

Margaret Esmond was the best skater among us, and she gave us the courage to skate faster. Once we were able to get up a good speed, she showed us how to lean forward from the waist, with one leg stretched straight out behind and arms spread out sideways in a glide. Altogether now, like a flock of birds. Or like Sonja Henie. We were all busy being Sonja Henie after seeing her in *Happy Landing* ('a show aglow with joy-laden wonder, winging from Gay Norwegian festivals to New York winter-time spectacles'). We had S H embroidered on our heart-shaped breast pockets.

It was an eye-opener when we were allowed into the evening sessions and saw the far greater speed of the older skaters, and the more complicated movements they performed with their partners. We danced the Skater's Waltz, girl with girl at first, still watching the other couples to pick up tips. But soon we danced with the boys, who were noticeably stronger. We could lie back on our partner's arm and have a brief free glide as dusk settled on the rink and the outline of the trees framing the edge grew softer to the strains of 'When the deep purple falls over sleepy garden walls and the stars begin to glitter in the night.'

2

From Dick to Olive

With my father

MY FATHER didn't work in our home town, Briton Ferry. He was a crane driver at the steelworks along the coast at Aberavon, the town where he was born and lived until he married. He had very good posture so you wouldn't have described him as short. Slim, thin even, but strong – he'd have passed for a Tour de France cyclist.

By the age of five I knew I would love my father for ever, and I can tell you exactly when I first knew it. It was when he took me out on the morning of Tuesday, 16th July 1935, my mother's birthday.

A saddle with two stirrups had been fastened to the crossbar of his BSA racing bike. He lifted me up and held the bike steady while I fitted my feet into the stirrups. Then he swung over, I rang the bell, and off we went for a pedal. Him doing all the pedalling. We rode down the main road which I didn't like since buses and lorries rumbled past, all hot and dirty and right up against us. But at the steepled Baglan Church, we turned left on to a stony, unmade road and then into high-hedged lanes. They became steeper and steeper, and my father's breathing heavier and heavier until we reached a plant nursery. The man who owned it, a stranger to me, obviously knew my father very well, which took me aback. I realised that my father had a life apart from me, and I became cross and sulky.

The man said, 'So this is your little girl, Dick.' And to me, 'I haven't got a sweetie for you but here's something better.' He gave me a tomato out of a basket he was carrying.

I wanted to smash it to the floor, especially since they were so obviously pleased to see each other. But I caught a whiff of that green smell of a fresh tomato, and I put it up to my nose and sniffed it. He saw me do it and said, 'She's all right, that little one there, Dick. What's her name?'

'Mavis,' said my Dad.

'That fits. A song thrush.'

So I liked him, and decided to like the tomato he'd given me.

We moved around his gardens and they talked about roses, which were my father's favourite flowers. But his friend said he'd feel disloyal if he had a favourite, and anyway you never knew with flowers whether or not they could hear you. Out of spite they might not grow for you if they thought you had pet likes. This made sense to me. I liked them all to look at, but I preferred some of the smells that came just at my nose height as we lingered along the beds.

'I've never regretted packing it in,' said my father's friend. 'I had bellyache from those furnaces.'

My father said he'd pack it in himself if he got half a chance. His guts were playing him up.

'You should be out in the fresh air,' his friend said.

'Don't talk bloody rubbish, mate,' my father shouted. 'Only a batch could say that.'

'Keep your hair on Richard John. A bachelor has no one, remember. Have another tom, love,' he said to me.

I didn't really want one after all that arguing, whatever it was about. I felt tempted but I moved over to my father and put my hand into his. And then I was sorry I'd refused, for the next second the two were laughing again, and my father said next time he was on the dole he'd come up and give him a hand and get himself some fresh air. So I moved off on my own, bored by this big dusty garden.

It was time to go. My father bought a bunch of sweet peas which his friend tied up with a piece of cord so that they could be fastened on the handlebars. But when he said he would help me up into the saddle, I held myself rigid.

'I haven't the right touch here, Dick,' he said. 'But then I never did have with girls.'

I felt briefly sorry for him. But we were off. And it was all downhill. The speed was either wonderful or frightening, I couldn't decide. Excitement seemed to me to be always teetering between something nice and something nasty. As we whooshed and bounced down the lanes the scent of the sweet peas wafted up in fits and starts, and my father told me they were for my mother. 'I didn't wish her happy birthday this morning. I wanted to pretend I had forgotten. I wanted to get her these first.'

That is when I knew I loved my father. And at that moment it was like being in love, as I was years later with Jesus Christ. Both were trial runs until I felt safe for the real thing.

It was not that I consciously preferred my father, but rather that I took my mother for granted. There came a time, though, later in the same month of July, when I saw my mother through somebody else's eyes and suddenly felt enormously proud that she and nobody else was my mother.

We had gone to Neath together, but as we stepped off the bus we did not head for the shops as usual.

'We're going to Jolly Court,' my mother told me as we walked under the railway arch and along the bank of the Neath Canal. She was taking me to see *her* grandmother – my *great*-grandmother. And she held my hand tightly in case I lost my footing and fell into the water.

'It's a dirty old canal now,' my mother said. 'Pity. It didn't used to be. People chuck any old thing in these days. When I was a girl I'd stand and watch people swim here, it was so clean.' Had she swum? 'No, your grandmother wouldn't let me be seen in my bathing costume, not in public like this. It was bad enough in her eyes to undress on the beach. I used to paddle, though.'

At first sight its still, deep-green surface was beautiful, but as we walked along the bank and past a works, smelly water spewed into it and oil and rust floated on the top. We began to list the rubbish. An old boot. Tins with half-open jagged lids. Bottles. A saucepan. A chair with its springs sticking out of the seat. And a dead cat slowly floating past, which I didn't want to see but couldn't take my eyes off. I knew I would dream about it that night and deliberately went on memorising it as though for the night's replay. Its bedraggled, sodden fur hid its face, and then I saw that it had no tail.

Jolly Court was a row of low, grey-stone back-to-back houses with rough cobbles outside their dark front doors. There was a big steep stone to step up and over to get inside, for the houses were not only near enough to the canal to catch the smells in hot weather, but close enough to the River Neath to be regularly flooded when the water rose after heavy rain. The high stone steps were an attempt at a flood barrier.

Inside, the only living room had an earth floor which hardly ever dried out and was covered with coconut matting. The light was dim, but I could see a dresser loaded with china and, in a chair in the dark corner by a smoky fire, a very old lady who did not alarm me as strangers invariably did.

She didn't get up out of the chair, but held out her two hands to me. 'You have beautiful eyes,' she said. Perhaps I looked shy, for she turned to my mother: 'They are the darkest eyes I have ever seen, and her hair, Olive Irene, is as black and shiny as a raven's wing. And you dress her lovely. Did you make her frock?' My mother said she had. 'Open your coat, *merch*, for me to see it.' I didn't mind at all doing that for her.

She turned back to my mother. 'Would the shade be duck-egg blue?' she asked. 'And her coat? Did you make her coat?'

No, not her coat, my mother said.

'Sky blue, I'd call that,' she said. 'And I love its deep blue velvet collar, don't you?' she asked me. I nodded, for I really did.

'Olive, you are even prettier now that you're a mother.' And then back to me: 'Between you and me, your mother is an angel. Love her for me when I'm not here to.'

She seemed to get upset by this, and then quickly suggested to my mother that she help me climb the ladder, for children always liked her ladder. It led up through a small square in the ceiling to what had been her bedroom when she had been fit to get up to it. The room did not have a window, just a bed with a cream cover. Where did she sleep now, I wondered. Apart from four upright wooden chairs around a table, there was only her armchair in the downstairs room.

We didn't stay long, and my mother seemed abstracted as we left, so I slid my hand in hers to remind her I was there. She told me she was sad to see her grandmother so very ill. I wanted to know who looked after her. Her other daughter, grandma's sister, lived next door, she said. Could we come back and see her again? We'd try to, she said, and added that she was really glad I had met her. This seemed to tell me that I would never see her again.

As we walked back along the canal my mother, usually so calm, became angrily indignant. It always made her mad, she said, to see how some people were forced to live. A shared cold-water tap out in the open. One lavatory, with no chain, between several houses, and the water flushed through only every so often. And look out – she added, not to be too solemn with a young child – if you were sitting on the lav at the time . . . whoosh! I remember wishing I had been sitting there when the wild water arrived.

I never went back to Jolly Court. The houses were condemned as unfit for human use not long after our visit – but long enough for my great-grandmother to see out what remained of her life there.

Left to itself, my memory of anything before that age of four is fragmentary. But I never left my memory to itself. I was always prodding adults to tell me about the past. Theirs and mine. So I could swear I remember my birth, but it is through my mother's recollections, after much urging, that I can describe it.

A pretty woman with loosened long brown hair normally pinned into a low bun on the nape of her neck had been lying in a back bedroom since Friday in great pain. It was now Sunday.

Apart from its double bed, with a black eiderdown embossed in a Chinese pattern, the room had a small wardrobe, very narrow inside, holding only three dresses and two suits. A dressing-table in the same dark wood, with a mirror you could tilt, and on it a glass dressing-table set. One bowl with a lid contained powder and a powder puff. The other without a lid held cuff links, shirt stiffeners and shirt studs, and hair pins. A ring holder bore an engagement ring with a row of three tiny diamonds. And on the glass tray containing them all were two expanding bands for holding up shirt-sleeves.

In one of its two drawers were a few ladies' things. Just a few, it was far from full – a blouse, pair of pants, vest, a pair of thickish stockings. And in the other drawer some men's underpants, a couple of ties rolled up, socks and suspenders. This drawer was always kept locked because it held the box of such documents as birth and wedding certificates, and a few sepia snaps. On the wall were two oil paintings. One was of a pond with two swans swimming from right to left. The other was of a pond with two swans swimming from left to right. They were painted and signed by O. I. Davies. O. I. stood, of course, for Olive Irene, the pretty woman lying on the bed trying to give birth to her first baby.

Tied to the bed rail was a towel in a noose onto which she could hold to help her push down harder. She had no clue about childbirth except that it was a painful necessity once you became pregnant.

There were no mod cons in the house. No running hot water. No bathroom. No inside lavatory; only a white china chamber pot under the bed. Her mother was around to see to meals. Her husband attended her anxiously, his headache getting worse and his stomach playing him up by the hour. He was home because he was on the dole at the time.

Nurse Abrahams would pop in or stay on when she hadn't somewhere more urgent to go to. This birth was getting more and more difficult. It was going to be a breach by the look of it. She couldn't shift the baby round and it wouldn't turn the right way so that its head would push out first.

Everyone did what they could, which was to wait around. No one had heard of relaxation exercises or deep breathing. There was nothing to take for the pain. Childbirth, as everyone knew, was meant to be painful. A screaming job. You just suffered it. It was a case of don't push. Now push. Harder. Harder. Stop. Leave it.

Eventually Nurse Abrahams had to ask Dr Dewgate to come and deliver the baby by forceps.

At quarter to eleven, as the church bells reminded the congregation that the service was about to start, a baby with rather a lot of black hair, because she was so late arriving, was born . . . tearing open her poor mother's body. Dr Dewgate then stitched up the wound as well as he could under the simple home conditions, but leaving a life-long ridge as a commemorative mark of bravery. The date was 19th October 1930. The baby was me.

I have no recall – they say you can have – of the knife being used on that tiny baby's body. But there is a line, a long indentation, under my left breast where they had to lance off some milk that had been left, so my mother explained later. Ages later in fact, for I was in my teens before I noticed it. If you don't have a bathroom, or a full-length mirror, you don't see your body. In any case, throughout my childhood and adolescence nudity was almost a sin, and most people averted their gaze even if there was a mirror handy.

I mean, we never saw our parents even partially bare. The most I saw was my father stripped to the waist while he washed under the cold tap. I once saw my grandfather naked at his bedroom door, though only for a second, as he scarpered immediately he saw me. I just caught the quickest glimpse of his white backside. That was thrilling enough to make me feel wicked.

So, into this full house, with its paper-thin walls, I arrived in October. Arms were at the ready to nurse me as soon as I murmured. My lungs had no exercise: one whimper and I was popped into a Welsh flannel shawl. This was wrapped round me and also round the body of whoever was nursing me. Lullabies and hymns were sung until I was bored to sleep.

Can I remember any of this? Not consciously perhaps, except that I certainly remember hating the sight of that rough flannel shawl later, and the atmosphere of the dark passageway where they rocked me to sleep.

If I wasn't indoors being nursed, my mother was wheeling me outside in my pram – up the park, round the woods, in all weather because daily fresh air was considered essential. On week days she would meet other mothers in the park. She would go for longer walks with my father at weekends, the one time when men felt free to be out with their wives and babies. Even though many were unemployed they didn't think it right to be seen loitering during the week.

Our longest walk was on the day my mother returned from her daily stint up to the park to find that my grandmother, Martha Jane had sold the piano. Out of the blue, sold at the door with no warning to my mother, whose piano it was and who loved to play. It had been a gift from an aunt. It was hers. Her very own.

My grandmother may have needed the money but what she curtly said was that my mother was not going to have any time to play now that she had a baby. My mother left without a word and walked and walked, pushing me ahead of her until it was dusk – and until she had calmed down.

The result was that my mother never again touched any piano. Nor, she told me later, did she utter a word to my grandmother about it. Nor did she even play the organ for the Craig Chapel, as she had done every Sunday for years. When my father was courting my mother he used to wait for her outside this chapel listening to her play the congregation out. According to him, she had a lovely touch.

The lid went down as the piano went out of the house. Even though as a child I pestered my mother to let me have piano lessons like my cousin Eileen, she never mentioned that she could play. All she said was that we couldn't afford a piano.

3
A Perfect Illness

With my parents

OUR CROWDED HOUSEHOLD included a dog for a time. Pincher. A short-haired terrier who walked round the park every morning on his own, stopping in turn at each of the park seats where the old age pensioners sat. Beloved by them all, it was said. But he was put down smartish when he bit me after I stuck my podgy finger in his eye. I had no memory of that, but for years I was unaccountably frightened of dogs.

No memory, either, of being hurt when my mother's flat-iron, straight from warming in the coals of the fire, slid off the stand and onto my hand. Or of a scalding from boiling milk. What I do recall vividly is falling backwards into the fire and burning my hands. I had climbed up on the back of my father's chair, while he was eating lunch, to put my hands over his eyes and scare him. He forgot I was there and got up out of the chair which toppled over, landing me on the hot bars of the open fire.

I remember, too, the first time the doctor came to examine me when I had measles. He had a hearty Scottish accent, which I found strange enough. He also had a cigarette in the corner of his mouth, but since my father often did, too, that didn't bother me. What made me furious was the way he got my mother to stand me up on the table and then, without asking me, lifted up my dress to see my 'tum-tum'. And the way he told everything to my mother with never a word to me. Where had I gone to I wondered? Did he think measles took away your tongue? Yet my mother was so polite and apparently so grateful to this rude man. I stood there sticking out my 'tum tum' and wondering how to rebel.

'Open your mouth,' he said. Here was my chance.

'Just let me see into your mouth. What's her name, Mrs Main-waring?' My mother meekly supplied it. What had come over her?

'Mavis, you say. The correct pronounciation in my book is *Marvis. Marvis* she is from this day on.'

I don't like it said like that, I decided, and knew it would take a major operation to get my mouth open after that.

'Mavis, we say, and it's up to you, I suppose, what you say,' my mother spoke up at last. The doctor had lost interest in the name by now, but still wanted me to open my mouth. I stared him straight in the eye. And kept my mouth firmly closed. He tried to force it open, and so, still standing on the table with my bare stomach in full view and my dress tucked back up into my collar, I bit him. Then I flung myself into my mother's arms and started to cry.

'I should cry, not you' said Doctor Imry. 'Keep her in bed. Don't let her near another doctor with teeth like hers. She has the measles. Call me if she gets worse. I wonder what I did to get on the wrong side of this dark lassie?'

He called in the next day, much to our surprise, and sat down right by me on the settee which had become my brilliant new bed for the daytime. '*Marvis*, I have brought you a sweety.' He gave me a wrapped Minto.

I looked at my mother, who was beaming. 'Say thank you, to Dr Imry.'

I said, 'Thank you.' I was slightly more interested in a doctor who came back to give me a sweet after I had bitten him.

'Now, will you open your mouth properly this time, not like yesterday.' I opened my mouth, and he placed a thin piece of wood on top of my tongue, which made me gag, looked down my throat with a torch and felt my neck. 'Say AHHHH,' he bellowed. 'Ahh,' I attempted.

'Her glands are swollen. Her throat's infected. She's got a bad attack of measles.' My mother told him, in case it was significant, that I was sleeping off and on all the time. 'Good, good.' He spoke loudly and enthusiastically. 'Natural body response to sickness. I'll call again in the next few days.'

He turned and said he wouldn't always have a sweet for me. 'Goodbye *Marvis* – to me you will always be *Marvis*.' But he went off singing loudly, 'I have heard the Mavis singing.'

After he had gone, my mother wondered why he had come back as though just to make friends. I didn't know, but the fight was still on between '*Marvis*' and Doctor Imry, him on his doctor's pedestal and me chiselling away at it.

For the next few days I wallowed in being ill. The settee where I lay was under the window of the small front room where my parents and I lived. The world unfolded through the sounds from outside. First I heard the men, heavy-footed, going to work, sometimes knocking at a nearby door to make sure 'Tom' was up and ready.

Then the older children went to school. One or two would be crying and their mother scolding them. There was quiet after the last had hurried past, and then I waited for the trains to go through the station at the bottom of our street. The ones which didn't stop were the goods trains. Fewer and farther between were the passenger trains which hissed to a stop and then huffed to a trundelling start.

My mother would hear the Co-operative bread van stop outside and go out to give her order. A small Hovis every other day for my father, who never ate white bread because of his bad stomach. We, the healthy, naturally ate white. Three custard pies and a meat pie, a half for me and a half for her warmed up for dinner. The custard pies would be for tea if my father was coming home then.

'Oh, go to hell, I'll risk one,' he'd always say. 'What's the point of living if you can't have a bit of grub?' Then he'd suffer and belch and go white and swear he'd never have another when all they did was play his guts up.

'Well, you know they do – you can't touch pastry,' my mother would say.

'Well don't buy them then and I won't be tempted.' I would like to have a custard pie for all the times I heard that.

That day she tried to tempt me with the usual meat pie but I couldn't eat. I only wanted to drink pop – left to go flat since my throat was sore. The kind I specially like was Our Boys' Dandelion and Burdock, though my mother tried to persuade me to drink Robinson's Lemon Barley which was regarded as medicinal.

When I was awake she sat and read to me. I loved her voice. It was a very good reading voice. You could tell she liked reading out loud because she put such emphasis into her delivery and the expression on her face changed as the story unfolded. I thought she had written the stories herself.

There were no books in our house except the Complete Short Stories of Edgar Allan Poe and the Family Bible with its elaborate brass clasp. And it was only as a privilege, now that I was ill, that I was allowed to look at these. I liked the psalms being read to me. But only the first couple of lines; then I lost the thread.

But the Edgar Allan Poe had me gripped. Scared stiff, I often begged my mother to stop and then, as soon as she did so, begged her to go on. 'I don't think they are suitable for a girl your age – or a girl my age, come to that,' she would say, dying to finish stories which were scaring us both. They were especially frightening if it was growing dusk and the gas light hadn't been lit.

Perhaps my mother thought the stories would not mean much to me. The horror of the one in which a live cat is bricked in behind a wall haunted me. Though perhaps no more than the wolf in Red Riding Hood.

Being ill was as near as I could imagine to a perfect state. The world stopped still. There seemed to be no housework to take my mother away. The goldfish in the bowl was really alive . . . I had a theory that when I was out, not there to stare at it, it didn't exist. It was I who loved it and sprinkled its feed in too freely and too often so that eventually it became bloated and keeled over. It couldn't be replaced until the fair came to town the following year. That was the only place we bought goldfish, which came in a jam jar with a piece of string around the top to carry it home.

The room was warm. I was utterly safe. And I was too young to feel any threat from being so ill. I dropped in and out of a feverish sleep all the time: mysterious naps, much better than night sleep which struck me as too long, too dark, too companionless. A short snatch of oblivion and then waking to a patch of sunlight reflecting from the silver shield of the wooden biscuit barrel on the sideboard, and to my mother asking me if I was feeling better.

When my older friends came home from school they would press their faces up against the window and mouth: 'Are you better?' The circle of their breath would stay on the glass and they would draw in two eyes and a smiling mouth for me. They would leave their comics for me. Their very old ones because they couldn't be returned in case they carried the measles (another rule was that we must not borrow library books while we were at the infectious stage of any illness).

Then they would drift off and play so cheerfully that they had obviously forgotten me, and I didn't seem to be missed. The games were just as jolly without me.

Plop, a large tear ran down my face. Suddenly a tap on the window and Muriel was there. My best friend. 'Okay? Soon be out again,' she mouthed. And in her misty patch left on the window she drew an X. And ran home for her tea.

4
Lipstick Traces

Auntie Dorrie with me and Grandpa Mainwaring

MURIEL LIVED five doors down from me. She had two sisters and a brother, all much older than she was. Her mother, Annie, was very short, four foot something, and her father was very tall. He was found to have such a bad heart that he had to give up work, and practically all activity, when he was in his forties. He just walked short distances very slowly and otherwise sat in his chair drawing on a pipe. It had little tobacco in it, but he'd tell you that he couldn't give up this one pleasure when there was so little else left for him. 'Can you imagine what it is like for a man to leave everything alone? Not to work and bring in the money? Not to lift the coal bucket for Annie? Not to join in anything? Can you imagine what it is like?' Muriel and I found it only too easy, and tears would come into our eyes as they did to his.

Muriel became very ill and had to stay in bed for months with a kidney disease, so I was in and out of her house very often. After school I would knock on her front door and if Annie answered she'd always call the same thing out to her husband, 'It's our Mavis. Muriel's best friend come to see her again, Will. Go up, old faithful.' If Mr Jones was coming to the door, because he could only make slow progress, you'd hear him call out, 'Don't go away. I'm coming, same as Christmas.' Then, on seeing me, he'd say quietly: 'Thank you for being such a loyal friend to our Muriel. Much appreciated.' It made me feel embarrassed but at the same time terribly pleased and proud of myself.

Muriel would ask what I had learnt at school and I would try to tell her something new. After a while she would look so tired, with huge black patches under her eyes, that I would have to leave.

On a Saturday night her mother would bring us up something to eat, and her brother Billy would look in when he was ready to go to the dance. He wore a white silky muffler which Muriel and I thought made him look like a gangster in the films. But he told us it was *the* McCoy, along with his Brylcreemed hair. After he had gone, we used to say that he looked a bit like Tyrone Power.

Billy had a good singing voice and he knew it. He'd sing for us with a little persuasion. 'Danny Boy' was our favourite because his voice, a tenor, had a quaver in it and made the song very sad. But then to cheer us up he would wind up the gramophone, which we were also allowed to use on a Saturday night, and put on the 'Laughing Policeman' record.

Then Muriel and I would play a crackly recording, which sounded as though it came from a long way away, of a man singing, 'You will never miss your mother 'til she's gone.' And she and I would discuss whether we would miss our mother or our father more. We told each other that we had to make a choice one way or another. And we would become really agitated about the subject, feeling terrible whichever we chose. Both of us got upset, but Muriel the more so with her father being so ill.

Gradually Muriel was allowed up and our Saturday nights changed. We would go downstairs to watch her oldest sister, Violet May, put her make-up on to go to the same dance as Billy. It was held in the Public Hall at the top of our street.

She started on the job at about six o'clock in the back kitchen by a small mirror on the front of a bathroom cabinet. Muriel and I sat together on a kitchen chair facing her with our backs to the mirror.

Out came a biscuit tin which held all her cosmetics. She began with her vanishing cream. Just a small amount rubbed in all over. 'For your skin not to age,' Vi told us. Then she'd take out a big powder puff wrapped in a piece of chiffon which she dipped into a box of powder by Tokalon. The shade, shown at the bottom of the box, was natural peach in the winter, but she would choose a darker shade for summer. She patted this on so generously that it came showering over us. It stuck to her eyebrows and lashes so that for a while she looked bald-faced. Then she brushed that away, or licked her finger and wiped it off, and on her eyelids and lashes she smeared some Vaseline. This made the lashes grow longer, she informed us, and you put it on your eyelids for allure. When a word was used with authority we didn't question what it meant. We just accepted that Vaseline on eyelids was for allure.

After that she applied her lipstick with bold upward sweeps to form a cupid's bow. With her little finger she smoothed over the lipstick. "Too much lipstick is common,' Vi warned us. The lipstick that remained on her little finger she smoothed into her cheeks.

The face was ready. Next the hair, which was hidden under a turban since she still had her 'Dinkie' metal curlers in. These took a while to remove and were put in another tin which also contained a hair net, for if she wanted to pin up her hair she would sleep in the curlers and hairpins and clips. But when she was going to wear her hair loose, she would simply comb it out and leave it frizzy – except for the two strands by her ears which had not been put in curlers. These she formed into two kiss curls at the side of her face, securing them flat with some more Vaseline.

Now it was time to go upstairs and put on her dress, then come back down in her very high-heeled shoes to twirl around for us to see how the skirt flared out showing a glimpse of a petticoat. 'How do I look, girls?' our star would ask. She need not have asked. We thought she looked 'it'. And off she'd waltz with the tip of her little finger still red from the lipstick.

She let us put her make-up away for her, and the scent of it in that tin had a vague smell of decay, a bit heavy and sweet to me, though I loved it. We never touched it because she had told us it would poison us until we were old enough to wear it. So instead we used one of our red liquorice torpedo sweets, smearing it on our mouths and rubbing a little into our cheeks, and wished we were past the poisonable age.

Like Violet, my Aunty Dorrie, my father's youngest sister, also wore make-up. And it was she who convinced me that make-up wasn't poisonous on my face. She was looking after me while both my mother and grandmother were out one day, a rare event. 'Let's make you up as a surprise for when your mother comes back,' Aunty Dorrie said. I was doubtful but I was very keen. So like a lamb to the slaughter I sat with my face upturned and let her apply it. 'Oh you look exotic,' she said, and showed me in the mirror of her powder compact the new me. A doll? A stranger. Did I like it? Aunty Dorrie did.

Then my mother returned. She went into a frenzy. 'Don't you dare do this again. She's a child. Are you mad to try to warp her in this way? Leave her innocent. For goodness sake, she'll have to be an adult too soon as it is. Take that filthy muck off her right away.'

Then she changed her mind: 'Here let me do it.' She dragged me down to the glasshouse scullery and under the cold tap she scrubbed off 'the muck', leaving my face raw and smudgy.

After Aunty Dorrie had left under a cloud, I realised that the cloud was now hanging over me too. My mother seemed cross with me. Face her then. Confess. I told her that it hadn't been my aunt's fault entirely. I had been only too happy to be made up, and I hadn't needed any coaxing.

'I don't care a hang. She had no business to do it,' said my mother – taking no excuse for my aunt and surprisingly putting no blame on me.

I dropped the matter and noted for future reference that weakly protesting some guilt seemed a good way of getting out of any blame at all. But she did still like Aunty Dorrie, didn't she? 'Oh, I won't alter my opinion of her just over that,' said my mother. 'I've always thought she was silly plastering on make-up. You only end up with a spotty skin. And don't you start to ever think that what Aunty Dorrie does is smart and that you want to copy her.'

I knew what she meant by that. Aunty Dorrie smoked. Too late, Mama, I thought. I had already rolled up a piece of paper, coloured the end red and sat in front of the dressing-table mirror to see what I looked like smoking. And I had wrinkled my face up as Aunty Dor did when she dangled her cigarette in her mouth while pouring us a cup of tea. I liked the effect and stored that away, too, for the future.

Aunty Dorrie had already shown me her cigarette case with *Dorothy* engraved on it in sloping joined up letters. 'Dorothy, that's really my name but everyone calls me Dorrie or Dor,' she told me – except for Jim, her boy friend, who had given her the cigarette case. 'I am Dorothy to Jim, who is a real gentleman. If Jim and I get married,' she confided, 'I might give up smoking altogether.' There was something I couldn't make out about them. They seemed very excited about each other. I longed to catch them doing whatever it was that Aunty Dorrie said they mustn't do, not in front of me. 'She has eyes everywhere,' I'd heard Dorrie say when she and Jim had taken me for a walk up the park.

She told me she was in love with him: 'It's wonderful being in love, you wait.' But Aunty Dorrie died very soon after this. She contracted TB. I went once or twice with my father to the convalescent hospital in Cimla to see her. I wasn't allowed in, for the disease was meant to be catching. So why did my father go in then, and Jim? I could only look at her through the window. She seemed very small and white-faced, and waved like mad to me, then sank back on her pillows. I cried and Jim or my father, who had stayed out with me, comforted me and said: 'Look, don't show Aunty you're crying or you'll make her cry.' So I waved and started to cry all over again.

That was the last I saw of her. And I never saw quiet Jim again either.

No one even mentioned her. I had no idea that she had died. Presumably because I cried so much when she was alive and ill, they spared me the grief of her death. But it was stranger not to know. If I asked about her, they would say that she was in hospital and I could see her perhaps next week. After a while I didn't ask about her any more. I secretly thought about her, but only briefly and, as time passed, less and less often.

But I never forgot her completely because she had given me *Snow*

White and the Seven Dwarfs – the book of the Walt Disney film. I adored it. I learnt to copy the drawings off by heart – especially Snow White. A heroine who had jet black hair like mine.

Then I found out what had happened to Dorrie one night when my father came home late from work and my mother let me stay up to see him. He'd had one of his sessions of letting his hair off as he put it. About the Tories. Something had got him going, and he declared they had no feelings for the man in the street.

His sisters Mary and Sara, his brother Tom and his sister Dorothy, all wiped out with tuberculosis – 'the disease of the poor, the disease of a government that doesn't feed the working class and houses them in damp homes. We're like flies to them.'

I knew at last that Aunty Dorrie had died. And the memory of my father's brother Tom came back to me at the same moment. He had looked a little like my father, but sadder. I had only ever seen him once. He worked away somewhere, and hardly ever came home. And that one time he had left me a drawing of a swan. So he, too, had slipped away and died without my knowing.

'Our Tom,' went on my father, 'if he had been given a chance with good schooling, he could have been a great artist.'

'Don't work yourself up, Dick,' said my mother. 'They're dead and best forgotten. Who is to know if Tom would ever have been really good.'

'I'm to bloody well know. If I don't remember them, no one will. They mattered, Ol.'

'They did, and now they don't, that's what I'm saying.'

'You had better vote Tory next time then. Because they have caught you with their propaganda. But they'll never get me to believe that I'm not as important as any of the bosses.'

Once my father started getting his hair off, and my mother started to argue back, I didn't like it. 'Dad, who was Sara?' I asked.

'Sara?' he asked, puzzled.

'You mentioned her at the beginning,' my mother explained.

'Oh, Sara, she was the sister who died when you were just a baby. You look very much like her,' he said. I did not like the sound of that. I did not want to look like somebody who had died. What hope of my surviving?

At times like this, when my father was tired and nervy, I would ask him if he wanted his hair combed. I would get a towel, put it round his shoulders and climb up behind him in the big brown leatherette chair and pretend to be his barber. And he would drop off to sleep with the soothing combing, muttering that his head was like a bucket.

My mother would bring in a bowl and fill it with hot water from the kettle boiling on the fire and wash up the cups and saucers and the basin which had held my father's supper. The same supper he had every night. Hot milk, a pinch of salt, and cubes of bread soaked in it. Having been affected by gas in the First World War, when he had joined up under-age, it was now all his stomach could take.

The fire would die down. The room would get cold. The gas light would flicker and go out, and my mother would say it was time to go to bed. She had no more pennies for the gas meter.

5
Bedtime

Sylvia, Graham and I with 'Jackie'

I HATED BED. The room was cold. Crowded. My big cot was along one wall. Right up against it was my mother's and father's double bed which we had to squeeze past. There was a chamber pot under it, which I very soon loathed.

It was a poor room. I knew it was even though I had no others to compare it with. In our street we hardly ever saw anyone else's bedroom because any spare cash to cheer things up went into the downstairs, and into food and clothes and toys. The bedrooms were left to bare essentials and that included the bedding, which was often supplemented with overcoats. People were ashamed of their bedrooms. I used to lie in my cot in the morning and feel bleak. Still, I'd forget all that once I had woken my mother and father and crawled in between them, and they had started to talk to me and tell me over and over again the nursery rhymes, pictures from which were transferred on to the sides of my cot.

My father, barely able to keep his eyes open, would bend his legs up under the bedclothes and sit me on the top of them and drop his legs down suddenly. 'Again,' and he'd lift them up and drop them down – sometimes to the accompaniment of my mother chanting 'I'm the king of the castle, get down you dirty rascal.'

I never wanted to go to bed. And when I got to bed never wanted to go to sleep. So my mother would tell me story after story to tire me. And when she had run out of ideas, then we'd go through the nursery rhymes. Little Bo Peep, she in a frilly bonnet and white lace leggings, and Little Boy Blue, and Tom, Tom the Piper's Son, in clothes the like of which I had never seen and didn't care for. It's what people wore in olden days my mother explained. So what did these people have to do with me? Repetition wore me out in the end. And I got to accept them sewing fine seams, sleeping under haystacks, sitting on tuffets – whatever they were.

And still I was wide awake. My mother would sit me on her lap with a blanket round me and open the curtains and sing 'Twinkle, twinkle, little star' to try to rock me to sleep. 'Count them', she'd say, 'quietly to yourself.' Or if that failed and there was a moon out, 'Look hard and you can see the man in the moon eating green cheese.' Not a restful request that one. The time I spent trying to make out the features with my mother saying, 'Can't you see his nose even? Over there on the right.'

There was a nursery rhyme that made at least some sense to me, the four and twenty blackbirds baked in the pie. The only birds you saw in our street were black birds. Clumsy big crows. For ages I thought birds meant these crows, and I couldn't imagine who would want to eat them. They looked ominous and unappealing. But they were clever enough to loiter near the chimney pots for warmth.

The one thing I admired about them was that they could fly. And I wanted to do that. I tried it out when I was about four. I sat on the top of our stairs which were steep and narrow and thought about it for quite a long time. I stood up with no faith whatsoever and jumped – feebly holding my arms up and out sideways. I landed at the bottom with my father rushing out to see what the bumps were all about. I was not hurt nor frightened, but furious. I still thought it ought to be possible.

I never gave it another try, though. If I was moping about something or other I would often sit on the top of the stairs. But not with the thought of flying. Just with the thought of falling and spiting my parents – that would show them.

The only other bird I knew was a canary in a cage which my father brought home from work one Friday – more for his sake than mine, I suspect. Its small cage was packed out with feeding bowls, perches, a mirror, a piece of cuttle fish and a bell, and it stood on the sideboard on top of the wooden canteen of cutlery used only for best. My father would let it out once in a while. He'd open the gate and we'd sit still and wait. Jackie would edge along his perch, his head to one side. He would pause, look quickly from left to right a few times, and then dart out of the small opening and fly crazily over to the curtains, where he'd cling, his droppings falling fast and furious onto the lino. He would bump against the walls and bang his head in the mirror over the mantelpiece. He fluttered above our heads creating a cold draft before he landed with his sharp claws tangling in my hair. Getting him back into his cage was an even bigger performance.

'Watch him with that fire, Olive,' my father would command. 'Leave him to me now, you two.' In fact he was far more flustered than either of us. Sometimes, when everything else failed, my mother would catch him in the tea cosy.

She said it wasn't fair on the bird. He had to be able to fly, my father argued. If you call this flying, my mother would say. Dad maintained it was better than nothing. He shouldn't be in a cage in the first place, she would persist and my father would say, ah, well that was a different story, but as long as Jackie was his pet he would let him try out his wings.

He used to clean out the bird-cage in the garden when it was fine. One warm summer evening I was helping my father, who had gone indoors to get something he had forgotten, when on an impulse I opened the cage door. It appeared to me at the time to be the only chance Jackie would get of a proper flight. He was away.

We searched. We went down the lane. We scanned the sky. Some of the neighbours, out in their gardens, looked among the foliage. Later that evening one of them called over the wall to my father that the bird had been found. A cat had got it. It lay in my father's hand with long scratches down its breast. Dad was crying, saying he loved the poor mite, and I was crying because I had killed Jackie. No, no, you didn't know any better, he said. You thought you were letting him out to have a nice time. But nature stepped in. Are you sure you can't save him? I asked. No, he's dead-and-gone-to-heaven. Cold as mutton.

My mother said, 'Come on you two. He's only a bird.' Wails from me. 'Stop it, Ol, you're upsetting her,' said my father.

'Look, we'll get another bird,' she said. How could she think that would help? 'There could never be another bird like Jackie,' I protested.

'We could get a budgie, this time, and teach it to talk,' my father suggested. And so we did, a blue one, and called it Jackie because we couldn't get out of the habit.

6
Lost and Found

At two

I WANTED TO GO to school long before I was old enough, so one morning I followed the bigger boys and girls from the street as they set off on their daily journey. But since I was following at a distance, so that they wouldn't see me and send me home, I lost them.

I turned the corner and walked behind them up the main road, all familiar. Post Office. The picture house. Then a part I had never been to in my life. I couldn't believe in the existence of a place that was so near home and yet so foreign.

The streets were like ours, but there wasn't a face I knew. I stopped, feeling sick, and with tears I hadn't tried for beginning to fall. Someone asked me what was the matter, and I couldn't explain. What was my name? Where did I live? I was too frightened to say anything. They were strangers and I wasn't to talk to strangers.

A voice said, 'Isn't she Olive's little girl?' And another, 'Doesn't

she live in Mansel Street? She's lost, poor little thing, aren't you?'
No answer possible from me. I was petrified.

I don't know how I got home. Someone must have walked me
back. But I remember that the reception I got was pleasing. Huge,
tearful hugs from my mother, and my father being told not to scold
her now.

'Just go down to the police station and tell them she's home safe –
that she was found up in the Grandison,' said my mother. 'You
wouldn't have thought she could have walked that far on her own.
She must have followed them to school.'

I felt a bit ashamed and very precious with all this fuss going on,
and then my father came back with the policeman who said I was
never to roam away from home again. There were naughty men
around. This meant nothing to me. All men were dads. 'The roads
are dangerous for little girls to cross,' he went on, 'Now aren't
they?' I didn't answer.

'Now aren't they?' the policeman repeated. I nodded. And we
would not ever go off on our own again, now would we? Next time
there might not be anyone to bring us back. Or we'd get run over
and be taken to hospital and we wouldn't see Mammy and Daddy,
would we? By now my homecoming had become horrible. I howled
and howled as I imagined getting run over and never seeing my
mother and father again.

My father told the policeman to lay off. She has learnt her lesson,
mun. She was scared stiff getting lost like that. That will be enough.

The policeman left, no doubt offended. My father and mother
went on arguing. 'You shouldn't have talked to the policeman like
that, he was only doing his job.'

'Doing his job? No, he wasn't, he was bloody well interfering past
the call of his duty.'

My mother thought this was most unfair. 'You were pleased
enough for the police to go and search for her.'

'And they bloody well weren't the ones, as per usual, to find her
first,' shouted my father, still on the attack. Getting his hair off was
the only way he could argue.

Getting run over wasn't something we worried much about.
There was little danger of it in the street where we played. Nobody

owned a car and scarcely any traffic passed through. The paraffin man had a small van which he drove at a snail's pace. He also had a bell that clanged to warn us of his approach when he rounded the corner, and we would all crowd round to see him turn the tap on and fill the oil cans through a giant funnel.

The Co-operative bread van called at fixed times in the week so we were ready for that. The greengrocer came with a horse and cart. Post was brought on foot, milk in a float. Ice cream came by a motorised bike ridden by the Stop Me and Buy One man. Window cleaners arrived by push-bike, one arm steering, the other holding the ladder steady. So did the lamp lighter carrying his long pole in the same way. The police were always on foot.

On certain Friday evenings in late summer and early autumn, we also waited for the arrival of one particular big horse and its wide and handsome wooden cart. They were driven by a farmer who came round the streets selling potatoes, swedes, carrots and cabbages from Pant Hywel Ddu farm. He weighed them out in large scales at the back of the cart, and we provided the bags to carry them home.

The cart was wobbly and smelt of earth and we used to beg for rides in it. Sometimes he granted the smaller girls a ride to the bottom of the street; this took a nice long time as he stopped at intervals to serve Mrs Vigars, Mrs Hill, Mrs Jones, the Misses Gethins, Mrs Harris, Mrs Lane, Mrs Farral, Mrs Hale, Mrs Pike, Mrs Southcourt, Mrs Evans, Mrs Hughes and Mrs Trimnel.

The bigger boys would hang from the back rail even though he shouted that he'd knock them flying if they didn't stop. Their weight was dragging his cart down, and they should think of his poor horse – *chwarae teg*, fair play. All the same, they hung on for as long as they could or until he leant over and pretended to swipe at them.

'Don't you hit me, or my mother won't buy any vegetables off you any more,' some boys would threaten.

All banter stopped, though, if by any chance the horse started to 'do his number one' as we called peeing. The amazing steam and stream which poured forth made us all stop in wonder, and then we would die laughing. If the horse did his number two, that was even better, and then it was laughing and holding noses and pretending to be sick. But if it happened near our house, that would produce another drama which embarrassed me. My grandmother, standing and watching by her open door, would dive back inside and emerge, flushed in the face, with a bucket and small shovel to scoop up the droppings for the good of the rhubarb (that being the only thing we had growing in the garden in those days).

It was a lucky day if she got there before the Gethin sisters who lived opposite. They were often nimbler and nipped in first. There being two of them, it was thought that one sister lurked in the passageway while the other ordered the vegetables, and as soon as the horse's evacuation started, out would come the lurker with her bucket to pounce. My grandmother then countered these tactics by taking the bucket and shovel out with her when she was ordering her spuds. So she was head of the queue.

Although I wanted her to beat the Gethins to it, I wasn't altogether on her side. It seemed a bit rude to me, this ungainly rush for horse manure. Especially since the heap dumped round our rhubarb seemed far and away in excess of what it needed.

This rhubarb was taller and thicker than any I have ever seen. It grew like palm trees. But it wasn't juicy like the thinner stalks we used to pinch from other gardens. Pinching rhubarb was one of our earliest adventures. None of us much liked its taste. The reward was the excitement of creeping in and out of back gates without being seen.

Since almost everything on wheels moved slowly from house to house, our street was as safe as most playgrounds. But I did manage to get knocked down on the main road up at the top. I ran out from behind a parked van and an approaching car had absolutely no chance to brake. I fell on my face and cut my mouth open. Blood poured out, but I refused to get into the car for a lift home because it had been drummed into me that I must never get into a car with a strange man.

I broke away from all the concern and persuasion and pelted down the street. The car followed and anxious women at the scene tried to keep up with me. I reached our door first, with this crowd close behind – quite a scene for my mother when she opened the door. I flung myself into her pinny and one of the women said 'Get a doctor. She's been run over.' My mother picked me up: 'There, there'. The driver of the car was saying it hadn't been his fault.

My grandmother was out by now. 'We're not interested in whether it's your fault at this precise minute,' she told the driver. 'Go for medical help. We will deal with you later.'

Doctor Imry thought my mouth probably did not need stitches. But for the next few days I couldn't eat and I was only able to drink out of a cup with a long slender spout that my grandmother dug out from the back of her cupboard. An invalid cup. She could not remember, not for the life of her, why she had it. Lucky she had kept it, wasn't it? My mother wasn't interested. She wanted my grandmother to go back to the kitchen, and leave us alone.

7
Whitsun and Other Treats

Weston-super-Mare, Mother, Father and me

M R AND MRS MARTIN, Carrie and Vernon, lived next door to us at number 7. They shared the house with Carrie's elderly married aunt and uncle and an elderly maiden aunt. Just as we did, they lived in the front room.

I used to stand holding onto my mother's skirt, face half hidden, when she paused from hanging out her washing to talk to them over the short garden wall that divided our two houses. One aunt, the married one, smiled a lot. The other didn't. The uncle would go into the outside lavatory, ducking his head at the low door, with his braces already hanging down over the seat of his trousers just like Pop did.

One day I wouldn't smile for the smiling aunt and my mother explained that I had earache.

'Oh, there's nothing worse.' The aunt picked a succulent leaf from a plant growing on her wall. 'Squeeze the oil from this leaf into her ear, that will cure it,' she told us.

'It won't. You want warm olive oil,' said the other aunt. The oil from the leaf didn't do a thing. The warm olive oil worked, but I still preferred the smiling aunt to the grumpy one.

Mr and Mrs Martin were Sunday School teachers at Jerusalem English Baptist Chapel, and once I was old enough, asked my mother if they could take me there each week. Carrie Martin was younger than my mother and wore very smart clothes. Spotless and crisp, as if they had just come from the cleaners. The Martins had no children, and as I walked hand in hand with them I used briefly and secretly to pretend they were my parents.

Mrs Powell in a dark overall – was it blue or green? dark anyway – stood there to greet us. She was our leader and I never got beyond finding her grim. So stern. Did she ever laugh? Smile even? I don't know. When I was ill at ease with people I wouldn't lift my eyes long enough to look into theirs. By dodging their glance, I felt I could hide from them my fear or distrust.

She was always described as a very good woman, deeply religious, spiritual – holy, even. And maybe she was. I was sufficiently impressed never to let on that I found her off-putting. But I was always relieved once she had finished welcoming us with a prayer and a hymn to God, and we were able to move our chairs into separate semi-circles around our own Sunday School teacher.

There'd be about six of these cosy little huddles in the vestry. We all sat on really low chairs and often you could see your teacher's petticoat – its lace edge peeping from under her skirt. She had on her best clothes and smelt flowery from the scent dabbed on the handkerchief tucked up her sleeve with just a triangle left out at the wrist. This she would lend if one of us suddenly sneezed.

It was all loving and gentle, and the teacher taught us things we could easily understand. In particular, that Jesus loved us. There he was on the wall behind the piano, his arm held out over the lambs which surrounded him, saying 'Suffer Little Children to Come Unto Me.'

Once we had learnt the words we would all stand up and sing our new hymn:

Jesus bids us shine
With a pure, clear light
Like a little candle
Burning in the night
In this world of darkness
We-ee-ee must shine
You in your small corner
And I in mine.

And at moments like this I would love Sunday School with my whole heart.

It came into its own on Whit Mondays. All the churches and the chapels of the town paraded through the streets of Briton Ferry carrying their banners and singing 'Onward Christian Soldiers' – especially loudly as they passed under the railway bridge which gave back an echo. My first Whitsun procession was on a sunny day, which meant masses of people turned out to line the streets.

We set off at 1.30 to congregate outside our chapel for the march. Mr and Mrs Martin in their spanking new outfits, and me in mine – new right down to the last scrap of underwear and right up to my wide, floppy, cream-satin bow, fastened – precariously as I was only too aware – with a hair clip. I had to hold onto it as a breeze got up, which rather spoiled the effect.

Mr Martin's shoes squeaked, as men's new shoes always seemed to. and mine still felt unsafe even though I had scraped them on the edge of the back doorstep, scuffing the shiny leather soles to make them less slippy.

My mother had told me exactly where she would be standing to watch the march go past. First at the top of the street, and then at the bottom on Rockingham Terrace by which time we would have rounded the corner where the new Lodge Cinema was being built.

When I did catch sight of her – she was waving and blowing me a kiss – I had a sudden urge to leave the ranks and run across for her to take me home. Not only because I was homesick, but because my new shoes were rubbing my feet. I wanted to change immediately into the new sandals and the as-yet-unworn Whitsun Field dress which I had been bought for playing games after tea. But the

Martins persuaded me not to run off. Teas and games had to be paid for by good behaviour on parade.

The tea was laid out in our vestry where rows of long white-clothed trestle tables wobbled under the mounds of triangular sandwiches. An industrious line of older women of the chapel sat in

Whitsun parade

front of another trestle table buttering and filling plate after plate with more sandwiches. Or they cut up slab cake. Or scooped trifle into dishes.

This was the first time I had eaten outside my own house and I was so self-conscious I could hardly swallow. It also dawned on me that every child there seemed to have a mother helping or an aunt serving at the table or a grandmother waving to them from the table where the elders sat. There was a strong thread of family running through the chapel, but not of mine. My only link was with the Martins. A chill set in then that I never fully lost. The feeling that I was not quite in the family of this church. That I was a bit of an outsider.

This was made worse because, simply through not knowing what to do, I had not gone up to get the bag of hard-boiled sweets which every child was given to take up to the Whitsun Field. Vernon Martin noticed this and hurried up to the man giving them out and said, 'Aye, this little girl's been missed out, Fred.' I almost wished he hadn't.

'And whose little girl is this who hasn't a tongue in her head to ask for her bag of sweets then?' Fred asked.

'Olive Davies's, lives next door to Carrie and me. We brought her. Tell Fred your name,' Mr Martin said cheerfully.

I said Mavis Mainwaring very quietly. Fred didn't catch it. So he asked me again and I said it again, and he said, 'Try once again. I must be getting a little bit deaf.' He held his hand up to his ear.

'Mavis Mainwaring,' I repeated. I could hardly speak, I so much hated saying my name for him.

'No sweets until you say that name loud and clear. Right let's hear it,' he persisted. Floors don't open.

'You've got a queue forming,' said Vernon Martin. 'I'll tell you her name – Mavis Mainwaring. Sweets please.'

This tease called Fred gave my hair ribbon a tug and handed me a bag of sweets. 'You don't really deserve them, do you, naughty girl?'

I had still not taken them from him. 'Here you are. Let's be kind. Off you go and don't go eating them all at once.'

The Whitsun Field was all to do with races – egg-and-spoon and sack races, three-legged race, relay, sprints and hurdles. All of them seemed to take a terribly long time to organise, and you were either boiling from just having taken part or freezing as you hung around waiting for the next race to start.

There was also a game in which young and old all joined together. We formed a circle, every person holding a partner by the hand. Or rather every person except one. And that one would pick out a person of the opposite sex to chase around the circle. Once touched, that person would become the chaser's partner, and whoever had lost their partner would become the new chaser. But if the one being chased got back to the original partner without being caught, then he or she was safe.

When we were young we were amazed to see our Sunday School teachers break into a run. And since they usually called each other Miss or Mr or Mrs So-and-So, we were equally delighted when the odd Christian name slipped out. It was a glimpse behind the curtain.

Later we became more interested in who was chasing whom, and took the chance to flirt with the boys.

The chasing game was always played at the end when the shadows were lengthening, it grew suddenly chilly, and you went to in search of your new Whitsun cardigan. You would eventually find it piled with others on the lap of some elderly woman who had been sitting watching the proceedings from the sidelines, and who now complained good-humouredly that she was going to feel the draught if we took the cardies off her all at once.

On my first Whitsun Treat my mother and father came to fetch me at the end. They knew the Martins would gladly bring me home, but my parents said they felt like stretching their legs. In truth, they came because this would have been our longest day apart from each other.

We walked home – me between my mother and father – holding hands. They swung me up, running a few steps forward, taking the weight off my feet when I started to moan that I was tired. Then my father gave in and lifted me up for a piggy-back and I laid my head on his shoulder and smelt his Brylcreem.

The Whitsun Treat was such a big event in our lives, I suppose, because nobody in our street went away on holiday. You might go off on day trips. And if you had an aunt or a gran in another street or town, you might stay with them for a while. I never did. Except for one weekend in Weston-super-Mare with my father and mother when I was four and a half.

I wish I could say that every single detail was etched on my memory. But that would not be true. I know we left from Swansea Docks by paddle steamer and I know it was crowded and that we stood near the funnel. And that's when I learnt there were other birds much cleaner-looking than our crows. The sea gulls. Whenever I see those birds hovering, their wings wide open, in the air stream above a boat, I still feel a little of what I felt on that first sight of them. A wave of pride and happiness swept over me as the ship's siren blew and we started to move. I now had my parents to myself for the first time in my life.

There had been excitement before this. My mother had been knitting me a swimming costume with a matching cape. Turquoise with a cream stripe around the legs and round the hem and neck of the cape, which also had knitted strings threaded through the top to secure it. When I tried it on I never wanted to take it off. My father bought new light-grey slacks and two short-sleeved Aertex shirts. And my mother bought two cotton dresses. They were the first clothes I ever knew my parents to buy.

My father made us a boat to take along, with a blue-painted wooden bottom and cloth sails which could be let down to lie flat along its side. We were going to find a quiet pond and sail it, my father told me. 'And if it works, who knows that it won't sail over the seven seas.'

'And back,' I insisted.

'And back,' he confirmed.

We stayed in a boarding house that smelt. A stinging smell of disinfectant which I had never come across before. Nor could I understand the landlady when she spoke. She had the first English accent I'd heard. I couldn't make out what she was saying. Keep smiling, I decided, when in doubt.

She said something and held out her hand to me. 'Mrs Warren has a surprise to show you,' my mother explained, but I wouldn't go with her, not without my mother and father. So they came, too, and the surprise waiting for us on a perch in the dining room was a parrot. It was red, green, orange and yellow, all in clearly-marked patches, like a parrot in a colouring book.

I thought Mrs Warren looked exactly like the bird, with her big, hooked nose (though hers looked blue not yellow) and her two wily, beady eyes placed close together on either side of it.

And the parrot spoke. It said, 'Pretty Polly'. My father was always telling me stories about talking parrots and until now I had never believed them.

One of his stories was about a vicar who dragged out his visits to people's houses in the hope of being given cups of tea and cake. A friend of my father's, an ex-sailor, got so fed up with the vicar's cadging that he taught his parrot to say: 'No tea today. Go to hell.'

Whenever my father and I could get into Mrs Warren's dining room alone, we kept on at the bird to say: 'No tea today. Go to hell.' But we got nowhere with that one. There wasn't enough time, my father said.

We'd come back for longer next time. Did I want to come back, he had asked me. Yes, I did. The most wonderful thing had happened that day. The boat my father had built finally sailed on the pond. The day before, it had capsized every time we had put it on the water and the sails got so wet we had to stop using it. My father had been really disappointed – there wasn't rhyme or reason, he insisted, why that boat shouldn't sail.

Today it had. It sailed right across the pond, proud and straight, and people had stopped and watched its maiden voyage.

This had been the first time I could remember my mother going into the sea and swimming. My father carried me into the water running and splashing. My mother followed very timidly. 'Come on, Olive, or it will have to be a ducking for you, I can see,' he called out. And he kicked some water in her direction which made her run laughing back to the beach.

At last she made it. And then she coaxed me to lie on my stomach while she held my hands and pulled me through the water while I kicked my legs. 'Look at this, Dick. Your daughter's swimming,' she called out.

They swung me into the waves and my mother put me on my father's back while he swam out a bit deeper. 'I'm off,' he said suddenly. 'Cramp in my calf. That's it. Finis.'

I was looking forward to watching my mother dress after seeing the way she had undressed when we arrived on the beach. My father had held a towel around her and there was a huge palaver while she wriggled out of her clothes, whipping her underclothes into her bag, screwing them up into small bundles before anyone got a glimpse of what was what.

She was no different from the other people, including the men, who were all changing in these cramped and furtive ways. It made me all the more curious to try to see what they were hiding.

The performance was more complicated now that she was taking her wet costume off. It took ages and involved two towels – a small one for drying herself which went under the big one my father was holding up. My father was losing interest. 'Keep the towel round me, Dick,' she begged. 'You're letting it slip down.'

I wanted someone to hold the towel for me but I was told it didn't matter. We'd soon get me dried and dressed with my cardy on. I acquiesced because I was very interested in the group of people next to us. One of the boys was going round tweeking at the towels which the girls were holding up for their friends.

'Okay then. I'm not ashamed. Pull it down,' invited one of the girls who was changing. He ran a mile. The girls laughed and he asked them to please, spare his blushes. Coward they called back at him. I crossed my fingers and wished the towel to drop.

We had our photograph taken by a street photographer on our first day in Weston and we collected it on the next. There was a woman on it, not with us, just someone who happened to be included because she was walking right behind us. She was the spitting image of my grandmother. My father commented on it.

'Hell flames, Olive, it's her ghost. We can't get away from her even for a day. She's everywhere we go. I've always told you that your mother has an evil eye.'

We spent the last hour before catching the boat looking for presents to take back in a shop that sold peppermint rock in all sorts of different shapes. For my grandmother, my father chose a set of false teeth. For Pop, a pipe. 'Damn, it's hard to tell that's not real.' He was in his element. He loved jokes. He found my uncle a pair of kippers; he reckoned Cyril would think they were the real McCoy. 'They'll be in the frying pan before he notices.' He bought a pink rock with Weston printed through it for my mother. And for me the biggest round lollipop I had ever seen. My mother sneaked back and bought Dad a black and white rock umbrella saying: 'Here you are, you're always worrying about getting wet.' He was highly de-lighted.

'Damn, Olive, I didn't see this one. What'll they think up next?' I stood between them both and put one hand in each of theirs and felt loved, united and safe. We had been so happy in Weston-super-Mare. The sun shone all the time.

And it was there that my mother and father, with some privacy at last, conceived my twin brother and sister.

8
Grandmother's Bed

Martha Jane

M Y MOTHER was sitting in the chair by the fireplace in our front room. She had her coat on and I wanted her to take it off. 'I have to go out,' she said, 'and I can't take you to where I'm going.'

But where was she going? I wanted to go too. She was going to hospital, she said. I decided that it must be something to do with her big stomach, which I'd noticed but which up to then hadn't concerned me. I thought she looked sad and worried.

She was waiting, she explained, for a car from the hospital to come. Then she would have to leave, but she would be back as soon as she could. 'Be a good girl while I'm away. Daddy'll be here to look after you.' He was, and it was he who took over my stories at bedtime. He wouldn't read to me. 'Wait till your mother comes back, for she's better than me at reading.' I am now convinced that my father could read only with great difficulty. He left school at fourteen, and while he was there the teachers spent more time rapping his knuckles for using his pencil in his left hand than teaching him to write and read.

He told me stories about his boyhood. Playing up at school. Putting tin tacks on the teacher's chair. Dipping flies in inkwells and letting them run over the paper. Mitching from school to go and help the farmer in return for some food.

When his father was out of work his family had no money. They would have to queue outside the soup kitchen for something to eat.

With Grandma Mainwaring

'People don't know they are born who have always had food in their bellies,' he told me.

Although I saw my mother's parents every day, my father's parents were far more remote. There is a photograph of me with my grandmother Mainwaring, who died when I was three. It used to make me feel forlorn to look at that snapshot of her; she had belonged to us and yet I hadn't even the slightest recollection of her. I felt better about it only when I persuaded myself that the little girl with her hands up to cover her face wasn't me at all.

While my mother was in hospital my father took me to see *his* father, probably not for the first time but the only time I remember. Although he lived only six miles away he had never visited our house in Mansel Street. He was white-haired and white-moustached and grim. He sat in a high-backed chair in the corner of his dark kitchen and, as I remember it, he did not speak. He looked exactly like the memorial statue near the library of a Great War soldier staring sadly down in stony silence. I stayed close to my father, but kept the shadowy figure in the corner under sly surveillance.

There was an American organ, a harmonium, in the room. My father opened the lid, sat in front of it and, pulling out the stops, began to play. He had such a lot to do. He moved his legs like mad against the two side pieces which were for the swell. His feet were at it nineteen to the dozen on the pedals. And his hands were pulling out and pushing in the stops. I couldn't believe this music was coming from my father. I hadn't had the faintest idea that he could play. Here he was, seriously engrossed. And the music which poured out in that small room sounded so carefree.

My father played by ear, and knew mostly hymns. Rousing tunes like 'Onward Christian Soldiers' and 'Guide me O Thou Great Jehovah', and others like 'Rock of Ages' which were mournful.

Then with gusto and the trumpet stops full out he closed with, ''Twas on the Isle of Capri that I met her, Beneath the shade of an old apple tree.' This he sang in a very jolly way, while I laughed and clapped my hands with joy that my father could play like this.

I can see the scene as clearly as if I were looking at a picture of it. No bright colour in the dark back kitchen, everything brown and grey. Flagstones on the floor, the door open and letting in a shadowy light. And I can still recall the contrast between that music and the feeling of gloom which surrounded that old man who had lost his wife and three out of five of his children.

Opposite my grandfather's house was the steelworks where my father drove a crane when the work was available. After we said goodbye to grandfather, he took me over there. We crossed the iron bridge at the place where the men clocked in and out. It was Friday, pay day, and although he was between shifts he couldn't afford not to come to the works to pick up his packet.

A couple of men working high up on what my father explained were the cranes called down to us. "That's your little girl then, Dick? One thing, she won't have to work in this inferno." My father said I was not to let go of his hand, or to move from his side, since we were going to see the furnaces and the crane he drove.

As we approached the furnaces, one of my father's mates gave me a pair of blue goggles: 'You can't look into the furnace without them.' I asked my father why a man who was working much closer to the furnace didn't have his on. 'Because he needs his head read,' he explained.

The furnace door opened and a huge shovel of molten metal came spewing out. I was caught in the heat and the glare. It looked beautiful through the blue glasses.

My father said there were men who had to walk in and clean out those furnaces before they had cooled down, and they were either bloody heroes or bloody idiots, he couldn't decide. One thing for sure was that they couldn't stay long in that job.

Then my father pointed to a crane high up in the steel rafters of the shed. It was picking up a ladle of molten metal and carrying it above our heads. You could just see the crane driver in the cabin. On another shift that would have been my dad.

The crane moved painfully slowly as we dots on the ground watched it until at last the big claw opened and dropped its red-hot cargo. My father told me that every single load a crane driver carried was a nightmare until it was safely deposited. I knew from waking in the cot next to his bed that he often swore and shouted warnings in his sleep.

He took me into the cabin where the men ate their food. They were all glad to see us, and I felt very proud of my dad. They told me he was a fighter. 'He speaks up when the rest of us shut our mouths.'

My father said to one small, thin, ghastly pale man: 'Tell her why you're called Wagner.' (He said it Wag as in wag of a tail, by the way).

'Oh, they are devils,' the man said in a whining voice. 'You see I

Father at the steelworks

attempt, in my small way, to play the violin. And they tease me. They are only jealous, methinks.'

He looked craftily at me, and the men roared. 'Jealous? Come off it, boyo. You play like a cat being tortured.'

'See what I mean?' whined Wagner.

Outside the cabin my father was still laughing. 'What the bugger doesn't know,' he said to me, 'is that we also call him Wigner behind his back because he wears a wig. He thinks we don't know. Everyone knows because once when he was playing his violin in a concert his bow caught in the wig and lifted it right off his head.'

On the bus going home from the works, my father told me that my grandfather had voted Tory all his life – even after all he'd suffered at the hands of his bosses. It made my father see red (and vote it).

A few nights later he took me to the next street to listen to a Labour Party electioneer who was standing on a box under the lamppost and speaking with great emotion. He had gathered a crowd around him, and my father hoisted me on to his shoulders so that I could see better.

My father called up to me that this was the only way out for people like us. We had no hope unless the buggers believed that workers were as good as the next man.

The speaker seemed to know the right things to say, for there were cheers all the time. High up on my father's shoulders I could see the dark shape of the nearby hillside covered in trees. We were all packed together touching shoulders, restless and excited. Especially me, since I knew I ought to be in bed.

When we got home, my grandmother was at the front door worrying that the child was out so late. Leave the worrying to me, my father told her. What she heard tonight will do her more good than an extra hour's sleep. My grandmother didn't agree. My father said she wouldn't, would she? She didn't vote Labour, did she? Her vote was secret, my grandmother retorted. That's as it should be, he said. But he knew even so.

I can recall my grandmother only in snatches before this occasion, yet she must have been there all the time. It was my mother who mattered, and my father when he was home. My grandmother was just a shadowy presence in the back kitchen sitting and waiting for the next thing to happen.

Soon afterwards, when my heroine, Brenda Charlton – an older girl who lived opposite us in the street – brought me home from school one afternoon she told me there was a lovely surprise waiting for me. What was it I wanted to know. You'll know soon enough she said. Was my mother going to be there? I begged her to tell me. I couldn't bear to suspect she might be, and then find she wasn't.

Brenda was torn between wanting the power of possessing a secret and the gratitude earned by the bearer of good news. She said she thought my mother would be there, and there was something else.

Something else did not matter to me. My mother was home. And she seemed younger and prettier than I remembered her being two weeks before. Two hundred weeks. Two thousand weeks.

'Look in the corner,' she said. And there in a pram were two babies. These were better than any doll I'd had. Especially the tinier of the two, my sister.

Where had they come from? She'd had them in hospital, my mother told me. How? Did she buy them? Not exactly. Did the doctor give them to her? Sort of. Did she ask for two? No, that was a surprise. A very big surprise.

And out in the street I went, to tell everyone. And one older girl said, 'You know they came out of your mother's stomach.'

Ugh. Don't be stupid. Yes, they did. How did they come out? Through her belly button. They couldn't, it's too small. One girl lifted her dress up and we all looked at her belly button really closely. It couldn't open.

'And,' said the big girl, 'your father puts the babies inside your mother.' How? 'With his Toby.' We decided she was too horrid for words, and I ran home to tell my mother. She told me I was to forget what the big girl had said. Babies did not come out of belly buttons.

But at that moment she was feeding one of these new babies with her bosom, which was astonishing enough to make me think that what the big girl had said might possibly be true.

The night they came home from hospital I was told that from now on I was going to sleep in my grandmother's bed. The little babies would have to sleep in my cot.

Without warning my world changed. As two umbilical cords were cut for the twins to be born, mine as an only child for five and a half exclusive years, was suddenly severed.

It was not considered a good idea to prepare children for new arrivals in the family. The very opposite, in fact. Grown-ups put off telling us anything for as long as possible. Neighbours in the street died and we all thought they'd moved or gone to hospital. Time enough to know about things when you had to. Until then my mother's day had been devoted to me. But she accepted that now, with two new babies to care for, she would have to let my grandmother look after me. It was not what she wanted, but it had to be. And it was only at the last possible moment that she faced up to it.

So, with no explanation really, out of the blue, I was put into another bedroom. A room I had hardly ever been into. The babies were in my cot with the sides pulled back up again. And I was in a big double bed with my grandmother. A figure who had always been in the background, and whom I distrusted because she made it obvious that she did not like my father.

Why on earth I wasn't given a single bed in my grandmother's room I do not know, unless it was that we simply couldn't afford it. But I do know why my grandmother wanted this arrangement. It was to keep her out of my grandfather's bed. She must have moved into this room, which had been my uncles' as soon as they moved out of the house to get married.

My mother left the twins to settle me into my new bed and read me my story from where she had left off. All the same, though I fell asleep quickly, I woke with a vivid nightmare. I dreamt my parents were being killed downstairs. I lay there listening. No sound now. I was too terrified to call out. I tried to shout and couldn't. I swung my legs out of the bed, but it was much higher than my cot and I couldn't touch the ground. They dangled there over the edge, chilled, and I was convinced that something under the bed was ready to grab them and kill me just as it had killed my parents.

I waited almost hopefully for that to happen so that the fear would end. I did not want to live without my parents. They were gone, I was sure. I slid off the bed, crossed the floor and came out on the landing, where I held my face against the banister railings.

Desperate, I stayed sitting there. No one was left in the world, now that the only two people I loved and who loved me were gone. A downstairs door opened and I heard my father say he would just go up and see if Mavis was all right. And as he started up the stairs he caught sight of me. He picked me up and held me to him. 'Damn it all, I thought you weren't all right. I wouldn't be all right if I was in a strange old bed, either.'

I tried to tell him how happy I was that he wasn't dead. And was Mam all right? To reassure me he took me down and put me to sit in her lap while she fed one of the twins. But my crying went on for ages. Bitter tears that hurt, followed by the odd shuddering sob. Although this time my parents had not died, I knew now that one day they would.

At this point my grandmother tapped on our front room door.

She suggested that since it was so late she would go to bed with me. I surprised myself. I was glad of the offer.

So up the sticks we went to mark the accession of the queenly Martha Jane Davies. And long was she to reign over me.

I forgot about my miseries as I sat up in her big soft feather bed and began to take an interest in my new bed-mate and surroundings. She propped the pillow up behind me to keep me warm around my back.

It was a nicer bed than my parents' and she told me that my old cot was too babyish for a big girl like me. This one had black and brass rails with round knobs which looked like door bells.

To one side was a big chest of drawers, and by the window a mahogany dressing-table. My grandmother now faced this as she took the clips out of the bun which held her hair, letting it fall down to her shoulders.

She took off her cardigan and dress. Underneath was a pink corset which took a lot of getting out of. It meant undoing the fasteners down the front, then unhitching the suspenders from her stockings which she rolled up carefully and put in her navy court shoes.

She threw the corset over a chair where it jangled as the metal bits hit the wood. I wanted to know what it was for. 'It is to hold your stomach in when you get older. It's a bit of a nuisance – like growing old is – but don't bother yourself with all that.' She remained in her vest while she had a bit of a scratch and then put on a long white nightie. I thought she looked very comfy. Now, she said, shift over, which I did into the cold patch of the bed while she got into my warm one.

'Now snuggle up to me, you'll be cold at first. I'll tell you a story by the candle. But I'll blow it out just before the end so that you can get used to the dark, and there'll still be some story left before you fall fast asleep into dreamland.'

9
A World Outside

The twins with me aged five

ALTHOUGH WE WERE overcrowded, I can't at first remember feeling put out by it. I don't recall the babies crying, and have only a vague impression of nappies steamily drying in front of the coal fire. I don't remember the twins crawling. How could they have done in a miniature front room filled with dining table, chairs, fireside chair and sideboard? Where was the floor space? I was so puzzled that much later I asked my mother about it.

'They didn't crawl. They sat up in their pram in the passage or, if it was fine, outside the front door or in the garden. When their legs were stronger I held them by their arms to kick and stamp and eventually they took a few steps. Or they stood by the settee and held on. The same as you did.'

What I do remember is being allowed to push their pram up and down the pavement on our side of the street. One blond, blue-eyed, round-faced boy baby; and one tiny, brown-haired, green-eyed girl

63

baby. Brother Graham gurgled, sister Sylvia grisled. He under the hood, she with her back to the handles of the pram because she was lighter and less likely to topple the pram over. Mind, I always worried that he had the more comfortable part of the pram.

They earned me great prestige among my gang of friends, for they were the only twins that had ever happened in the street.

But really they were my mother's business. And full-time that business was, with no hot water in the house. I got out of the way

Mother with the twins in the garden

and perhaps because of the circumstances I was given a fair amount of freedom. Anyway by this time I had started school. Every afternoon they were there to meet me. My mother with my mac and wellies if it had started to rain, and twins sitting up in their pram comical as anything. Something about two of them in one pram outside school used to delight me mightily.

Even more vivid than that scene is the memory of my first day at school. That was in September 1935, one month before I was five. I had longed for it so deeply that surely it would have to disappoint. It did not.

I can see the giant rocking horse, painted grey and white with a black tail of horsehair, real horsehair, and proper leather reins. I can see the shiny canvas alphabet chart which unrolled from the top and was so tall that Miss Jones had to use a wooden pointer to reach the top line: A a for apple. B b for bat. C c for cat. And I can see a little girl bend down to pick up her crayon and she didn't have her knickers on. I had no explanation for this then. You might dream you went out without your knickers on and wake up with a terrible start, relieved to find that, thank goodness, it wasn't true. But there she was in real life. I never saw her without them again — although I often checked after the astonishment of that first day's discovery.

There was our teacher who told us all that her name was Miss Jones. She clapped her hands a lot to get some quiet. Eventually she persuaded all of us new arrivals to sit in our tiny chairs by our tiny tables, and tactfully managed to usher our mothers out of the classroom. Only the odd child was still noisily breaking its heart, with its clinging mother remaining outside, face pressed up against the window, mouthing, 'Darling, don't cry. Mummy won't be gone for long.' And there was Miss Jones mouthing to the mother, 'You go. It will be all right.'

She started to make up her class register, and it was she who told me this next bit many years later. A voice by her side piped up, 'Please, Miss, I want to learn to read today before I go home.'

Miss Jones went on to tell me: 'I bent down and hugged the little mite. These words were music to my ears. They were what I had hoped to hear in my previous job, which was in a run-down school in Birmingham. But I never did. And now to hear this on my first morning — I was thrilled. I told her that as soon as I had entered all the names in my register we would start learning to read. Go back to your table now, good girl, and wait for Miss Jones. What's your name? I'll put you down first in the register.' She had retired by the time I met her again, many years later, but she had kept the register as a souvenir. And when she showed it to me, there was my name heading the list, out of alphabetical order: Mavis Mainwaring. It didn't bear out my conviction that I was very shy and backward-in-coming-forward, but there was no disputing the evidence.

School was wonderfully fixed and safe in its routine. I sat next to a boy who was shy and blushed easily. Godfrey White. He was always neatly dressed in a shirt and tie which was as clean and tidy at the end of the day as at the start. He didn't run wild in the playground. He knew a lot of the answers and put his hand up promptly – so did I. Miss Jones loved him. So did I. But it was ages before he would talk to me. He'd answer if I asked him a question. But he only spoke when spoken to.

What broke the ice was my being away from school ill for a few days. Godfrey was responsible for winding up the gramophone which played the music to which we marched into hall for assembly. On my first morning back it was 'Marche Militaire'. Godfrey caught sight of me and his face lit up. He forgot his duties and let the brisk march slow down to a dirge before Miss Jones called out, 'Attend to the gramophone, please.' He quickly wound the handle which sent the music slurring back to its correct tempo.

When we were seated at our desk, I put my hand in his. He turned and kissed me, and we bumped noses.

School for the first three years was Toy Town. Learning was a gentle process, and if ever you felt sick there was a little bed you could go and lie on until your mother came to take you home. Half way through the afternoon – and this was not just in the first class, the babies' class as it was called, but went on until you were nine – your teacher would say:

'Now put your arms on your desk, lower your head down onto them, and all of you have five minutes silence and rest.'

At first we obeyed, but by the time we reached junior school we used to peep to see what Miss Collins was doing. She, too, was motherly, but smarter than we expected a teacher to be. Sometimes we caught her popping a throat lozenge into her mouth while she leaned on the radiator to have a warm. Or maybe she'd be taking a quick glance into her powder compact mirror and giving a tweak to her immaculate head of deeply-waved black hair. Or checking the bottles of milk which she had put to warm on top of the radiator for those children who preferred their milk with the chill off.

At the end of school we all stood in the aisles by our desks, hands together and eyes tightly closed, to sing:

'The day Thou gavest Lord is ended,
The darkness falls at Thy behest
To Thee our morning hymns ascended
Thy name to sanctify and bless.'

And on a Friday afternoon we could take sweets to school and our own books and just one comic each. It was a long free period when, as long as you didn't keep your nose stuck in a comic all the while, you could do pretty well what you liked. Unless you were in Granny Morgan's class. She was the school ogre, and stories about her abounded. She thumped you in the back for nothing. She caned boys and girls very hard across their hands if they talked in class, and some could show you the red marks to prove it. Everyone in her class had to do sums on Friday afternoons and if she found you with sweets she would confiscate them – and not even give them back later.

When there was a school concert coming up, some of us went into the hall on Fridays and stood round the piano where Miss Howells taught us the song we were to sing. Soft spoken, Miss Howells wore thick rouge and a gallon of scent and would never have used a cane. So of course we played up in her class.

To teach us the words and music she would first sing the line herself, putting a lot of expression into it. That did it. Helpless giggles. Grown-ups singing always set us off. If she caught you giggling she would send you off to stand outside the headmaster's room where eventually you would be told off and sent back. Then you'd catch the eye of one of your friends and collapse in giggles again. This time the punishment would be 20 lines of 'I Must Not Giggle in Class', to be brought in the next day in your best handwriting.

Miss Howells was determined to get the best out of us and wanted us to think carefully of the meaning of each and every word. So 'Gather the roses, beautiful roses, Gather them early all heavy with dew,' had to be sung quickly, in a jolly way. But when we came to the next line, 'Lightest of breezes,' we had to whisper the words. And the last line, 'Which do you love best?' very slowly because it was a question. 'Pause while you think of your answer. Now all together with a lot of spirit: "Say you can't tell".'

All the while she put her heart and soul into conducting us with her face, at the same time thumping out the notes on the piano. She played with her hands coming up very high after each note, and never sat on the piano stool until she had first smoothed her skirt down under her and made sure the hem was well below her knee. At the end of the lesson she always thanked us for trying to give of our best for the sake of the music.

She wore an engagement ring and remained engaged for years while she stayed at home to look after her parents, and it was not until they died that she married. She was very happy, but only briefly, for her husband died soon afterwards. It wasn't an uncommon story at that time, but we found it sad.

One girl in our class, who played the accordion in a concert party, had permission to wear a scarf round her head on Fridays whenever she had an engagement in the evening and had to come to school in curlers.

Once she brought her accordion in for us to see. It was highly polished and had keys of mother-of-pearl. Accordions were all the rage (and so, because of George Formby, were ukuleles). Audrey played while she danced to the music. The accordion sounded very loud in our classroom and looked enormous strapped onto her, especially when she was dancing. She had red shoes with bows on top and tips on the soles for that lovely tap sound. We all rushed home to ask for steel tips to be nailed onto our shoes so that we could tap dance in the yard at play time. Audrey was our tutor and she soon had us in a line a-tapping to 'Rise and Shine and say Good Morning'.

It was during one of these sessions that Esmo Prothero Lewis accidentally tripped me over and knocked me out on the hard concrete of the playground. While he and another boy tried to carry me to the staff room I, half-conscious, was worrying that my navy blue Shirley Temple dress with white spots was torn. What if Shirley went away on holiday! How would I be able to take over from her in that film and dance and sing in her place?

It was a boiling hot day and my teacher took my dress off and laid me under a white sheet in my vest and knickers. At least I knew they were clean. In our house my grandmother believed in spotless underwear just in case you were knocked over and had to be rushed to hospital. Would I be rushed to hospital?

No, such luck. No dramatic ambulance with loud, clanging bell. When my mother came for me at home-time with the twins, I was crammed into their pram, while my brother and sister held onto the handlebars on either side, tottering slowly all the way to Mansel Street. I felt a clumsy clot, too big to be sprawled in their pram but I was still too woozy to get out and walk.

I wasn't an infant any more. By now I was hell bent on reading and allowed to go on my own down to the public library to borrow books. Muriel, Glenys, Maureen, Margaret and I would call on each other to make sure we all went at the same time. Or we would arrange to meet at the top of the steps which led up to the library. Then we could be sure of swapping over books between us.

We were proud of our library. In our eyes it was historic. In fact it had been built as recently as 1902. Big brass knobs and a letter box always brilliantly shining on its double doors. A musty smell inside the tiled hall with its grand sweep of wide stone stairs and mahogany banisters up to the Council Chamber.

'You ought to value your library books,' my mother stressed to me when she saw me drop some jam on a page and wipe it off carelessly. 'Let me get that off properly or the pages will stick together. And it will be one less book for the library. Mind, this one looks as if it's on its last legs. Might even be one of the books I borrowed when I was your age. It would have been as new as the library then.' I was dismayed. It meant my mother was as ancient as that building.

She went on to tell me the library was broke as soon as it opened and had hardly any books to lend. The Council appealed to every man in the town who was in employment to contribute one penny a week from his wages towards a fund to stock the shelves. The men agreed to pay a penny a month, and ten years later our library had four and a half thousand books.

As soon as we went in through the big doors of the building, we stopped talking. Miss Parfait, our librarian, who had her legs in irons, managed to be kind and helpful and terribly strict at the same time. Silence was the rule. She liked to be able to hear if a pin dropped in her library.

Once we had given in our old books at the counter – which was too high to see over and only just possible to reach – we had to walk around the shelves without a word said. There was a stuffed crocodile in a glass case on the top of the first book case. Just staring up at it silenced us for ages. Rumour had it that if you stared long enough you'd see the crocodile yawn and tears spring to its eyes. And if you stayed in the library after dark you could watch it get out of its case, slide down the shelves and roam round.

One night we made a feeble attempt at getting back into the building. Fat chance that we'd find any of the mighty sash windows open. But we crept round the back and peered in to the darkened library and, naturally, one of us saw a shadow move. We all ran away yelling that it was the croc. Mind, we entered on these adventures with our tongue in our cheek. None of us believed the crocodile tale, but we yearned for something to happen as it did in books. We longed to be scared – though not by anything that would really hurt us.

As soon as we were big enough to see over the high counter where Miss Parfait stamped our books, we started to take out Mills & Boon books, searching the shelves for their red covers with MB in black in the right hand corner. These romances were in great demand. One gent with bleached hair (should we tell him that we'd heard Jean Harlow died from peroxiding her hair?) waited bent like a vulture near the entrance for us to arrive with our M & Bs. But we had already bagged each other's. All the same, we were open to bargaining with him since he often got hold of the new ones just out and he took books away by the armful. He must have been borrowing on eight tickets.

How come, we wanted to know, that he had eight when we were allowed only two. They were his mother's, his aunt's, his lodger's and his own, Miss Parfait told us, and anyway it was none of our business.

It was about this time that we'd get to hear of a book with dirty parts in it. One of us would make our way to the shelf where it was supposed to be while the others kept guard in case Miss Parfait was on one of her rounds. I was often the first to track it down and find the right page, and I'd stand there trying to make sense of some incomprehensible passage. A man threw grapes into a woman's lap. And . . . then he picked them up with his mouth. And . . . then he passed them from his mouth into her mouth. I stood trying to work this out – it was unhygienic all right, but not dirty in the way I'd expected – while the others grew anxious for their chance to read it. 'It is juicy. Page 34 half way down,' I'd tell the next girl as if it had all been clear to me.

Opposite the library on the ground floor was the Public Reading Room, the Holy of Holies, since you were not allowed in unaccompanied until you were over twelve years of age. So on tiptoe we used to peep through the glass in the top of the door to watch all the old men puffing at their pipes, blowing their noses, and standing up to read the papers which were fastened down on the stands with brass rods. There were spittoons for the old gents to use, and we waited ages for one of them to go red in the face with coughing and then march over to the receptacle and land a great gob of phlegm in the hole.

Why was it only men who used spittoons? Because they smoked and women didn't. We knew there were some women who smoked. They were flighty and wore make-up like Aunty Dorrie. Mothers certainly didn't. One of the girls from a rival gang told me that my mother smoked and I pelted home in a panic to hear from her lips that it was a lie. She denied it. But she also said that if men took up the filthy habit, why shouldn't women, if they wanted to? If I didn't mind my dad doing it, why not my mam? I had no answer, except to beg her never to smoke.

At the same time as I was allowed to go to the library on my own, my grandmother let me take my grandfather's club money down to their hall a few streets away on a Friday evening between six and seven o'clock. The Odd Fellows' Club was for the welfare of working men. If they fell sick and couldn't work they'd be given a small amount every week. Their hall was twice the size of our middle room. Bare boards. Dusty smell. School clock up on the wall – always telling the right time so that people would pop in on club night just to set their watches by it.

There were wooden chairs round the wall and a big heavy table in the middle with green felt on it. On one side facing you was Mr Len Williams, a kindly-looking man with a pipe in his mouth who was also the School Board Man who called if you were absent from school. He filled in the club books. Opposite him with his back to you was a fat man with a deep, pink fold of skin hanging over his stiff, white celluloid collar. He was also puffing on a pipe and he took the money. Right next to him was an empty chair.

When it was my turn I was invited to take this seat, and with slow ceremony Mr Williams went through his weekly routine. He asked how my grandfather was. 'Ah yes, Joseph Morgan Davies,' he would say as he looked down at the card. 'And how are we doing at school?'

Very well thank you, I'd answer.

'Are you any good at sums, Marvis?' I never minded him pronouncing my name like this.

Not very, I'd say. 'Oh, oh, so now then. Are we going to be able to count how much money we are handing in today?'

Yes, I'd answer, ready for the next question, which was, 'If you are not good at sums how can you do that?'

'Because it is ten shillings and it is only one note,' I'd answer triumphantly as I did every Friday night.

'She has caught me out again,' he'd say to the room. He was always the same. I loved him.

Mr Williams would then fill in the card with his fountain pen, very carefully which meant very slowly. And just as carefully and just as slowly he would turn it over and press it onto a folded sheet of pink blotting paper.

Meanwhile I handed my money to the fat man, whose name I never knew, and who turned to take it from me. And once again I'd force myself to look into the empty socket of his lost eye. He'd put my money into a wooden bowl and when my card was handed back to me he would empty the money from that bowl into another identical one which fitted underneath.

At this I used, almost masochistically, to hope he would do one of his spits into the spittoon at his feet which was also very near mine. If he did I'd call him ignorant under my breath as I withdrew my foot to avoid the splash. Otherwise I had to make do with watching him draw on his pipe, which made bubbling sounds, and taking a quick look at the hand holding his pipe which had lost half a finger.

Mr Williams would send his good wishes to Grandpa and Grandma and his thanks: '*Diolch yn fawr i chi*. And by the way, how is your Welsh coming on?' I'd tell him I wasn't learning any.

'Oh dear, and it was your grandpa's first language once upon a time. But then your grandma has only ever spoken English,' he'd add as though it might be news to me.

I'd say my goodnight in Welsh just to finish off our teasing. '*Nos da*.'

'*Oh da iawn*, very good, *merch*,' he'd say, laughing.

All this, including waiting for my turn, would have taken about an hour, and I'd have stayed there all night given a chance. If I couldn't be the one filling in the cards, I'd have liked to be the one who took the money. And since I couldn't be either, I wanted to watch.

IO

Fearless, Tearless Gwyneth

My aunt's teapot

ONE GIRL IN OUR SCHOOL, called Gwyneth Ward, was more daring than the rest of us and cheeked the teachers. One of them smacked her in class and Gwyneth did not give a hint of being sorry or angry or hurt. Not a sign of a tear, either.

She always hung about on her own, would stand up to anyone and could fight even the boys. I had a sneaking admiration for her. But she was forever taunting me. 'Gipsy. Your real name's Rosanna.' I didn't mind being called Rosanna. It struck me as a more romantic name than Mavis. I was half-and-half about being called a gipsy, for gipsies, we were told, stole children and kept them to beg and steal. But they were also the people who arrived with the fairs in brilliant caravans, and when they were in town came round the doors selling wooden pegs and white heather 'for luck, love', and told your fortune if you crossed their palm with silver. In books their children were allowed to run free in bare feet as brown as their faces. Their hair was long and dark and curly, and their clothes were bright and embroidered. I could quite see myself like that.

So I ignored Gwyneth. When that had no effect, she changed tack. She called out, 'Fatty like your granny.' And I called back: 'Skinny like your mother.' And this cutting wit went on all the way home.

The next day she had had time to think. She was ready with, 'You haven't got a mother. Only a fatty granny.' She was standing by the wall of a house in a silky elastic-waisted floral summer dress, a big slide holding back one side of her short bobbed hair. I charged at her. I was instantly out of control. Unafraid of her and furious because what she was saying was partly true, I caught her by her shoulders and shook and shook her while her head banged up against the wall.

I stopped in horror as Gwyneth-tearless-Ward burst into tears. And we were both holding each other and crying and saying we were sorry. While one of those alarming, egg-shaped lumps appeared on the back of her head where I had banged it, Gwyneth asked if we could be friends. I couldn't say yes quickly enough. I was now scared stiff at what I had done, and was only too keen to be forgiven.

We walked home hand-in-hand, each little paw getting clammier and clammier and stiffer and stiffer, but neither daring to be the first to sever connection. This was our small betrothal.

Gwyneth wanted me to come in to her house and meet her mother who had, including Gwyneth, seven children (none of them twins, which was my only way of scoring in such competitions). I said I had to go home first. 'Why?' she wanted to know. 'Your mother won't miss you.'

So I went. Mrs Ward seemed pleased when Gwyneth told her we were friends. But would she be when she noticed Gwyneth's lump?

'What have you been up to my naughty girl?' she asked Gwyneth. 'That's a nasty bump. She's always in scrapes. She ought to have been born a boy,' she told me.

'I did it,' I blurted out.

'Only because I called her names,' defended Gwyneth. Much to my relief, Mrs Ward seemed uninterested. I said I had better go home now.

'Well, ask your mother if you can come back after tea and play here,' said Gwyneth. 'I'll come with you half way. You will be my friend now won't you? My best friend?'

'Well, one of them,' I promised for I had to consider Muriel.

That wasn't enough for Gwyneth. All or nothing. But I couldn't promise more. 'I haven't known you for as long as I've known Muriel.'

'Well I'll give you a week to decide. If I can't be your best friend, I won't be your friend at all.' And off Gwyneth ran.

There was a row from my mother because I had not gone home straightaway. She had been frantic with worry. 'Don't ever do this again. Come home first and ask. You know the answer is usually yes.' And she warned me that I was going to have to be firm with Gwyneth, and not be easily led, as Gwyneth was a very wilful girl.

I rushed my tea and went back to see Gwyneth. We played for a while in her garden and then she had a suggestion. 'Let's go over to your great-aunty's opposite. She's got a lovely house hasn't she? I've never seen inside it.'

You didn't get asked into people's houses round our way. You stood talking for ages at front doors craning to see in. You were privileged if you were allowed to step over the threshold. If it was raining and your friend wasn't quite ready to go you'd be asked to wait in the dark passageway while she finished her tea.

I tried to explain that my aunt wouldn't like us just turning up. I had been there only once with my mother, and it had been a very stiff occasion. 'Oh, come on,' Gwyneth said, 'she's not going to mind you turning up and bringing your friend. Come on.'

It took her ages to persuade me. I wouldn't know what to say to my great-aunt, I protested. Gwyneth said just to knock her door and when she answered say, 'Hello, I've come to see you, Aunty.' It was easy. Nothing to it.

I wanted to go, for on that previous visit to my aunt's house I hadn't liked to stare, which meant I had not taken much in at the time. So, now with Gwyneth egging me on, we went up to the big, panelled front door with the kind of spanking, shiny knocker and letterbox which ours didn't have. We couldn't reach it. And Gwyneth, without a by-your-leave, picked me up by the legs and shoved me up to it, just as the door was opened by my aunt who was even more doll-like than I remembered.

'*Nawr te*. (Now then). To what do I owe the pleasure of two young ladies trying to climb up my door? I presume you were going to knock and run away.' I was dumbstruck. Gwyneth wasn't.

'She is Mavis, Olive's daughter, who has come to visit you.'

'*Merch fach*. (Little girl). I didn't recognise you. Come along in, but does your mother know where you are?' I had lost my tongue. Gwyneth said my mother knew I was playing with her in Osterley Street.

'Well, come along in then, and you will wait outside for her, good girl, until she comes out again.' With this she took my hand and left Gwyneth on the other side of the firmly-closed door.

Once inside I had to negotiate carefully the polished hall with its shining, slippery floor. It was not like walking. It was more like finding your way through hazardous territory on skates. Past the front room where the curtains were drawn in case the sunlight faded the furniture. Where every chair stood to attention. Every cushion at a stiff salute. The glass vases shone even in the dim shade. And the polish stung my nostrils.

Through the middle room which was as formal as the front room. It had a piano which was never played in case the keys were dirtied. My aunt apologised for my finding her in such a state. 'I haven't cleaned in here today.'

'I love your house,' I blurted out as we walked into the back room which had a dresser laden with china, and a blackleaded hob, immaculately clean even though a coal fire burned in it. No ash seemed ever to land on the hearth; it must have been suspended there with fright. The fire irons shone. The brass trivet and the iron fireside stool gleamed. Two spotless white Staffordshire dogs stood high on the mantelpiece. We had two of them in our house always slightly covered in coal dust. Did she sit in front of the fire dusting every minute the fire glowed?

The clock, in between the two dogs, tick-tocked but time was standing still. I began to imagine that under my aunt's endless dusting the dogs, clock, gleaming steel poker, coal shovel, brass horses, fire stool with its curved, bandy legs, would all come alive as soon as I left the room. And they would dance a crazy dance led by this neatly-shod, tiny-waisted, full-bosomed, white-haired lady who would wave her golden duster to keep them in line.

What did she dust in? Her clothes were spotless. She had a black dress with a sweet white collar and a starched white pinafore as though she were in service at a grand house. And it was a grand house as far as I was concerned, but an uncomfortable one. I was asked to sit down on her leather chaise-longue, and I felt myself slipping off, it was so polished. You had to perch upright, not touching the back, and with your feet held hard to the floor in order to stay on. Was that why my aunt had such a straight back?

We must have a cup of tea, she said to me. I was dying to do so since she had a teapot in the shape of a house which was kept warm inside an embroidered tea cosy also in the shape of a house. And her cups were so thin and the handles so small, and she kept sugar lumps in a dish shaped like a rose with silver tongs to pick up the lumps. My grandmother had sugar tongs, but we didn't have lumps of sugar so we never used them. Even so I said I wouldn't have tea because Gwyneth was waiting outside.

'Well, come again on your own and we'll have a nice cup of tea and a slice of aunty's *teisen-lap*. And come when your uncle Tom is home from work, for he'd like to see you. He's good with children, you'll see. It is our tragedy that we have none of our own.'

My aunt spoke slowly, formally, picking her words carefully. She was, like Pop, from Carmarthenshire. Welsh was her first language. Her husband Tom was Pop's brother. The sober side of the family, though he worked in the thirsty tinplate works too. As did Johnny the youngest brother who lodged with them. He always wore a brown leather glove on his right hand because he had an artificial hand. He'd lost the real one in some accident on their farm. 'You are not able to speak Welsh?' she stated rather than asked me. 'Your mother never picked it up, even though she used to come over here and clean for me.' My mother used to clean for her?

'You'll come soon then?'

I said I would and walked out feeling like Alice in Wonderland – out of place, big and clumsy.

Outside Gwyneth was seething. My aunt was a snob, she fumed.

And she was daft. People said she washed the coal before she put it on the fire.

I welcomed Gwyneth running my aunt down. This perfect little lady. She really was little. Not as tall as us and we were not anything like fully-grown yet.

Gwyneth proved a perfect companion for me. I was too solemn for my own good. Too eager to please. Afraid to be disliked. There was a daring streak in Gwyneth which I longed for.

We planned two robberies in Woolworth's. With or without disguise? Without, we decided. If we were caught, then acting innocent as ourselves would be the best ploy. Gwyneth was to do the actual pinching and I was to keep a look-out for the police outside the store, which was her suggestion. It didn't seem to me to be of any practical use. But she insisted.

I was so nervous on the bus going up there that when the conductor asked for our fare, instead of asking for one Return to Neath, I asked for a Return to Woolworth's. Gwyneth nudged me and the conductor said 'Woolworth's' just to make conversation, 'And what are you going there for, eh?' I was so terrified I couldn't answer. Gwyneth could and did so with obvious enjoyment: 'Just going to look round. We haven't any money to buy anything.'

Her suggestion that I act merely as look-out was clearly more practical than it had sounded. She must have thought that she was safer alone inside, with me outside where I wouldn't draw attention to her.

Our loot was to be framed photos of Deanna Durbin and Stewart Granger, and the raid was to be made in two stages. Gwyneth stole Stewart's photo first. And the next week we came back for Deanna's, and a packet of sweets to eat on the way home on the bus for good measure.

The thrill had vanished. We were not keen on the photos once we had them and we didn't know where to keep them out of sight from our mothers. We decided it was not worth stealing again and even toyed with the idea of sneaking the photos back. But one was already broken and it didn't seem worth the bother.

11

'Come unto the Lodge Today'

Morfydd

WHETHER I STAYED awake late, or my grandmother came to bed very early, I'm not sure, but most nights she lay next to me not reading stories but making them up. The one I liked at first was about a litle girl who had been asked by an old lady to carry her shopping bag home for her. 'It isn't far, good girl. Just across the way,' said the little old lady.

They started to walk until they got to the woods on the edge of the town. 'Just over the field,' said the dear old lady, who gave the little girl, one by one, her favourite sweets. Over the field they went, the old lady telling such marvellous stories to the little girl that the little girl didn't notice that the field had become another field, and that they had crossed a river bridge and yet another field, and now were entering some woods. 'I must turn back,' said the little girl.

'We are there now, and I have a lovely little present for you. Come in.' From the outside, the house looked like a sweet cottage but as soon as they were inside it became dark and dirty, and the old woman – not a dear little old lady any more – barred the door and grinned an evil smile and said, 'Now you are my prisoner and my slave. You will never see your mother again.'

'She does though, Gramma, doesn't she?' I begged to be reassured. My dramatic grandmother would say, 'Well you will have to wait until tomorrow night to find that out. It is time for sleep now.' And however much I tried she would not budge. She left me only with a hint that it would be all right.

I might have been more anxious if by then I hadn't already got used to cliff-hangers from going to the pictures.

The Lodge Cinema first opened its doors in 1938, and was billed as:

'Briton Ferry's own luxury cinema, the newest and the best in Wales. BALCONY: Adults 1/6d & 1/3d, children 9d. STALLS: Adults 1/-, 9d, 6d, children 6d & 4d. Continuous performance daily commencing at 5.15. Matinees on Mondays and Saturdays at 2.15. This modern and artistically designed cinema, this palace of fantasy, seats 1012 patrons.'

It wasn't the Ferry's first cinema. There was already the Kinema, known as the Kin, which was in a converted chapel. Its seats didn't match, and some were benches. It had no carpet on the floor, so that people stamping in and out constantly drowned the actors' voices. And there were other interruptions. The manager would stop the film to give messages – 'If Bobby Davies is here, his mother wants him' – or in winter would clatter down the aisle with a coal scuttle and thunderously fill the stove. The beam from the projector was so low that at critical moments some joker could cast a hand shadow of a rabbit or a butterfly on the screen. Or at other moments a shaft of light from the Gents would shine on the screen as the door was opened. Boys made loud kissing noises and wolf whistles in love scenes. Paper bags were blown up and burst in ghost films.

The Kin had been good fun. But now the Lodge had come into our lives with its velvet blue tip-up seats and matching blue runners down the aisles. The usherettes wore grey and blue uniforms and had torches to show you into your seat. So we gave the Kin a miss for a while except when we were enticed back by horror films like *The Mummy's Hand*.

No one under the age of 18 was allowed into the evening performance at the Lodge unless accompanied by an adult. That was normal at the time. But there was another rule peculiar to our cinema: any patron who had a child with him should leave the performance before 9pm because (in the view of the Management) by that hour children should be in bed. The owners were conscious of their social responsibility, which is why the Lodge stayed open right throughout the war.

There was a special Saturday morning children's programme with Flash Gordon, Jungle Jim and Zorro serials. The episodes always ended like my grandma's stories with the hero in grave danger. Danger so dire that it was impossible to see how he could be rescued. At first we racked our brains all week trying to imagine how Flash Gordon could escape from the spikes which were being lowered to within an inch of his head. But we soon caught on to the fact that his escape was always a bit of a swiz, and we used to let out a huge bored groan. Altogether now.

The next development at the Lodge was to turn the Saturday morning into a proper children's club with Uncle Terry as our host. He was the son of Mr Hancock, owner of the picture house.

That was what finally did for the Kin in our eyes: the fact that the Lodge had '*Uncle Terry*'. Uncle Terry in his navy blazer, white shirt, navy-and-red tie, grey slacks, walking stick and – even a straw boater. He would jump up onto the narrow strip of stage in front of the curtains, announce the forthcoming attractions, crack a joke and lead us in the singing. The words of the songs would come up on the screen and he stood in front pointing to them with his stick.

We had our own club song, 'Oh come unto the Lodge today,' sung for some reason to the tune of a German drinking song, 'The Stein Song', and our favourite words were the finale:

> That's why we all cry Whoopee
> The Lodge is the place for me.

And it was the place for me . . . from the moment the house lights dimmed and we saw the Lord Chamberlain's certificate through the illuminated curtains. They clinked before they opened with a whooshing sound. We cheered. Then silence fell as the film titles came up. Sometimes I'd squeeze my friend's hand to share my devotion to the beautiful, dark world that was about to envelop me.

My father took me to the first adult film I ever saw, picking the early evening performance so that we wouldn't have to wait outside for so long. Even so you always had to queue. There were queues all the week, and particularly long ones on Saturday.

We went to see Jessie Matthews in *Evergreen*. My father got us places in the back row so that I could tip the seat up and sit on the edge of it. He rolled up his coat and put it under me to make me more comfortable and give me an even better view of the screen.

I adored the singing and dancing parts of the film and concentrated on my sweets when there was only talking. I didn't know quite where to look when they kissed – certainly not in my father's direction.

Our gang was soon going to the pictures twice a week, three times when our mothers could afford it. If the cinema was a bit empty and the usherette was in a good mood we saw some films twice over. The first time this happened Maureen's mother was waiting outside scolding us that it was far too late to be out on our own like this. No one had known where we were. We were practically living in the pictures. Had we thought of taking our beds and making a thorough job of it, we were asked.

I had made a new friend at school, Morfydd Davies, who lived in a house with a bathroom and with bookshelves, and a piano in the front room. Her house impressed me no end. As did Morfydd. She was undoubtedly the prettiest girl in the world, I thought. Prettier than Maureen O'Hara but with the same rich dark-reddish hair and blue eyes with long lashes. She was mad on the pictures as I was. She cried and laughed in them even more than I did. There was a competition as to who wept the most in Lassie films and in Greer Garson and Walter Pidgeon films like *Blossoms in the Dust*. Morfydd won by a very short margin.

In the matinées we sat with the gang of boys we went round with. I was still meant to be 'going with' Godfrey White but his parents did not allow him to come to the pictures. Nor out to play in the evenings. So I only saw him in silence at school.

If I was in love with G.W. then R.M. was in love with me. He was as dark as I was and as soon as the sun shone his skin went a deep brown. He lived in a white-washed cottage in the woods at the edge of our park, with cobble-stones and a pond in front of it. He knew the names of birds and wouldn't tell the other boys where the nests were in case they pinched the eggs.

But he would let me into his secrets. He would show me a bank of violets on condition that I didn't show anyone else, because if you picked them, he said, they wouldn't grow again. He took me to the spot in a field just above his house. We could see the smoke from his chimney curling up. And there were the shy violets, tucked away and beautiful, the first I had ever seen growing naturally. I wished then I could fall in love with R.M. instead of G.W. who wouldn't be kneeling down with me gazing at the flowers in case he got his knees dirty.

He asked me if there was anything else I'd like to see.

'I have to go now,' I said, 'because I'm meeting the girls in the cemetery.' He said he'd take me out again and show me lots of things he knew. I told him he was very nice to show me the violets, and I would come out with him again. 'When?' 'Soon.' 'How soon?' 'I don't know. Just soon.'

The cemetery, on the edge of our park, had become a craze with us. After school, once the fine weather started, we were always there. We liked it when there was a funeral, so that after the mourners had left we could go and look at the wreaths and read the cards. And feel sad.

Then we would wander round the graves just reading the inscriptions. If a grave was very neglected we would tidy it up, and go round to the better cared-for graves, taking a flower or two out of the big bunches in the urns and placing them in jam jars on the poorer graves.

We made up a game to play. We would find the grave of someone who had died young, and one of us would lie down on it while the others came round and pretended to read the inscription on the headstone: 'Mavis, Dearly Beloved daughter of O. I. and R. J.

Mainwaring, died at the age of 7 years. Whom the gods love die young . . . not lost but gone before . . . safe in the arms of Jesus.' And so it would go on until one of us – usually the one lying down – became too upset to continue.

We were reported to the police. Someone said he saw us pinching flowers from graves. It was hard to explain to the policeman who came to my house that we hadn't pinched them. We had only moved them to the poorer graves.

My mother was angrier than I had ever seen her when she heard how we had been following funerals and standing near the mourners and reading the wreaths. 'Those funerals, that person's death is a private affair. And so are graves. Would you like it if you found a child lying on my grave? Following my funeral? You would want to be on your own at a bitter time like that. For shame on you all.'

I ran upstairs and cried but no one came to comfort me. So I decided to run away from this home where no one loved me. I tied up my pyjamas in an old piece of sheeting, meaning to find a stick so that I could carry it like Dick Whittington. And then sat down to write my goodbye note. It took ages to compose because I wanted to make a list of who was to have which of my toys. My black china doll was for my little sister, Sylvia. She would love it for me even though its head had been broken; I had dropped it getting it out of the box on Christmas morning. My father had stuck the many tiny pieces with Durafix, and my mother had knitted a bonnet to conceal the network of cracks.

By the time I had worked out my will, my mother was calling me to go up to the chip shop if I wanted chips for supper. And off I went, deciding I would run away next day instead.

Getting a basin from the cupboard for the chips, I ran up to the shop at the top of our street. Mr Ellis, the owner, had a notice on his shelf: 'Our Motto is Cleanliness and Civility'. He wore a clean, white, starched apron every day. The counter was spotless. The fryer had not a splash of fat on it. No one dropped chips on the floor. If you had done you could have eaten them off it. It was said that Mrs Ellis ironed the sheets of newspaper which Mr Ellis used for parcelling up the chips. His greaseproof sheets which went next to the chips were in a pile on the counter, and with a smooth piece of wood he would fan them out so that the edges were separate and all the easier to pick up.

In the corner of the shop was a potato slicer. It had a lever like a beer-pump handle, and a pale girl called Muriel used to operate it. Her hands were purple and her nose was red. And she never came out in the street to play. Was she a relative or was she adopted? We decided she was a prisoner.

We made up our minds to call on her and ask her out to play, after which we would probably help her to escape. Quiet Mrs Ellis answered the back door and we asked for Muriel. She called her and then lurked just behind her while we asked her would she come out and play with us. She said no, but thanked us for asking. And before she could say more Mrs Ellis called her in.

Some time later she disappeared from the chip shop. We reckoned that the Ellises must now be holding her prisoner in the back room never to see daylight again. Being fed on bread and water with the smell of fish and chips to torment her.

But when we plucked up courage and asked Mr Ellis one night where she was, he said she had gone back to her family in Newport.

We learned that she was one of several children, and her parents thought Muriel would have a better start in life with her childless uncle and aunt. But she was so homesick that they had come and taken her home. Then we felt rather sorry for the Ellises.

12

Getting to Know Pop

Pop

IT MUST have been summer time because the front doors of the houses were open, and we were out very late playing in the street. I saw my grandfather coming down Mansel Street from the main road.

Why I ran up to greet him I do not know, for he kept himself to himself in our house. When he was around he sat in the back kitchen in a big wooden armchair with an old overcoat draped over the back. He smoked a pipe and when he spat from time to time the gob of spit would land on the hot iron bars of the fire and sizzle. He was always nodding off to sleep, when he wasn't upstairs in bed or out working as a night watchman. I scarcely met him eye to eye. Everyone seemed to ignore him. So I followed suit.

That evening, then, at about ten o'clock, quite out of character, I ran up to him to say, 'Hello, Pop,' and nearly screamed. His glasses were smashed onto his face and he was covered in blood. He lurched towards me and I fled to call my mother, sobbing that Pop was hurt and bleeding. She said to go into the front room, and she closed the door on me. Then all hell broke loose. My grandmother was shouting and my grandfather mumbling something in reply. I heard my mother shout that this was too much for anyone to stand. 'You've frightened the child. Have you no respect even for children? No, you never had for your own, so why should you have for anyone else's.'

I could hear him crashing upstairs, and my mother came into our room. What had happened to him? Why were they sending him to bed. Pop was bleeding. Was he all right? My mother told me he was. He had always been all right so long as he had a skinful of beer.

My grandmother came in and said she would pulverise him if she got near him, doing this to the child. My sympathies were with my grandfather who was hurt, and I wished I hadn't gone home crying.

'Why doesn't someone go and look after Pop?' I asked.

'Just stay out of this,' I was told. I didn't understand.

How could these two women who were loving and kind to me be hateful and unkind to him? His bedroom was up above our front room and I could hear his boots being dropped onto the floor. He was singing a hymn to himself. Was he really all right, or singing to God for help? Then you could hear him pee into his bucket, as loud as a horse.

'He is just like an animal,' my grandmother muttered. 'No better than an animal. Like all men.'

'Not like all men,' said my mother, as though not for the first time. And then to me she said, 'You stay out of Pop's way from now on. He's a drinker.' This was totally inexplicable to me. I was. She was. Everyone was.

But it meant that I kept a look out for my grandfather after this. And I noticed one or two things. I liked his face. It was a good-looking, handsome face. He was often humming under his breath, 'When I grow too old to dream.' He was always on his own.

I went up to him on the road and said, 'Hello, Pop,' one day soon after this bleeding face episode. He peered down through an old pair of spectacles mended with sticky plaster and said, 'Hello, *merch.*' I asked him if he knew my name. And he seemed not a bit surprised by the question.

He said, 'You tell me it.'

'Do you know, though?' I persisted.

He winked and said, 'Perhaps I do and perhaps I don't.'

'You don't anyway. Do you?' I was shocked that my own grandfather, the man I knew as Pop, was a stranger to me and didn't know my name even when we had been living under the same roof for going on for seven years. I was affronted and puzzled.

'You see, *merch fach*, they keep me in the dark.' He winked.

He didn't ask me my name so I didn't tell him it. As I began to move away from him, he brought his feet together in a shuffly way and drew his hand up to the side of his temple and saluted me. That tickled me.

This was how we went on greeting each other, even in the house. He'd wink and salute me silently. And I began to wink and to salute back, for we both understood, without saying it, that we could only be very secret communicators.

I noticed he was given different food from us. He would have his meals served in the back kitchen, at the dark end of the table and without a table cloth. My grandmother would sit at the far end, away from him, with her arms folded, not eating.

Bread and cheese, it seemed to me, was what he mostly ate, with a big cup of tea which he made a noise drinking while my grandmother would tut tut and mutter, 'Pigs slop.' He would not even look up.

'Pigs slop,' she would repeat, looking at me. 'Don't they?' she'd ask, but I did not want to be on her side against Pop so I'd drop my eyes.

'And ignorant people don't answer. Or do I find myself with a couple of deaf mutes, I wonder?'

I was staring at the flowers on my skirt as if their pattern held the secret of life. Pop was chuckling. And he'd say, 'What's that you were saying, Martha Jane? Speak up. It's rude to mumble.'

'Tell him,' she'd say to me, 'that I said pigs slop. Perhaps he will hear what you say.'

'Grandma says she said pigs slop,' I'd tell him.

'And cows chew the cud, tell her.' By now my grandmother was eating her tea. He couldn't mean my grandmother? My mother had said it was beyond the pale to call anyone a cow. I was dying to say it. But Grandma was there before me.

'You b. off to the Harp' – that was his local – 'There won't be one where you'll end up.'

And he'd throw back his head and roar with laughter. 'You're a funny woman, Martha Jane, I must give that to you.' I'd be staring from one to the other for signs that they were going to be friends.

I asked her once why Pop didn't have cake or tart like the rest of us and she said he couldn't taste good food. Not with all the drink he drank and all the tobacco he smoked.

I didn't believe this, so once when she was out I sneaked some tart from our front room at tea-time and took it down to him. He was nodding away in his chair so I hissed, 'Pop,' and he turned round and made a drowsy attempt at a salute.

'Here's some tart for you.' I slid the plate down the sloping table. He stopped it. I slid a spoon down after it. He chuckled and got stuck into it, while I stood there feeling chuffed. And my grandmother caught us.

She tore into him for taking my tea. And she pulled me to her slightly smelly pinafore and said, come, good girl, and I'll give you another piece. I didn't want another piece and I certainly didn't want to be a good girl. And I hadn't wanted to be caught and I was very glad that Pop had finished the tart before she came in.

I went through the whole operation again, sneaking him a slice of cake next time, but he held up his hand to stop me sliding it down to him. He said it was much appreciated and thank you, but truth to tell his stomach wouldn't take it. (Every man I knew seemed to have a bad stomach.) Eat it yourself, he'd said. It was too rich for him.

Too rich for him, when he could put away a dish of cockles from their shells with no trouble. The cockle woman who called at our house every Saturday morning in the summer, was a brown-faced woman in a voluminous skirt covered by a heavy navy apron with large pockets across the stomach. She walked with majestic slowness and an utterly straight back, for on top of her head she had swathed a white cloth, and on top of this she carried a round basket of cockles in their shells. In the baskets which hung from her arms were boiled cockles already shelled and sometimes mussels. These were covered in soft white muslin cloths – like the bags my mother soaked the dried peas in overnight on a Saturday ready for Sunday dinner.

The woman sold them from tin mugs by the pint and half pint. Her money she kept in the pockets of her apron. Silver in one and coppers in the other. Pound and ten-shilling notes in a little purse in one of the larger pockets.

My grandmother bought the live cockles in their shells, taking an enamel bowl to the front door for the woman to measure them into. Afterwards she poured cold water and salt in the bowl and left the cockles to stand overnight out the back. I used to take my brother and sister to watch the shells part and the cockles gradually ooze through the opening. A bubble came out of their shell as they tried to get rid of the sand inside. We stood there for ages waiting for the bubble and the oozing.

We thought they were wonderfully awful. And were delighted to be horrified that anyone could possibly eat them, as my grandfather did, boiled up for breakfast on Sunday morning and taken with vinegar and pepper and bread. He would suck the little monsters out of their shells with the three of us staring from one end of the table – me holding my sister up to give her a good view. We'd lose interest by the end and I'd show Graham and Sylvia how they could grip the top of this solid table and give themselves a swing.

Having now made contact with Pop, I wanted to buy him a present for Christmas. My mother said she had never had a present from him when she was a girl, but she supposed that ought not to stop us. What should we buy him? A tin of tobacco for his pipe, she suggested. Not a pipe? No, he liked his old one. Not a tobacco pouch? No, he never used one. But perhaps he would if we bought him one. I wanted to impress him with a more personal touch. Well, get him a pouch, if you like. It won't get used, she maintained.

So, on Christmas morning, after we had opened our presents, we went to take our tobacco pouch up to Pop. The drawn curtains made the bedroom dark and eerie. My brother and sister and I crept in to a funny stale smell and our grandfather lying snoring on his back, mouth open with his spectacles still on and askew. We tried waking him but he wouldn't wake up. So we put our personal touch on the pillow by him. And left him.

I had pictured it so differently. The least I had expected was a wink or a salute. And perhaps a tear? I had imagined this left-out old man so grateful for our present that he would have gathered his grandchildren into his arms and sung a carol with us.

He didn't appear all day. No Christmas dinner for him. And on Boxing Day when his two sons, Uncle Crad and Uncle Cyril, came to tea with their families, he passed through the house and out of the front door saying hardly audibly, 'Compliments of the Season to one and all.' And that was his family Christmas.

I wanted to run after him. Preferably with snow coming down outside. Two orphans in the storm.

I heard one of my aunts say quietly to my uncle, 'Oh, poor dab. I do feel sorry for him going out on Boxing Night.' And my grandmother picked her up — keen hearing, when it suited her, had Martha Jane — and put her down with, 'You must be joking. Try keeping him in with one glass of sherry like ours. Live with him before you say "poor dab". We were the poor dabs.' Under her breath was my aunt really saying, 'I wasn't talking to you'?

I almost enjoyed the tension of this gathering amidst my grandmother's best furniture in her small middle room. It positively crackled with powerful personalities, all at various odds with each other. Or maybe they were only at odds with Martha Jane.

Meanwhile the third generation was getting on surprisingly well together. Ken, the oldest son of Gladys and Cyril, played with Graham; they were roughly the same age. 'They've both got the same blond hair as me when I was their age,' said Uncle Cyril. 'Two little snowballs,' as Aunty Gladys described them. Their daughter Ruth, the youngest, and just as fair, tagged along with Sylvia. Really these two wanted to be with cousin Eileen and me, but we were absorbed in our own secrets.

My father never settled in this gathering. He ate his Boxing Day tea in our front room saying there wasn't enough room for all of us to sit. My mother made the same excuse. But Dad bobbed in and out and was very jolly with my uncles. When they told a joke, my grandmother laughed. Forced was not the word for it. When my father cracked his jokes, Martha huffed. Was it a huff? Or a tiny snort. A condemnatory noise, anyway.

She raised her eyebrows secretly to me when one of her daughters-in-law said anything. If she had seen more of them, they would have come in for the straight cold shoulder treatment my father received. And even though she tried a bit harder to be on her best behaviour at this time of goodwill, she only just pulled it off. Even her polite face was insolent, and at the same time inscrutable. Martha Jane was Queen of the Ice Maidens. But she had competition. Nobody in the room was at all prepared to be her servant. At the most the family were willing to be courtiers — just for the day and with no lasting loyalty.

I always found Christmas tiring. For weeks before I had a permanent headache of excitement. There was all the business of Jesus in Sunday School, where we had to remember the true message of Christmas. Presents were not the point.

And yet they appeared to be entirely the point. Ever since October, mother and father and aunts and uncles and grandmother and friends were asking us what we were going to ask Father Christmas to bring. After all that checking up, one year I had six bottles of scent. I oiled my three-wheeler bike with most of it.

After hanging up my stocking at the end of the bed for Father Christmas to fill, I couldn't go to sleep. I always wanted to stay awake and see him, even though I had been told that if I did see him he wouldn't leave me any toys.

I would fall alseep eventually, waking up when it was still dark to feel the stocking and check if he'd arrived. This was when I slept in my parents' bedroom. If the stocking was full I woke them to tell them he'd been. And then got into their bed and untied the cord at the top and put my hand in, and then my arm, trying to reach down to the toe.

The toe always had a tangerine in it which I asked my mother to peel. This she'd do, keeping her hands under the blankets as far as possible, because our bedroom was always freezing in winter, and also because she was trying not to wake up fully yet. Tangerines, in their silver paper wrappers, only appeared in the shops in December. So the smell of that exotic little fruit as the skin was broken was Christmas in itself.

Opening my stocking posed a problem when I slept with Martha Jane. I wanted to be with my mother and father and Graham and Sylvia. The first Christmas I galloped in to them before my grandmother had opened her eyes, quickly scrambling over her to get out from my side of the bed which was up against the wall.

But the next year she was ready for me. And as I stealthily crawled over her mound, she grabbed my ankles and said: 'Merry Christmas, Gran's sweetheart. Don't leave me on my owny. Show Gran what Santa Claus has brought you.'

She spent a long time looking at every single thing until at last my mother came in with the twins, and said to come and show Dad what I'd got.

I was too guilty the next year to dash out. I stayed but rushed through showing her the contents of my stocking. And then when I was older and could tell her I did not believe in Father Christmas, I began to decide for myself how to allocate my time.

My brother and sister partly solved the problem for me. They still believed in Santa and would come and show me their things. Once they got into bed with me, Grandma would get out sighing heavily, conveying to me that she was being usurped.

13
Through Road with Diversions

The Docks

As I became more independent and was able to go further afield, Briton Ferry seemed to expand. I counted the streets on the way to the library in Neath Road, the main road. After Mansel, and parallel with it, there were four: Vernon, Grandison, Caroline and Regent. After the library were Ritson, Tucker and Villiers, and if you walked right down Villiers Street there was a low bridge which we called the tunnel. Once through that and we were at the Docks – the outer edge of the town. Although we learned at school that they'd been designed by Brunel and had done a flourishing trade in coal in their day, that day had long passed. Only rusty, unromantic sand boats called there now, though the place still had other, unexpected uses.

The Docks were where, for the good of their health, all babies were wheeled if they had a cold. When I got whooping cough at the age of five I walked round the Docks with Valerie, an older girl who also had it, because the air down there – especially by the wall facing out to sea where the receding tide left great mud banks – was said to be immensely medicinal. When you were older you went down to the Docks because it was a lonely place for kisses.

Before that we thought of the Docks as adventurous in other ways as we picked our way over the tangle of railway lines from the steel and tinplate works, peering into the parked trucks, stopping to watch the dolly engine pulling its loads. Beyond the tracks was an area where we could gaze out to sea and think our own thoughts about pirates and romantic voyages on the high seas, all borrowed from books. The coast around the corner brought you to Aberavon, about six miles away, where we went by train for a day out with our mothers in school holidays. And that was the farthest that most of us travelled until we were well into our teens.

We liked the touch of danger about the Docks. Men who worked there were always warning us to go and play somewhere else, and we ended up being chased when one of them lost patience. All the same, we kept going back until a boy our own age fell into the water and was drowned. That halted us for a little while. But the Docks remained a magnet even after some of the works closed down and they grew more and more deserted.

I had the idea of walking from the Docks along the sands to reach Aberavon by foot. Four of us set off. It was to be an adventure, which meant not telling anyone else. We could have been no more than nine years old, with no idea of direction or distance. We had sneaked some small refreshments from home which we had eaten before we reached the beach. And once on the sand we half-buried an empty bottle with a message sticking out of its top. It said S O S GONE TO ABERAVON. I had written it (wanting life to resemble exactly the stories I was reading), and we all signed our names in case we were captured or lost or cut off by the tide.

It was a very windy day. We whooped along, laughing and collecting shells. Finding a rare conch to put up to our ear to listen to the music of the sea. Then it started to cloud over, and we found it harder than we expected to walk in the fine soft sand which was whipping up against our legs and stinging our bare flesh. There was rain. Hard big drops. Distant thunder. An eerie light.

Maureen said she was scared. Immediately we all were – except Gwyneth. We started to pelt back, holding onto each other, frightened of being left behind. The sea was much nearer. Best run towards the dunes. Then we saw a figure of a man just standing looking down at us. A murderer.

'Oh, Mam,' Maureen was really crying. We started to scramble up the dunes, at an angle away from the distant figure. Maureen couldn't. She kept slipping back with fright. She was howling. Her fear was catching and we all sat down in a tight circle at the foot of the dune clinging to each other. Some were crying and some just trying to get Maureen up on her feet so we could start running again. I was sneaking looks over my shoulder at the figure who was walking nearer us. But since I felt I'd been wrong to suggest this outing, anyway, I kept quiet about the advancing threat. Suddenly I noticed we were sitting near our bottle. I could see it sticking up in the sand: 'Look, we're nearly back at the Docks. Come on.'

Maureen was still letting out the odd sob. But I gave her a big stone to hold in her hand for safety. And I held her other hand – it was the least I could do, even if it slowed me down.

Once out of the docks our spirits rose enough to sing 'London's Burning' as a round. I cautioned everybody not to say a word about where we had been, remember. We had just been up the park. If anyone did tell I would never speak to her again. I made them lick their finger, make a cross under their chin and say, 'God's honour. I will not tell a single person.' And now that we were home safe, we all vowed we would make the trip again and next time we would get to Aberavon.

Briton Ferry was not at all a bad town in which to be brought up. It was near the seaside. Near woods. Small enough to feel safe in and big enough to find new places to explore. But you could never by any stretch of the imagination call Briton Ferry a pretty town. It was simply an industrial sprawl beside the main South Wales road from Cardiff, Bridgend and Port Talbot to Neath, Swansea, Carmarthen and Pembrokeshire. (Nowadays it isn't even that, since the town has been by-passed by a bridge across the mouth of the River Neath.)

Briton Ferry had moved away from the river bank where it first nestled. We couldn't recognise our town when we read a description of it written by a travelling clergyman in 1804:

> The country now put on a pleasing rural garb as we passed through large groves of oak and chestnut . . . an avenue nearly two miles in extent defended us from the oppressive heat of the sun. Here is the justly admired spot called Briton Ferry. The advantages which nature has bestowed on this place baffle all attempts at adequate description.

We were loyal to our version of what that admired beauty spot had become. We called it the good old Ferry. Its poverty aroused our solidarity – 'them' against 'us'. It was largely classless. Or rather it was one class – pure working class.

The Ferry had two jazz bands of its own, the Mexican Promenaders and the Juvenile Romany Kids. They competed each year in a Jazz Band Contest and would rehearse by marching through the town in their black-and-gold and red-and-white satin outfits, gold coins dangling all around their boleros and headscarves. All puffing like a horde of hamsters, at their gazookas (tin instruments a touch more sophisticated than paper and combs). And we would line the main road to cheer them on and wish them luck.

We were never allowed out to play on a Saturday night after ten. Pubs closed then. The drinkers were on the loose. We didn't see them but we heard a good deal of their slurred singing on Saturday night. But some of the stories made drinkers out to be good fun. A friend's uncle was locked out by her aunt when he came home drunk one Saturday night. He'd tried to get in by climbing down the chimney. When that failed he fell asleep where he was on the roof, and was still there when someone spotted him the next morning on their way to chapel.

Two of us went up to Neath one Saturday, which our parents had stressed was strictly out of bounds. Defying them, we saved the fare and went. It was quite early in the evening when we got off the bus. Even so, there were men lying in the gutters and leaning heavily against lampposts with a splodge of vomit at their feet. They were staggering along the pavements to the next pub. Peeing great crooked streams up against walls in full view.

We held onto each other giggling like mad but really we didn't know what to make of the things we saw, and suddenly we were feeling let down. 'Let's just buy some chips and go back on the next bus.'

That night in bed, I told my grandmother not to tell Mum where I had been. I described it to her. She said to save the fare next time, or give the money to her and she'd show me all that without my having to move an inch. And I knew of course that she meant Pop.

At the beach with Gwyneth, centre

14
A Second Home

Uncle Crad, Eileen and Aunt Flo

THE ONLY PLACE I knew beside Briton Ferry was Llandarcy, the village where my cousin lived. Every other Sunday my grandmother made us an early dinner and we caught the Richmond bus to Neath, then waited outside the bus station for the ten-to-two United Welsh to take us to Llandarcy. It was a journey of about ten miles to see my Uncle Crad, Aunty Flo and cousin Eileen. The village had been built by the oil refinery to house its employees and Llandarcy stank of bad eggs when the wind was blowing in the wrong direction.

Eileen was one year and one month younger than me and we were like sisters, everyone said – especially so since I had the same colouring as my Uncle Crad and could easily have been mistaken for his daughter. She was fair, curly-haired, even-tempered, very good-hearted, and we were extremely happy with each other. I can't remember that we were ever spiteful towards each other, and we never quarrelled. In fact, just to see what it was like, we wrote a play in which the characters fell out. But we only giggled when we came to act it: we couldn't say harsh words even in pretence.

Eileen was always waiting at the bus stop when our bus arrived. A big beam lit up both our faces and I couldn't wait to get off. Neither of us hid the confident pleasure we felt at being together, as we might have done had we been older.

Now the only question was whether her mother was going to let us dress up in her clothes so that we could perform our concert after tea. This was for the benefit of our regular audience of three grown-ups, with an occasional fourth, Eileen's Aunt Gwenny. She was the quietest woman I had ever met, with the gentlest face in the world, and I thought she was the spitting image of Rupert Bear's mother: a maiden aunt about the same age as our grandmother, with crocheted lace triangles in the V-neck of her dresses.

They all sat and clapped and were endlessly patient during our concerts. We recited poems and sang songs and performed a short play usually involving a spy or a murder. Our grand finale was always the same, a mysterious (to us) song and dance. We did not have a clue where it came from, who had taught it to us, or what it meant:

> Two model Quakeresses
> Wearing our stylish dresses
> You may not know it
> I may not show it
> Hiding our face from the golden west.

We would sing this to actions, bringing the fifth line to an end by fluttering our home-made paper fans in front of our faces, while at the same time pointing with our free left hand in the vague direction of this golden west.

Concerts were organised by me. Outside activities were Eileen's province as she was more athletic. There was a marshy piece of ground at the back of their flat and we'd go there and jump the ditches while my uncle tended his allotment. There we ate his peas from the pod. Eileen could jump effortlessly across really wide ditches and I admired the style with which she did it. I stood and watched her and knew exactly where I had to jump, but just as I was about to take the leap I'd pull up short and funk it. Eileen and Uncle Crad would coax me from the other side to do it. But I couldn't, wouldn't and longed to. I dreamt of jumping the ditches. I practised them in my sleep. The next time, I vowed inwardly, I would soar over them like a racehorse. Then when the time came to try again, I'd take a run and almost scream to a halt. My feet were fastened to the boggy grass as if in irons.

One day I did jump but fell backwards into the muddy water, and Eileen came in to rescue me. I wished I could have laughed. Instead I sat there like a solemn prig pretending I had twisted my ankle so they couldn't laugh either. With their help I hammed it onto my feet and continued to limp.

We went back, stinking dirty, and were put in the bath in their kitchen. This was hidden under wooden boards which acted as a working surface when the bath wasn't in use. The water was heated by a ferocious geyser. I didn't think that their fixed bath was so much better than our portable one, though without doubt it was socially a cut above ours. I hadn't come across even a two-star bathroom yet.

Our own bath had to be unhooked from a nail on the garden wall outside our glasshouse and carried into the back kitchen in front of the fire. To fill it we needed kettle after kettle of boiling water or fewer bucketfuls from the boiler. And someone also had to keep guard so that nobody walked down into the kitchen. The water cooled rapidly as you washed yourself, though as you sat up in the bath next to the fire, the upper part of your body became baking hot and lobster red.

I came to like our bath more after I saw a film where a cowboy bathed in a similar one. He was surrounded by heaps of white soapsuds which we could never get out of our heavy bar of germ-killing carbolic, though my mother had taught me how to blow hand bubbles with it. And while she scrubbed me she taught me how to spell by tracing letters in the soap suds on my back and getting me to guess from the touch what they were.

During the war Auntie Florrie had a worker from the oil refinery billeted in their flat. Her name was Gwen. I think she was from near

London – somewhere like Ilford. Eileen idolised her. I didn't see so much of her, didn't know her as Eileen did, and had a suspicion she wouldn't have been quite my type for full-time idolising. But certainly she had allure.

Not on all Sundays but on many, Gwen would join us at the end of the evening. I was fascinated especially by her hands and nails which were just like the ones they drew in nail polish advertisements. Pale and tapered. She was the only person we knew who wore coloured nail polish. The shade, she said, was Old Rose and it showed up her ten perfect half moons. We tried for the same effect by wetting pink rose petals and sticking them on our nails.

Gwen had pale hair and wore it in a loose bun at the nape of her neck. She played the piano. And we thought she looked very tragic sitting there, particularly when she played one song we loved and which she would keep to the end – just before my grandmother and I went to catch the last bus. Eileen and I would stand behind Gwen at the piano stool while my aunt and Martha Jane sat on the two brown leather easy chairs. My gran would already be wearing her hat, gloves and coat (not fastened so that she would feel the benefit when she buttoned it up as she left), and would have her handbag and fox fur over her arm. My uncle would be by the window keeping his eye on the bus. And arranged in this customary tableau we would tremulously join together to sing along with Gwen's pretty average rendering of:

> 'God send you back to me,
> Over the mighty sea,
> Dearest I want you near.'

Then with Gwen's foot pumping the loud pedal, and great swoops from her left hand as the tempo slowed slightly, we'd take a deep breath to end with the even more emotional burst of:

> 'God dwells above you,
> He knows how I love you.
> He will send you back to me.'

We always waited for a moment before we clapped and then Eileen and I would go away and confer. We knew that Gwen had a fiancé in the forces. Would he return to marry her? We thought not. We thought somebody as gentle as Gwen might be destined to be left an Old Maid, on the shelf, cruel fate killing the one and only love of her life.

We decided she would have made a perfect wife and mother, though I was always slightly anxious about her perfect hands. She could never keep them looking lovely if she became a housewife. Perhaps for the sake of her pale hands fate was not playing such a cruel trick.

Our little stories about Gwen were far from the truth. Her fiancé, Cliff (whom we thought handsome enough to be a film star) turned out to be her secret husband. The refinery would not employ married women during the war, so to get her job Gwen had to pretend to be single (though she declared herself engaged to be married). No one knew this at the time, not even my aunt, who had Cliff to stay on one of his leaves and put him to sleep on the settee while Gwen slept in her virgin's bed.

One weekend when I stayed overnight with Eileen I saw Gwen next morning just after she had got up. I was mesmerised by how different she looked without her make-up and wearing a well-worn dusky pink dressing gown with a turban round her head to hide her curlers. She smelt of Germolene, which glistened in patches all over her face, and she was dyeing a jumper in the kitchen sink. Eileen told me afterwards that Gwen was always dyeing jumpers. They began as white, then proceeded through the pastel shades until they became a deep ruby and finally black. Clothes were short in the war and this was one way for a working girl to ring the changes.

My uncle and aunt always made me feel at home. We all knew that Uncle Crad adored Eileen. 'Worships the ground she walks on,' my aunt would say. But to his credit, he never let me feel anything but cherished too. He made us laugh and Aunty Florrie made us think. She was clever and sharp and unsentimental. Uncle Crad, on the other hand, was incredibly sentimental and would cry at good never mind sad news. I loved him for that. My father was the same. Tears fell fast down his cheeks whenever he heard a record of Gigli or Caruso sing something like Handel's 'Largo'. So I grew up thinking it was manly to show a kind heart, and not at all cissy to shed tears.

We took the last bus home from Llandarcy at about nine at night. And even in summer it had to be to lit up. But the conductor never switched the lights on while the bus stood killing time at the terminus. I loved getting into the lower deck of this twilit double-decker. The conductor and the driver sat on the long facing seats at the back smoking a cigarette and drinking tea from the cups which screwed on to the tops of their vacuum flasks. And Eileen would jump in, too, neither of us wanting to say goodbye.

We would go right down to the front of the bus for privacy, huddling together for our last exchanges. The driver would slowly get up and stretch and say, 'Dai, it's time we were off.' Then, with a big wink at Eileen, he would call out, 'Any passengers on board who do not intend to make the journey, would they kindly remove themselves forthwith.' Off she'd scamper. Then I'd turn and kneel on the seat to wave frantically until Crad and Florrie and Eileen were dots in the distance. After thinking about the day, I'd join Grandma who always sat in the middle of the bus. She said you got more warmth there.

For several stops, we were usually the only two aboard – we two and Martha Jane's fox fur. This was almost like another presence – so important was it to her and so impressive was it to me. After a while, I would put my arm through hers, and my head on her shoulder, snuggling up to the old fox, with its hairs tickling my nose, and inhale its strong smell of moth balls.

One night on the bus a big chap got on. Dark and very good looking. 'Don't look now,' said my grandmother, 'but here comes Bruce Dargavel. Wonder if he'll still have the time of day for me.'

I wanted to know who he was. 'An opera singer. He went to the same school as your Uncle Cyril. But he's moved to London with Sadler's Wells, that's a big jump for a singer to go there.'

With that he saw Martha, and greeted her with genuine affection. 'Oh, it is nice to see you after this long time, Mrs Davies. Is this your granddaughter? You look too young to have a granddaughter.'

'Thank you, Bruce,' said my grandmother. 'How are you getting on up in the big city?'

'Can't complain. No complaints. It's treating me very well. You have a wonderful gran here, you know,' he said, bending towards me. And then turning back to my gran, 'I'll never forget your kindness to me, Mrs Davies.'

The bus conductor was asking him to move down the bus and take a seat. 'Lovely meeting you. Best of everything,' he said enthusiastically, and with a touch of theatre, maybe.

'Lovely seeing you too, Bruce,' said my grandmother. Then, under her breath and with her lips hardly moving, while still with a big smile and nod of the head towards Bruce, to my utter astonishment she added: 'He thinks his shit is sugar.'

'He what, Gran?' I wanted to know, shocked but shaking with laughter.

'You heard. He thinks his shit is sugar. Don't laugh or he'll know we're talking about him. Not that he'd mind so long as we *were* talking about him,' she said grimly.

'Well, all I know is that he's obviously fond of you. Has he got a good voice?' I asked.

'Fair play to the devil,' she said grudgingly, 'he has a wonderful baritone voice for opera and it was a big thing for someone from his background to get into Sadler's Wells.' And for someone who found it so hard to give anyone credit where it was due, that was practically a standing ovation.

When we got home to Mansel Street my mother would bustle me up to bed because of school next morning.

One of these Sunday nights I went to comb my hair by the dressing table and couldn't find a comb, so I went into my grandfather's room to look for one. I knew he was out working as a night-watchman.

I opened the tiny drawer in the dressing table and in it was a cardboard box, which I opened. In the half light I couldn't see what was inside. I put my hand in, and touched something very soft and silky, quite heavy and curled up. I let go in fright and it slid easily out of my hand. When I made myself look again, I saw it was a coil of hair. Rich dark, almost black hair. I was transfixed. It lay like something live. I forced myself to pick it up, then I bundled it back into its box and fled.

It was my grandmother's, I found out. She had kept it ever since she cut her hair, which had once been down to her waist. I meant not to tell her I had found it, but even stronger than my worry about being told off for snooping, was my anxiety to discover the story of the hair. She explained she was keeping it in case she ever wanted to wear a bun again. I said I thought it was creepy. She said she was not the least bit interested in what I thought on this subject since I had no business to open drawers in other people's rooms without asking. But the next time I made it my business to open that drawer in another person's room without asking, the hank of hair had gone.

15
Eileen and Martha Jane

I wanted to be a missionary

LLANDARCY was a step up the social scale from our house and street. But Eileen loved coming down to stay with us. Uncle Crad would bring her just before dinner on a Saturday morning. I knew he would miss her, but he wanted her to have company her own age. So, after a good deal of lingering, he'd eventually leave and return for her early the next morning.

My parents let me play outside and go off on my own quite a lot. It set me wondering whether I wanted them to be more like Eileen's parents. For didn't their behaviour mean that they loved her more than mine loved me?

Eileen and I had a game we made up, Detectives, which we played in Grandma's back kitchen. Pop, who would be snoozing in his armchair, was always the spy in our games. Or else the crook. And because he was often half-drunk and half-deaf we could say what we liked about him without his hearing, which made him a perfect foil.

My grandmother would be persuaded to lend us her stemmed trifle glasses and to give us a bottle of American Ice Cream Soda as champagne. We borrowed two pairs of her gloves, made cigarettes out of rolled-up paper, and sat opposite Pop at the table pretending to be indifferent to him. We were disguised as idly-loitering ladies of great wealth. Little did he know that we were really top agents employed by the government to trap a dangerous, filthy German spy. Or on another day, when we had decided that Pop was an Oriental, that we were detectives whose job was to catch him red-handed smuggling drugs. Smuggling opium, to be precise, since that was the only drug we had heard of. This was our favourite game, ever since I had seen a film in which the hero had burst into a room where a Chinese was smoking a pipe of something evil and deadly. The pipe which Pop smoked fitted the bill admirably.

I was a great cribber of B-movie plots and because Eileen wasn't allowed to go to the pictures as often as I did, she thought I was a genius at making up stories. I basked in her praise, and found her a wonderful partner. She loved the plots unfolding and took them every bit as seriously as I did. And she fell in with all the clichés: 'We shall have to move fast' . . . 'Speed is of the essence' . . . 'Let's beat a hasty retreat.'

What Pop thought we were doing, I'll never know. He must have noticed something about these two little girls sitting there in his wife's hats, scrutinising him from under heavy lids or through a black veil darkly. Or squinting through a pair of Grandma's discarded spectacles, and offering each other a 'ciggie' out of an old cigarette case. All the while sipping lemonade out of trifle glasses and nudging each other knowingly when Pop stirred his tea. And saying in a stage whisper, 'That's undoubtedly a signal for someone in this room. But who?'

At night we'd sleep either side of Martha Jane in the big double feather bed. Martha, a huge soft and spongey mound between us, and a convenient ledge for our elbows as we sat up and listened to her talking. Having Eileen there was the perfect chance for Martha to show off and play the part of the funny, risqué lady who taught us cheeky rhymes:

Once upon a time,
A dog shit lime
And a monkey chewed tobacco.
The little chicken run,
With a feather up his bum,
To see which way the wind blew.
The wind blew north,
The wind blew south,
The wind blew the feather
From his arse to his mouth.

And she let us play a curious game, where we would pretend to be pumping her up as she lay in bed. We'd lift and lower her arm and, as if she were being inflated, she would raise herself up by her bum until her stomach looked like a small mountain. Then suddenly she'd flop back to our giggles.

And she was sure to be up to her favourite trick of showing that Eileen was her real favourite.

I never minded people I loved sharing out their love and loving someone else as well. But like most people, I had a streak of jealousy ready to come to the surface if preferences were spelt out. Most orders of preference, after all, are kept secret. It's enough that you are part of the love of someone you love.

It ought therefore to have gone without saying that our grandmother loved Eileen, since she was her grand-daughter too. You would expect her to make an extra fuss of Eileen since she did not see her every day as she did me. But the old devil was never satisfied unless she was creating a stir.

As long as Eileen was there, my grandmother would give me the cold shoulder, not too obviously but just enough to make me feel bewildered and put out. In response I'd try to get more of her attention than I ought to have needed. There was one ploy so subtle that I couldn't even accuse her of using it. The old schemer would avoid catching my eye, as though I had offended her, while turning all her attention and charm on Eileen. She'd tell us stories and not look at me, only at Eileen. I think the reason she made such a play for Eileen was that while my cousin was around she didn't have my whole-hearted attention. I was being paid back.

As soon as our Eileen had gone home, of course, she would want things to go back to being as they had been. If, to spite her, I turned my back, ready to go straight to sleep, with no talking, she would ask if she could tickle my arm. No thanks. Was I sure? I always liked having my arm tickled. Oh, all right then if she wanted to . . .

Eileen and I went to our first classical concert together. Though once again Martha Jane's jealous scorn almost ruined our enjoyment. It was held in the vestry of our chapel. The pianist Cyril Dunn came from England with a black baby grand piano which took six of the deaconry all their strength to move. 'I'll never be the same again,' Mr Martin told me.

It began as another excuse for Eileen to stay the night. On the way home afterwards we were full of it, competing to find the words to express the effect it had on us. Brilliant. A revelation. Stunning. We would never be the same again.

Back in the old feather bed that night, Martha would have none of it. She mocked classical music. And, funnily enough, so did my father in spite of his fondness for the Mozart arias on his gramophone records. Orchestras, they'd pontificate, pronouncing the word as or-chest-rahs, sounded as though somebody was playing on Jacob's ribs.

'Chopin –' deliberately pronounced 'Chopping' '– I cannot for the life of me see what people see in his music. They must be putting it on when they say they like it,' my grandmother said, looking straight at me.

'Martha Jane Davies,' I said, looking straight at her, 'the music gives people beautiful thoughts and feelings. And you could do with some of those, by the sound of it.' I was cheekier with Eileen at my side. And besides we still felt glorious after the concert. Nothing could squash our spirits.

We lay in bed whispering over the corpulent body of our grandmother, who was sighing and thumping up her pillow and making loud snores, until she fell into some genuine snoring. Not loud snores but small puffs – she was quite ladylike in her sleep.

Quite different from Dad, who was a very noisy sleeper. We

could hear him quite clearly through the walls arguing out loud in his sleep. Shouting out, 'What the hell', 'You need your head read', 'You think that's fair? As a blackman's hair'.

I had grown so accustomed to his almost nightly discourses that I hardly heard him any more. But Eileen was trying to make out the words and was asking me who he was having such arguments with? The bosses at work mostly, I told her.

'The bosses, you say,' chipped in Martha, wide-awake at the mention of my father's name. 'I've often wondered. I have never been able to make head nor tail of his rantings. They say you are only restless if you have a guilty conscience.'

Eileen, chirped up, 'Well that can't apply to Uncle Dick. So bang goes that theory.'

I lay back in the dark with 'a fat grin on my chops' as Martha would have termed it. She couldn't get at me with Eileen there, so I was able to react without my usual solemn indignation, even for once with a touch of light-hearted benevolence.

Eileen and I went on talking dreamily about the music, and then in my case more solemnly about religion and what it meant to me. She said her father, my Uncle Crad, was dead set against Chapel, so she had never come under its influence at all. He'd be livid if she so much as mentioned Christianity to him.

At that point I made the mistake of trying to live out my fantasy of becoming a missionary. Eileen would be my first convert. I bored her until two in the morning with the richness that faith could bring to her life. Towards the end she could scarcely keep her eyes open any longer. In a last bid, I made the disastrous mistake of asking her if she would like to join me in prayer.

Her eyes opened wide at this suggestion. There was I already kneeling on the cold lino by the side of the bed, hands together, eyes up to heaven. Something I rarely did at night unless it was to infuriate Martha Jane. Eileen couldn't believe it – all she wanted to do was giggle. And far from bringing her round to my way of thinking I only succeeded in widening the gap that had already begun to grow between us.

16
'O Voice of Magic Melody'

Father with the twins

THERE WERE two possessions my father valued. One was a Kodak camera which he kept locked up in his drawer, protected in an old navy sock. It was pushed gently down the leg part only. The matted, baby-sized foot hung loose; it had shrunk too much even to take the compact little camera. I was as proud as Dad was that he owned this camera. It impressed me, particularly the way it sprang out on bellows when you opened it. It was definitely 'posh'. Like Martha Jane's fox fur.

When the camera came down to the beach with us, my father wrapped it up in several pages of the *Daily Herald* for fear of the sand getting into the works. And because of this danger, he would not let his Kodak see the light of day if there were the slightest breeze to scatter the fine sand. Or if there were a grey cloud hinting that a drop of rain might fall.

When he took a photograph, he held the camera as gently as if he were protecting a baby's head. Well, this was a once-in-a-lifetime purchase as far as my father was concerned. I don't know how he had come to afford this one. It took him years to use up a whole film. Then it was ages before the developed film was ready for collection at the chemist, and further ages before my father had the money to claim it back. But when he did have the snaps in his hand, he would be newly amazed and lost in wonder at the magic of the whole process. There was one of him on all fours with the twins on his back. I had been allowed to take that and on seeing my snap, I fully understood his amazement.

The other pride of his life was his gramophone. A wooden case, wind-up, His Master's Voice beauty. He did eventually let me put on some records, but only when he was there, too, and only after I had served my apprenticeship in the mystifying workings of this source of his endless delight.

I knew the number of turns of the handle required to wind up the machine without putting a strain on the spring. And how to clean the needle. This did not require an expert's touch – you just picked the ball of hard dirt off the point every so often. Yes, but remove the dust carefully now, he'd warn. That needle is important. His records he handled even more tenderly. Like the snapshots they were miracles of science which never ceased to impress and move him.

He and I would sit and listen to Mozart's *Magic Flute* 'best arias of', *Fingal's Cave* 'extracts from', 'Vienna, Dear City of Dreams' and 'You are my Heart's Delight' sung by Richard Crooks. And the tearful finale, Handel's *Largo* sung by Gigli.

I was rarely as moved at this moment as my father, for I'd have been busy playing the piano on the table edge. Or conducting the orchestra. Or mouthing the words of the song with arms outstretched. Dad's great contribution was when he whistled like a bird to that part of 'In A Monastery Garden' when all the birds sing in chorus to 'Through the distant twilight calling'.

When he wasn't working on a Sunday, my father would take me and the twins in their double pushchair to visit 'our Gwilym', his youngest brother. He had helped bring Gwilym up. They shared a love of my father's records from the days when they had lived together. My father used to say proudly, before their big quarrel, that Gwilym was deeper than him about music and could appreciate the real classics.

Very slim, handsome Uncle Gwilym and plump, pretty Aunty Lizzie lived in a house similar to ours in a street further down the Ferry. Three children like us – Thelma who was older than me, Norah, my age, and a baby, Cynthia, who was the same age as my brother and sister. We often called in for an hour on Sunday morning before dinner-time to give my mother a rest. Their joint would be spluttering away in the oven and their kitchen windows misting up from the boiling vegetables. My head would be swimming with desire, and my mouth watering. I longed to be asked to stay because we always had cold meat on Sundays. The whole world had a hot dinner on Sunday except us. Martha Jane had recently decided to cook our hot dinner on Saturdays. This was not from any religious conviction about not working on the Sabbath. It was simply that she felt we could get by with warmed-up left-overs on Sunday, so that she could have one whole day off. Off from what? I once dared to ask. Where did I inherit my cheek, asking such a question, she wanted to know. 'As if I neded to ask,' she added.

I hadn't had time to get to know my cousin Norah really well before the quarrel erupted. It came out of the blue. One Sunday we were down there. The next Sunday never again. I couldn't understand it. Why did grown-ups not say sorry and make it up as they told us to? When I was older, I'd pester my father to tell me why he didn't see his own brother any more. All he'd say was that he was no longer his brother. He had wiped him out of his life.

'I once had a hell of a lot of admiration for our Gwilym. He's entirely self-educated and, give him his due, he could knock spots off many a man with letters after his name. But for all his learning, he's turned out to be a bloody fool.'

So what had he said? What had he done? I begged to know. It wouldn't be fair to say, my father maintained. After all it was a private quarrel and I would only be hearing his point of view. Uncle Gwilym would no doubt have another.

I ended up knowing only that they came to words up in the woods, and that it had something to do with Uncle Gwilym's injury and being off work. I got as much from my mother who wouldn't say more. I suppose it was typical of my mother to keep family affairs private. Although she would back up my father if he fell out with someone she never wanted to discuss family quarrels.

'Your father believes his reasons are valid. I'd say he has flown off the handle, but it's not any of my business. Come to think of it – it isn't your father's either. But there you are. I believe that once people leave home and have their own families, they should get on with leading their own lives. Otherwise it's trouble all the time.'

I asked my mother why we never really saw much of Dad's family? She told me there was no ulterior motive. They lived in Port Talbot and six miles was a long way if you didn't have much money to spare.

'Mum. You and I will always be friends, won't we?' It was a statement rather than a question.

'Oh, we're quite different, darling,' she said, and neither of us thought that there was anything inconsistent about that.

17
Little Women

Street games (me on left)

WHEN I WAS TEN I began to want to help my mother in the house, which inevitably made more work for her. All the girls my age in the street had a brief craze for washing the pavement outside the front doors. Not all of the pavement, just a semi-circle – like a hearth rug – as far as you could stretch while you knelt on the doorstep. We wanted to take this hard slog away from our mothers, having been told at Sunday School that we did not have to look out in the wide world for people to help. Charity began at home.

Our mothers had to stop whatever they were doing to get us a bucket of hot water. A scrubbing brush. A cloth. A bar of soap. A piece of slate – this was optional. They tied an old pinny round our waist, which still reached down to the ankles even after it was tucked up. They carried the zinc bucket to the front door. Then all four of us – Muriel, Glenys, Maureen and I – opened our front doors dead on eleven o'clock, the appointed time. We knelt down, keeping our legs inside the passage. We stuck our heads out, waved to each other and began. We washed and soaped and scrubbed our semi-circle. We rinsed it with a clean bucket of water. Some people then liked to rub a piece of flat slate all over it while it was still damp. This lightened the paving stone, leaving a dove-grey half-moon rug lying on your dark-grey fitted pavement.

For us little madams pretending to be housewives it was an enthusiasm that lasted all of two Saturdays. But when did the real housewives stop scrubbing their bits of pavement, I wonder? Perhaps the war put a halt to it. At any rate something brought them gradually to their senses and except for throwing a bucket of water over a patch some dog had fouled, they never washed their fronts again.

I played at being domestic by looking after my brother and sister. Not for long. But I'd have them with me in the street, take them up for a walk to the park in their pushchair or I'd sit them down in the house and play school with them. I was teacher. They were soon bored, and wriggled off the chairs where I had forcibly placed them, and toddled away while I went on chalking words on the little blackboard painted inside the lid of my desk, chuntering away to myself. The twins were still a comical contrast to each other. Graham, white-haired, blue-eyed, chubby, would barge ahead rather than walk. Sylvia, brown-haired, green-eyed, spindly, wobbled forward with her arms outstretched for balance.

When my father had a day off work in summer, then all five of us would set off for a picnic. And on one occasion we took a new length of thick rope which smelt of oil to make a swing. My father told me not to tell anyone, but he'd smuggled it out of work. So shouldn't he wrap it up in something, instead of carrying it openly over one shoulder? I imagined a Bobby stopping us and taking him to the police station.

My mother told me not to worry. Dad was being dramatic. He hadn't pinched it. He'd taken it because it was lying around not wanted. Same difference, my father told her. But she winked at him and said, 'But it wasn't pinching, now was it? Mavis is worrying you'll be put in jail.'

As usual, it took us some time to find the right picnic spot – it had

Family picnic

to be a field with a tree near a stream and with no fresh cow pats
close by. But once all these conditions were met, my father threw the
rope up over one of the high branches to make the swing. We sat on
the knot with a cardigan rolled up as the seat, and Dad pushed us.
Gentle pushes for the twins who couldn't quite keep their balance.

But when it came to my turn, I called, 'Higher.' And I got the
feeling, as my foot touched the thick leaves in the top branches, that
I might carry on until I disappeared into the sky.

That became the pattern of our picnics with the swing. After
pushing us all, my father would lie down and instantly fall asleep
with his hanky on his head; it had a knot at each corner and a dab of
TCP to fend off the gnats. We would wander off and pick daisies for
my mother to thread into a chain. I'd put one on my wrist and one
on my sister's, and another on our heads as crowns. And by now Dad
would be stamping around waving the smelling salts he carried in his
pocket for his 'fat head', and trying in vain to get rid of the 'flaming'
gnats that were in a persistent halo around him. It's the cream on
your hair that attracts them, my mother told him. They're not after us.

Other times we made a day of it to the Baglan or Aberavon

beaches with our buckets and spades. We would bury our father up to his chin in silvery sand, though it was so soft and dry that it always fell away from him. With a bit of coaxing he'd be a good sport, and let us do it with the cold wet sand nearer the sea. This stayed on, encasing him like a mummy until he, with a roar, would break out of it, chasing us into the waves. Men, paddling with their trousers turned up, their braces on over their shirts, and ladies, with their dresses tucked into the elastic round their knicker legs, would tell us to watch out or we'd splash their clothes.

Sylvia and Graham and I liked to join the circle round the Salvation Army who were all in hot serge uniforms and carrying little concertinas and triangles and their big bass drum. They taught us the words of the hymns which we sang with gusto and, where appropriate, with actions:

'Dig deep down
In the Salvation Well,
Fill your buckets
To the brim,
Then draw them up with joy,
Joy, Joy, Joy.'

Another regular family outing began on the ferryboat down at the Docks. This was a large, creaking rowing boat which seated about ten at a squash and charged a penny or tuppence to take us over the River Neath to Jersey Marine. Muriel often came with us as her mother was too tied at home with her invalid father to take her out. Once over the ferry, it was a slippery walk up the gangplanks past the Ferryboat Inn, a suspicious place to our minds. Muriel had heard that smugglers in hiding hung out there. It was then an even longer walk across the golf links and the sand dunes to the sea. The beach was near the estuary and had a funny smell. This came from the mud which stuck and squelched between your toes as you walked through it barefoot. All these visits to the seaside ended of course, when the war came. And by the time the war ended, there was no longer a ferryboat.

Mind you, the family wouldn't see me for dust when somebody my own age called for me to go out to play. I was off. I hardly ever went to call on other people. I waited painfully for them to come to me. I could never make the first move. But once my friends were there, I was full of them and whatever we were going to do. If they didn't call, I moped in the house. Every day, I felt I had to start from scratch. As if just by being away from me overnight, by morning by friends would have forgotten that they liked me.

Eventually I would skulk out onto the doorstep, waiting for them to call across to me. My feet were in concrete, unable to run over and join in like the rest. I couldn't get rid of this paralysing need to have their liking for me reaffirmed every single time. I longed to be lighthearted and take friendship more for granted.

Once begun, the games we played out in the street rescued me from my self-consciousness. In the winter, we grabbed our skipping ropes and started, 'Salt, vinegar', two slow skips, 'mustard', faster, and then 'pepper', and we were off to the counts of our rivals. Over a hundred skips was easy for some. By the end of the contest the rope was so hot that it sometimes burnt our hands.

Just for a rest, two girls held a rope either end and turned it while one of us skipped to everyone else chanting: 'Vote, vote, vote, for Neville Chamberlain, Here comes Winston at the door.' At that point another girl jumped under the rope and skipped next to you while the chant continued, 'For Winston is the one to give us a bit of fun, And we don't want Neville any more.' And then the new girl would give you a shove and you had to get out of the rope. So it went on and on.

I loved the game of statues. One person was *it* and stood with her back to the rest of us who were over on the far side of the street. The point was to advance and touch the person who was *it*, without her ever catching sight of you moving when she turned her head. If you succeeded, then you became *it*. But it wasn't easy. *It* could turn round unexpectedly at any time. And when she did you had to stand utterly still – which meant not even smiling or making a face. *It* could even come right up to you and try to make you laugh, and if you twitched in any way, you went back to the start. But there were, besides, a lot of stealthy manoeuvres and daring breakaways to this game.

Boys joined in this one until they got bored, and then we played

Hide and Seek or, our favourite version of that, which was Kick the Tin. This was a chase game between two teams. A rusty old tin was placed in a chalk circle, and the first team would kick it as far away as they could, before scattering and running into hiding. The second team then had to fetch the tin and replace it in the circle before they could hunt down their opponents. It meant running like hell with chests aching and eventually ending up gasping under the lamppost.

Up to 1939, and before the blackout brought his job to an end, a lamp lighter used to come round the street to turn the gas lamps on with his long, hooked stick. If it was autumn or winter his appearance was generally the signal to stop the more boisterous games and settle down to ghost stories. They were not inspired but anything frightened us since we wanted to be scared.

My grandmother wasn't bad at the old chillers, which I immediately related to the others because one thing none of us wanted was to be scared alone. Martha Jane's stories always began by her swearing to me that what she was about to relate had actually happened to her. And that made her stories creepier. If these things had happened to her, then they could happen to me.

'See that part of the wall over there? It's like a small alcove?' she began, pointing over to the corner of the bedroom. 'One night when the moon was full – like it is now – and its beams shone through the curtains, lighting up that part of the wall, I saw the wall open and a strange-looking man beckoned to me. I felt myself drawn over and as I got nearer and nearer I got colder and colder. The air was chilly and damp and I shivered. I stopped. He went on beckoning but I did not move. I nervously put my hand up to my gold chain with a cross on it.'

I interrupted her. 'You haven't got a gold cross.'

'I had one like yours. I lost it. Where was I? Oh yes, and he cried a dreadful eerie cry and vanished into that alcove saying, "I shall return."'

I lay there wishing I had worn my rolled-gold cross to bed, and I stared at that alcove sure he was going to appear. I couldn't sleep even though my grandmother said I was safe with her there. And it was ages before she let me off the hook by admitting that she had made up the whole damn thing.

I told my friends but they were not impressed with that one since they didn't have to sleep in the room where it happened. So instead I told my little brother and sister. They had started to come into my bed after my grandmother got up on a Sunday morning. We used to tie the blanket onto the bed posts like a tent and pretend to be a gypsy family. Or we would turn it into a military hospital. Or we played mothers and fathers. Sylvia and I wanted to play very seriously, but if we gave any part to Graham he'd spoil it by laughing. He couldn't keep a straight face when he was supposed to be Dick – Dad – coming home from work. Or a soldier badly wounded in the war.

Anyway I wiped the grin off his face, poor mite, with Grandma's ghost story. I frightened him and Sylvia so badly that they went off crying to my mother. She was livid with me, and accused me of having a warped imagination.

'It isn't my story, so there,' I told her.

'Whose is it then?'

'It's not a story. It's true. Gramma told me it happened to her.'

My mother flew downstairs to see her mother and there were ructions. My grandmother was firing back, telling my mother she kept her twins in cotton wool, and what was a bit of a scare amongst friends?

'What do you mean I keep my twins in cotton wool?'

'You don't mind that Mavis heard the story. It is just your precious twins you're worrying about.'

'They're a lot younger. And, anyway, I don't think it's suitable for Mavis either.'

My grandmother told me in bed that night that I should learn to keep some things to myself. Such as, I wanted to know. Such as this next story I'm going to tell you. But I said I did not want to hear a ghost story if it was anything to do with our bedroom. I still stared over towards that alcove afraid to fall asleep.

In the fine weather we were 'up the woods'. Not playing so much as roaming and pinching apples. Creeping up on an empty house that was rumoured to be haunted. Sitting in the park shelter waiting for the rain to stop. Persuading one of the boys with a penknife to cut our initials into the back of the seat. Making pipes out of acorns with tobacco from fag ends we picked up in the street gutters – when we got them before a tramp.

We knew tramps were out of bounds to us. It was instilled in us that we must not talk to strangers. Nor go near them or we'd catch fleas. But if one managed to sneak past the park attendant for a rest in the shelter, then we – keeping a safe flea distance away – would ply him with questions.

'If I told you, you wouldn't believe me, the sights I've seen. The worlds I've travelled. I have been on pirates' boats on the seven seas. I have seen the sun rise over the highest mountain in the world. I have been up the Amazon and nearly got eaten by a crocodile. I have dined with sultans who have given me golden brocades . . .'

'Show us your golden brocades,' we begged. We were not trying to catch him out. We believed him.

'Another day. Another day. Today I shall be fasting with Jesus, the Saviour of Mankind. In the wilderness we shall be together. We shall share visions . . .'

He'd start to lose our attention after this. We'd just try him out on a few catch questions like had he ever encountered Jesus on any of his travels. Yes, he had. No, you can't have then, because Jesus is dead. We knew this would get the tramp going on and on, becoming noisier and more excited until finally the park attendant shooed him off.

If bluebells were out, we went home carrying armfuls. Such huge bunches that their perfume clung to us. We were innocent scavengers since no one told us that we shouldn't pick them. At least not until word got round that the white lower part of the stems was the food of the flower, and if we destroyed that none would ever grow there again.

We were keen on animal funerals. Any dead bird we found in the park was given a grave. Butterflies, and bumble bees lying with their legs up, were given a coffin, an empty match box, and later a short burial after we had shown teacher what we had found.

The biggest funeral in our house was one I conducted, with a congregation of my brother and sister, after the death of our pet rabbit. I led them in a proper service – trying to get my brother to read a psalm but he giggled. We sang hymns and prayed and we mourned with real tears, giving a good send-off to a pet we hadn't bothered with, except to feed it, after the first novelty of ownership had worn off.

We killed it not with kindness but over-indulgence, stuffing dandelion leaves by the fistful through the wire mesh. It grew bigger and bigger in its small hutch until one day my mother announced that it had died. We howled inconsolably. How had it died? It probably burst from eating too much, my mother said. The thought of it having burst with all that food inside it was too horrifying not to be seen. Could we see the poor thing for the last time?

No we certainly couldn't see it, my mother said, thank heavens. But she pointed to a spot at the bottom of the garden where she had already buried it, and there we congregated to pay our last respects. 'Dear God we are gathered here to ask you to take into your heavenly home, Blacky, our rabbit, who is not really lost, but gone before. Bless us all for thy son Jesus Christ's sake. Amen.'

Drained of emotion we went into the house and there was rabbit for dinner. I ran screaming upstairs.

'It's Blacky. I know it's Blacky.' My mother came up and said of course it was not. She would never do that to us. 'I promise you. This is an absolute coincidence.' And although I believed her, I never ate rabbit again.

My grandmother, in her usual way, cast a shadow of doubt over the incident by saying that pets were daft. People should only keep animals if they were able to lead a natural life. And when their time was up, they should be killed for food. You shouldn't eat meat if you can't stand the thought of an animal being killed.

So I ate vegetables and gravy and no meat for a while, since I knew I could never kill an animal. It was a good excuse, as I didn't like meat.

And here a further doubt was planted by Martha Jane who added, 'I'm sure when you are a mother, you would kill to feed your children.'

I've never met such a dab hand as Martha Jane at sowing seeds of suspicion. Or anyone like myself for fertilising them. Encouraging them to grow and grow in my mind. We were a fine match for each other.

18
My Father's Shed

The back garden

MY GRANDMOTHER allowed my father, as a huge favour, to use the corrugated iron shed at the top of the garden by the outside lavatory. She didn't use it any more herself, though she still kept her old iron mangle in it. However much she thought of it as her shed, in my eyes it was Dad's. It measured, I suppose, 10ft by 8ft and was windowless. For daylight he left the door open, and at night he hung a paraffin lamp from a nail on a beam. It smelt of its earth floor, of old sacks and of lubricating oil (Dad was a great one for oiling everything that moved or didn't). He it was who painted the outside with black tar when it started to show signs of rust. This was where he kept his bike, and mine once I had one, under a large sheet of tarpaulin borrowed from the works. He loved that old shed. It was his – and mine – definitely. And it was where we went to be together on our own.

His beloved tools, with their smooth well-worn handles were

hanging up between large nails sticking out of the wall. These tools had been his father's. He also had a small sack of rusty nails which he would empty out on the floor so that we could sift through the odd collection of bits and bobs which had found their way in there. We rarely found exactly what we wanted, but I often came across interesting things.

'This is a funny button, Dad.' It was heavy and made of brass. 'Off a soldier's uniform,' he told me. His own, I asked. 'Hell, if I know.' He looked and handed it back. 'Could be,' he admitted.

'Can I keep it?'

'Take what you like, love,' he told me. 'Wash your hands, that's the only thing after handling all this rust. But let's keep up the search.'

We were looking for a nail the same size as the one he had in his hand. He laughed when we couldn't find one: 'Can you bloody well believe it? I ask you. All these nails here – must be a hundred, easy – and not one in the damn size we want.' I was happy pocketing a rusty pair of scissors, a medicine bottle with a cork that smelt of winter-green, the spring from a torch, a broken piece of dark blue china and a cigarette card of a footballer. I collected film stars, but I could swap this with one of the boys.

Out in the shed he repaired our shoes – 'tapped' them as he always put it – and I would go and watch him. We'd have on our coats and scarves. It was freezing cold out in the shed on the earth floor, and Dad always criss-crossed his scarf through his braces. He said it protected your chest this way. In his mouth, while he worked, there was always a Woodbine.

He'd place a shoe on one of his heavy iron lasts which were in three different sizes: smallest for a child, next up for a lady, the biggest for his own shoes. But as soon as he started work he began to grumble that repairing shoes was a job for a 'trained man'. He couldn't be expected to do it anything like as well as it should be done.

The sound of him tapping would be sure to bring out Martha Jane. My grandmother's cuban heels were always working themselves loose on her court shoes.

'Who's out there hammering?' she'd enquire in the dark.

Under his breath my father would say to me with a wink, 'The King of England? Who does she think it is?'

'It's us, Gran,' I'd call back, watching my father's huge shadow, with its big nose, hover on the wall, cast there by the light from the lamp which hung near where he was working.

'Oh, am I in luck's way? Are you mending shoes,' she'd call out, 'by any chance?'

'Crafty did you say? Wait for the bit of scrounging coming up next,' he'd whisper. I wanted to tell him off for calling Gran crafty and I didn't like him for saying that she was scrounging.

'My heel has come loose on my shoe, Dick. Can you help me?'

'Leave it there. I'll have a go,' he'd say, not looking up.

'Oh you'll do it now, will you?' And before he could answer, she'd shake her shoe off and fling it over to him. And then she'd hop away on one foot. 'Careful, Gran,' I'd call out.

'She'll be careful. She always looks after number one,' my father would say.

'Who is number one?' My mother had just appeared from the house, having put the babies to bed.

'Not me, so I'll give you one guess. Mind, I've been promoted tonight. Your mother addressed me by my name.'

'What did she want you to do?'

'Her heel again. If she lost some weight, her heels would get a better chance.'

'Come on now, Mave,' my mother would say. 'In we go. It's getting cold and late. Let's have a read on my lap. Don't forget you want to become a teacher when you grow up.'

19

1939

Martha Jane's precious wireless

WAR WAS DECLARED on Sunday September 3rd and I heard the news down in the back kitchen on my grandmother's wireless. It was a big wooden set run on accumulators which were very dangerous, I was told, full of acid and not to be touched on any account.

I was sitting, aged nearly nine, on the top of her table watching my father sharpen his razor on a leather strop ready for shaving. He was in his vest, with braces dangling over his trousers and a leather belt round the waist for good measure. He stood in front of the mirror on the door of a small metal cabinet, the kind of thing which would have been in the bathroom if we'd had one, but instead hung on the wall near the tap in the glasshouse.

He probably planned to be shaving just at this time so that he could hear the announcement without having to ask Grandma. We didn't have a wireless of our own. He never used any of her belongings if he could help it, and would have cut out his tongue rather than ask her for anything.

I was only half-paying attention but I gathered the news was not good, for my father, as he heard Chamberlain's words, nicked his face with the razor. I slid off the table and ripped a piece off the corner of a newspaper without any print on it so that he could wet it and stick it on the cut to stop it bleeding.

'What's war like, Dad?' I asked, resuming my seat, swinging my legs nonchalantly. Any moment I expected my grandmother to tell me to get down as she believed that sitting on a table brought bad luck.

He flicked the last streak of lather off his face. And pointing with his razor he said, 'Don't ask me about war.'

I knew he'd say that. For I'd tried many times before to get him to tell me about the Great War, when he had cheated on his age so that he could join up. I knew he had fought in rat-infested trenches. And that he thought animals were better off than the soldiers had been. He did not wish to be reminded of it. Now he said he was bloody glad he was too old to be called up. He pitied the poor buggers who would go off believing, as he had done, that this was the war to end all wars, that they were risking their lives to create a better world for the future generation to grow up in. 'No, make no mistake about it, Mave. War is an insult to human dignity.'

The thought of war didn't bother me for the rest of that day, what with Sunday School and having tea with Mr and Mrs Martin next door. Very thin bread and butter and cake and tinned peaches and cream. And a pretty, immaculately ironed table cloth with embroidery on all four corners that Mrs Martin told me was from out of her bottom drawer and hardly every used.

And then in the evening I played cards with my gran because there wasn't much on the wireless on Sundays except religious programmes and Albert Sandler which we both liked but only as background music. Martha Jane would sing quietly along with her favourites like 'Dream Lover, fold your arms around me'. And I'd hope that Pop had once been her dream lover.

She knocked that bit of wishful thinking on the head when she told me her real favourite. It was her signature tune, you might say:

'The Merry Widow Waltz'. I asked her what widow meant and she told me it was a wife whose husband had died. So why, I wanted to know, was it her signature tune, since she had a husband. She touched the end of her nose to tell me to mind my own business.

It was not until I was coming home from school the next day with the older girls that the message about the war got through to me. My mother and father had probably deliberately played down the news in front of me. But the big girls were very dramatic about it and I thought we were going to be attacked any minute. I burst into tears and ran the rest of the way home in order to be with my family in case the Germans invaded us then and there.

After that our gang started to weave its own stories of horror. We went down to the cenotaph and sat on the steps underneath the statue of the Great War soldier with his head bowed. And there we worked out which of us would be brave under torture when we were captured by the Huns. And which torture would be worst? If they brought a snake into the room that would be it for Glenys. Spiders would do for Margaret. Gwyneth, we thought, would be bravest under physical torture. They decided I could hold out best against constant questioning.

When we heard that one of the tortures was by tap water dripping on your forehead, we took it in turns to try that one out. We stayed under the tap for all of five drips.

We expected to be invaded any day. Sandbags had already been stacked up outside the police station. We were told that we could no longer go down to the Docks for fear the Germans would arrive in their U-boats. The beach was barricaded off with big rolls of barbed wire and minefields which sometimes blew up stray dogs who got through the defences.

Fathers, we believed, would disappear to Germany and mothers would be forced to have German babies which would then be taken from them. We planned where to hide out in the woods.

My grandmother was full of thoughts about spies. She told me to watch out for anyone who had a beard. It was probably a disguise. Rita Lewis asked me if I was worried for my grandfather's safety. I asked why ever should I be. Because, she said, he was known as Joe Belgium. I said that Belgium was on our side, and, anyway, Pop wasn't foreign: 'He's Welsh. It's just because people round here are ignorant, and have never learnt their own language, that they call him Joe Belgium. It was just a nickname.'

We had much more to go on when they issued us with gas masks. They were so horrible to put on that some girls said they would rather go fast with the gas than linger inside those hot, smelly things. Shops were soon selling black or brown leather cases, which made them more attractive to carry around than those square cardboard boxes with a string in which they were issued. But it wasn't very long before we put our combs and pencils in the cases and left our masks at home.

The blackout was a much more permanent reminder of the perils of war. We knew that a chink of light seen at the window could mean a direct hit. 'Put that light out,' was said with great relish by the people who volunteered to join the ARP as air-raid wardens.

Criss-cross sticky brown paper on the windows also kept our minds on the dangers of bombing, and this was even more alarming because it seemed so useless – how was that going to keep out bombs? And so was the helmet my father was given for fire-watching. What good was that when he wore it with his pyjamas under ordinary working clothes? My father said it wasn't even steady enough for a chamber pot. As protection it struck us all as of no more use than a toy.

After being scared we all became cynical about these paltry war measures. The philosophy round our way was that there was no protection: if you were going to go, you were going to go. 'Look, if the bomb has got your name on it, you're not going to be able to change its direction.'

In the early days of the war we went dutifully under the stairs whenever the air-raid sirens sounded. Under-the-stairs was a cup-board so low that you could only stand up straight at the doorway. It smelt of dust and had no light and little air. But at first it was a bit of fun and when we were all squashed on a settee in there, it was cosy enough. If I was going to die, I wanted my Last Moments to be with My Family.

But very soon my grandmother and mother decided that if we were going to go, we might as well do so comfortably in our beds.

And we gave up under-the-stairs. Though there was one night when the action was close. A night when they bombed Swansea and an incendiary bomb fell in the Old Road nearby. My grandmother woke me up and bundled me under table in the middle room as under-the-stairs was now full up with coats. My mother brought the sleepy twins down and pushed them in with me among this forest of legs. Like three monkeys we crouched together with huge grins and hugs.

I was desperate to see what was going on outside and, dashing to the front door, I had a quick impression of a brilliant red sky criss-crossed by searchlights before my father declared he was bloody sure he had just seen a swastika sign on the wing of the plane overhead and to get back in at the double. My grandmother told him she wasn't coming in for she couldn't see how he could tell it was a German plane.

'I'm not arguing with you,' said my father. 'You commit suicide if you like. But Mave's going in with me.'

Not everyone in our street ignored the air-raid sirens. Some people were very keen on precautions. They loved their Anderson shelters as they might a caravan, turning them into homes from home with bunks and little oil cookers and shelves with spare tins and first aid equipment. They planted flowers on the roof to trick the Germans into thinking they were harmless patches of garden. Someone reckoned that the Rosens, who knocked through their Anderson to make it twice as big, could last out a year with the amount of foodstuff, beverages, crockery, blankets, battery lamps, candles and spare clothes they kept in it; and a powerful wireless which, so we believed, kept Reggie Rosen informed of all sorts of hush-hush messages.

My father was particularly impressed by Reggie's radio and made contact with him once a week for the latest low-down on the war.

I wish we had an outside shelter, I told my grandmother, for it was Martha who had announced that she wouldn't have a shelter in *her* back garden. As if her back garden was some special plot. She had never tended it, so nobody else could either, and it took the war effort to persuade her that my father should grow vegetables in it.

'If a bomb lands they're in the same boat only worse,' she used to say about the people in shelters. 'Who wants a corrugated iron coffin, I ask you? Do you think a shallow dugout with a tin roof is any safer than our house? The house might land on their dugout and they'd have longer to wait to die. At least we'd go out like lights. That's how I'd like to go, and I don't mind . . .'

'. . . if I die tomorrow,' I finished the sentence for her. 'You're always saying that.' I was lying on my back, eyes up to the ceiling, waiting for an end to the rigmarole of Martha Jane getting into bed. All that scratching after the layers of clothes had come off and the corset had clanked to the floor.

'I'm always saying that because I have seen all I want to and' – I knew what was coming – 'there is no one who is going to miss me.' That was my cue.

'Except me. What about me? How can you say that, Gram?'

'Well, yes, good girl, you would miss me for a little while, but you are growing up and one day in the not too distant future you'll be out of sight and I'll be out of mind.'

'When I leave home, why don't you go back and sleep with Pop?' I suggested. It was something I had wanted to bring up for quite a while. Actually, I had been hoping to put the thought of her rejoining Pop into her head long before I left. Sharing her bed was beginning to grate on me. I had nowhere to go in the house to be private apart from the outside lav which became my reading room with a candle or my bicycle lamp for light. And now, with the war, there was a chance of us all being blown up and I thought romantically that my grandparents ought to be side by side.

I would quite often wake up in darkness to find her flashing a torch onto the wall behind the bed and pressing things with her thumb. I'd ask her what she was doing and instantly she'd switch the torch off and say she had been looking for something. What? Oh, nothing. I couldn't get back to sleep because of wanting to see if she did it again and to get a better explanation of what she was up to.

I got one eventually. She told me she was killing bed bugs. They gave me the real shivers. But, at the same time, watching her prompted the daft desire to catch them myself. So for a while, like two mad hatters, we hunted them by torch light, topping each other's scores.

But I began to get nervous, and would lie awake, sore-eyed, thinking of these blood-filled creatures which popped and left their dark smudges on the wall. When I could stand it no more I told my mother and she fumigated the feather mattress and the bugs disappeared. My mother assured me that the powder had done its killing, and that there were no dead bugs even under the mattress. But I couldn't be convinced that they had gone for ever, and I still remained wakeful and watchful for weeks after this.

One night, both of us were unable to go to sleep. Martha Jane said with a chuckle that she thought we were missing the old bug-hunting. Let's check, I suggested, that there aren't any more. Out came the torches which we kept under our pillows in the blackout in case we had to get up. We trained them slowly over the wall. Our beams criss-crossed.

'Mave,' she said shaking with laughter. 'Can you make the sound of an aeroplane? And we can play searchlights.'

20
Nightmare Stories

With the twins

BY TEN YEARS of age I really did not want to hear my grand-mother's made-up stories any more. And she did not like my reading a book in bed. For one thing, she maintained, it was a waste of gas light. We had moved from the middle bedroom to the front bedroom which was the only one upstairs that had gas light. And she claimed she paid for the gas. I wouldn't let her get away with this. I said I saw my mother and father put more pennies in the meter than she did any day of the week. So, she said, who's counting? Anyway, I was ruining my eyesight. And books were full of lies.

But then sometimes she would ask me to tell her about the story I was reading. Like a fool I did. And invariably she would yawn and say it was childish and not half as good as hers.

I had started to be irritated by her constantly wanting everything her own way. She never liked anything that I liked. But if she liked something then I was supposed to follow suit. She had a trick that if

I were reading late, she'd turn over suddenly and catch my leg and kick it quite hard. It was a victory to her if I said, 'Look out, that hurt.' Victory to me if I ignored it.

I had also rumbled her little game over the stories. In fact, I had begun to help her along with them. 'There was once a little girl . . .' 'What did she look like, Gram?' '. . . short, not pretty, with straight black hair . . .' 'What was her name Gram?' '. . . I don't know. Something beginning with M. I think. But her name doesn't matter . . .'

And the story would continue, always with a little girl disobeying her mother and ending up with an old witch. And this old witch was often so kind that for ages the little girl forgot all about her home and was utterly happy. But after a while the little girl would start to pine for home, and the little old lady would be sad and let her go. But it was always on condition that she return very soon – or else, said the old lady, 'I will die.'

The little girl named M would go back to her mother and forget about the old lady until one day, while playing in the woods, she would stray upon an overgrown house. She would peep into the window and spy the old lady lying on the cold floor, dead of a broken heart.

In another version the girl was kept a prisoner, a poor slave made to work every hour of the day while chained to a ring on the floor. Her only happy time was when she sank asleep at night to dream of her mother and father and her cosy life at home with her little brother and sister.

Then one day, by an oversight, she wasn't locked in her chains. So, when the old hag fell asleep in her rocking chair, the little girl ran away . . . over the fields with her ragged long skirts billowing in the wind, the old woman pelting along behind her, black skirt and white apron hitched up into her waistband, and slowly but surely catching up with our little black-haired girl.

She would reach a high wall and start to climb it with the witch in hot pursuit. Below them was a railway line or a swirling river.

'Ha ha,' cackled the witch. 'Gotcha.' And balancing on the top of the wall, she began advancing on the terrified girl. But the old devil would miss her footing and fall screaming onto the railway line or into the river. At which moment an express train would tear through crushing her body or the cold waters of the river would drag her struggling into its swirling depths.

Now this may be run-of-the-mill stuff as far as Grimm is concerned. But when you know that the child is you and the old woman is your grandmother, the stories take on an extra force of their own. For me they were part of a crash course in learning to uncover the hidden ramifications of love and jealousy. I reckoned Martha Jane gave me a degree in it.

It was strange that she invariably depicted herself as a nasty person. Perhaps she didn't like herself. Perhaps she expected people not to like her, or not to like her for long, anyway. This old lady, the image of my grandmother, was lonely and bored. But then who wouldn't have been – hanging around the house as much as she did?

While she and I were playing the cat-and-mouse game of these stories, I would sometimes, just to twist the knife a little further, ask about the little girl's father. Where was he when the hunt for the little girl went on? He never appeared – not even at the rescue. My grandmother would say, 'Oh, he didn't care. He was working.' Dismissed. As was my father by her.

The main fault of my father in her eyes was that he did not touch liquor. If he had, she would have gained an ally in my mother. They could have been two suffering grass widows sharing their sense of disgust and injustice.

My mother appreciated how hard my grandmother's life with a drunk had been. No money in the pay packet by the time he came home on Friday. As a child of five she had had to walk to her own grandmother's, four miles there and four miles back, just to borrow some money so that the family could eat over the weekend.

And she remembered times when Christmas dinner was cooked, table laid and waiting – and Pop came home from the pub and pulled the whole damn lot off the table. No wonder she was bitter, my grandmother. So bitter that she could not bear to accept that my father was a good husband.

Some Saturday nights – perhaps once a month at the most – my mother and father would go out together to a dance. The twins would be asleep in their cot. I was allowed to stay up until my parents got back.

Down in the back kitchen I'd be, Martha Jane having bought me a bottle of pop. It would be on the table with two of her best glasses right next to where she'd be sitting. She'd dole it out.

'If you drink too much in one go you'll be filled with gas and, up-a-daisy-dando, you'll float out through the window like a balloon,' she'd say. She often used phrases too young for my age.

We'd settle to listen to the the 'Happidrome', a variety show which began with a song which baffled me:

> We three we're all alone,
> We're living on our memories,
> Ramsbottom, and Enoch and Me.

While it was on we sometimes played cards. If I won, Gran would produce a sweet from her pinafore pocket. And if I lost she'd still produce a sweet from her pocket.

'This is the life,' she'd say. 'How lonely it would be without you here.' I'd feel so glad I was with her and I'd put out my hand on top of hers and she'd put her hand on top of mine and I'd put my other hand on top of hers and she'd bring out her hand from the bottom of the pile and we'd move hands faster and faster for the game of towers.

The clock would strike ten and she would spoil the fun by saying something that bothered me: 'Wonder if your father is dancing with his blonde? It's the last waltz by now.'

I gave up asking her what she meant because her reply was always the same: 'I didn't mean anything except I wonder if your father is dancing with his blonde?'

You must mean something, I used to say. What could I mean? she'd ask. Some women who go to the dances are blondes. And your father might ask them to dance, she'd say in a theatrically off-hand way. So, I'd prompt, why do you refer to his blonde? So, she'd say, did I say his blonde? No importance. I knew it was important, and it made me anxious.

Martha had many of these small wiles to poison my mind very subtly against my father. She never succeeded because I never accepted that I had to choose between the two of them. It was only later that I realised she was putting me to a test.

She was quick to protest complete innocence if I ever tried to confront her. And if ever she felt she had gone too far, she would think up some treat. She'd send me on ahead to bed and bring a surprise with her.

Her favourite was a ripe pear, which she peeled and cut in slices and which I never liked as much as she did. 'No,' she'd say, 'perhaps a pear is an acquired taste.' Next time it would be an apple – more to my liking. Again she would peel it, trying to keep the peel in one long, unbroken curl from the stalk at the top to the bottom of the core.

Again, too, she'd slice it thinly and we would eat it sitting up in bed, she in her hair net and the steel Dinkie curlers, me in my pipe cleaners for softer curls. But after finishing the peeled fruit in our genteel way, we would attack the cut-off peel. Invariably a bit got stuck in my grandmother's throat and it ended with my bumping her back to get her to cough it up. Afterwards, with streaming eyes, she would say, 'That was a close one. I thought I'd breathed my last with that piece.'

Sometimes she would let me take the little top drawer out of the dressing table and I'd spill it out on the bed and go through her brooches, fastening them on my pyjamas. I wanted to know if they were real jewels. There was one huge one with multicoloured stones which flashed. Surely that was real.

'Put it this way,' she'd say, 'the Queen has *not* got any like these.'

Perhaps that is what first made me think that my grandmother was secretly rich – the beads and brooches. She had far more clothes than my mother. Many hats. A new one for practically every season. And her fox fur.

Once I heard her tell a neighbour that she wore all her riches round her neck, and I got it into my head that the fox fur was filled with gold and jewels. So one day when she went out without me I started to unpick the lining, opening it enough to put my hand inside to search. Nothing there. Now what? I couldn't sew it together, so the only thing was to put it back in its bag with the camphor balls and hope she wouldn't notice.

She didn't notice for ages that the lining was a bit undone. When finally she did, I had convinced myself I knew nothing about it and stared her out without dropping my eyes.

21

The Faraway War

Victory celebrations in Mansel Street

ALL THROUGH the war we were encouraged to buy National
Savings stamps at school on a Monday morning. My mother
either did not believe in saving, or said she didn't because she was
short of the spare cash. Whichever way, it was the devil's own job
to get her to give me some money for savings, although I felt
desperately that it was the right thing to do to help the war effort. A
soldier had turned up in assembly and said if we wanted to show our
gratitude to the men who were fighting for us, then we should save
more. And he saluted us, which put the tin lid on it.

I wanted to be up there with the big savers in our class. And I
begged my mother on the next Monday morning to give me just
sixpence, then, for just one stamp. But please some money. She
really couldn't give me any. Why not? I wasn't going to school
without it, I threatened. She went to the sideboard drawer and
brought out her purse. It was one of those with several compart-

ments, which opened up like a concertina. Every pocket was empty.

'See? Now do you see? I can't make money when there isn't any.'

I felt I had violated some part of my mother's privacy when I forced her to open up her empty purse like that. But of course it didn't stop me feeling inferior when the savers marched up to the teacher's desk to have their stamps stuck in their books. I realised it was not the cause I cared about at all. Not the soldiers fighting for me. I simply wanted to be posh.

At first we tried to observe war as a serious business down our way, but the reality of it seemed to fade pretty fast from our lives. We practised school evacuation but it took so long to empty the building that it was more frightening than reassuring. You felt you'd be under six foot of debris before you could get out. That kind of emergency training dwindled and then stopped.

We went to see a Spitfire on a stand in Victoria Gardens, in Neath. A shop window in the centre had a torpedo display. A Union Jack over a long torpedo and a swastika over a small torpedo. The swastika sign was what caught our imagination and we had a mania for drawing it on everything including the backs of our hands, forgetting by then what it stood for.

Then there were lots of concerts and get-togethers in local halls to take our minds off the war. And always including a sing-song. We knew all the words to popular songs, which we learned off the music sheets sold in Woolworth's. We couldn't afford to buy them, but we became very nifty at taking the words down before an assistant shooed us away.

Soloists in the concerts weren't always as quick off the mark as we Woolworth's swots in learning the current favourites; we knew 'White Cliffs of Dover' almost as soon as Vera Lynn did. Mainly they stuck to older ballads, like 'Shine Through my Dreams' and 'Because', which we liked all right, but we wanted the new ones. When we shouted for an encore, we'd ask for 'Russian Rose', knowing they'd have to say they were sorry they didn't know that one. Then we'd start to boo. We were awful little back-row hecklers. Or we'd clap slowly. Or stamp the floor. Or giggle. Yawn loudly. And – lucky soloists – we never missed a concert. There we were whatever the weather.

This was the time when allotments came into their own. And people followed the instruction to 'Dig For Victory'. Our apparently sterile garden was suddenly full of orderly rows of beans and radishes and lettuces. Many people kept chickens and pigs, but that didn't make much difference to the rest of us. We had to stand in line for everything, and once a rumour got around that such-and-such a grocer had tinned fruit or tinned salmon, the queue was a mile long.

We also made the most of what was to be had for free in the countryside just behind Briton Ferry. There were great expeditions to gather blackberries. My father would carry my sister Sylvia, who would never walk a step. My mother and I followed more slowly behind them keeping pace with brother Graham's dawdling, and whiling away the time playing I-Spy.

'Mum, do you know everything?' I once asked her as she guessed first go that 't' was for 'tree'. She said she wished she did. I told her I thought she knew more than my teacher and I thought my teacher knew nearly everything.

'There's something I really wish I had been. A teacher,' she said almost to herself. So I decided there and then that was what I'd become.

I told her she would have been the best teacher in the world. But if she had, would she also have been my mother or not? Come to think of it, probably not, she said, which is why she didn't mind one scrap not being a teacher.

We were good blackberry pickers. Having stripped the bushes we returned home with enough fruit not just for bottling and making tarts but also for turning into blackberry jelly which used up pounds and pounds of fruit. We usually ended blackberry afternoons waving ferns above our heads to ward off the hordes of circling flies. But that was on the good days. Sometimes the rain caught us, and we'd shelter under the trees until eventually we had to make a dash for it.

Some years later, for no apparent reason – it happened out of the blue – my grandfather asked me (and my brother asked himself) to go and pick whinberries up Whinberry Mountain. This wasn't its official name, but it was what we knew it as.

It was on a Saturday morning just after the cockle woman had called. Pop was wearing a shabby old suit, still with its matching waistcoat, over which his gold chain straddled. He took his fob watch out of his top pocket and noted the time. 'Ten o'clock. Let us see, shall we, how long it will take us to pick enough berries for two tarts? Starting from now.'

Off we trotted. Pop carried his blue enamel tea can for the fruit. Graham and I had a jam jar each. Pop also brought a walking stick. We wanted a stick too. So as soon as we left the town for the rough track up to the mountain, Pop hacked down two sticks for us with a thick sharp knife which I hadn't seen before. My brother was delighted with his and tried to walk like Pop, taking long strides. He was eight years old and had a tuft of hair on the crown of his head which always stuck up. I thought he looked like Just William.

After we passed the farm of Hywel Ddu, we were in the open countryside. Pop had been silent all the way up. It was like being with a perfect stranger. And the thought flashed across my overactive mind, what if he were a secret murderer?

From eleven plus, when there were men around, I always felt this slight hint of danger lurking – not necessarily an unpleasant feeling.

We were now on the springy, heather mountain. No person, and no house in sight. I had never been in this part before. I felt nervous. Pop told me that, because the whinberry bushes were so low on the ground, it would be easier for me to pick the fruit sitting down in the bracken and shifting along on my seat. Even then it wasn't as simple as picking blackberries. The leaves were tinged with dark red, which made it hard to see the tiny purple berries. I sank down and felt even more nervous. The bracken was so tall that now I could not be seen nor could I see my grandfather who had also sat down further along. Graham was somewhere, I could hear him crashing around. I could hear a rustle near me – could it be a snake?

My jar was nearly full when I saw Pop standing up, clear against the sky, stretching his arms up straight. The wind was blowing his hair back. The sun was on his face. He took a deep breath and said 'Ah.' Caught my eye and said, 'Ah,' again. 'This is where I feel more myself,' he called back to me. 'Up here with the birds.' And it was only then I noticed the small brown birds which were swooping round us.

Pop had been brought up on a farm in Carmarthenshire. His father had died young and he and his mother had moved to the town to find work.

I looked at him now and thought what a shame. He'd never liked the change, nor working in the tinplate works. My mother had told me that when she was a little girl, she used to take his dinner down to the works at mid-day, along with his enamel billy-can (maybe the same one he had with him that day) filled with tea, and a clean towel. Pop's other towel by then would be wringing wet with sweat.

I stood up and saluted him. He saluted me back. My brother, jumping from one hump of heather to another, missed his footing and landed half way up his legs in a small bog. We decided to call it a day. We had enough berries for two tarts and it was half past twelve and dinner time. We made tracks for home with Graham's shoes squelching and all our hands and our mouths stained a deep indigo.

The war affected people in different ways. A lot of women went out to work in munitions factories. They wore turbans and siren suits and looked as if they were really onto a good thing. On the surface, anyway. We didn't think of their partings from husbands and boyfriends. Not many mothers with young children did war work. My mother didn't and she wasn't unusual.

And some refused to support the war at all, which for all my new patriotism I never questioned. Carrie and Vernon Martin were conscientious objectors in the war. Vernon was made to work away in London where all the bombing was, and Carrie soon followed him. I couldn't understand why they had to move so far away. Some others at Jerusalem English Baptist – which many local people referred to as the conchies' chapel – had been more leniently treated, and were working on the land or in the coal mines nearby and came home to Briton Ferry every night. But I thought I'd never see the Martins again, London being as remote to us as Siberia. Even if they didn't get killed by a bomb, I couldn't imagine how they'd afford to come back. My grandmother said it was expensive enough to go to Llandarcy; going to London must be a hundred times worse. She and I between us had no clue.

Because materials were short we made shopping bags from cardboard milk bottle tops covered in raffia and sewn together, and knitted blanket squares for hospitals from odd scraps of wool, and socks for soldiers from khaki wool which was more plentiful. I started to knit a balaclava for my father at the start of the war but it still wasn't finished by the end. Clothes were in short supply and there was a lot of make do and mend. Wide inserts of different colour bands were put into skirts to lengthen them for growing girls.

The young accepted without blinking that during the war no church bells rang out on a Sunday. Older people felt it just wasn't Sunday without them. They rang only once. A very naughty boy – not all there, I was told – started them off, and everyone nearly died of fright. The bells were supposed to be kept for emergencies, and people thought an enemy invasion had begun.

All iron railings were cut down to go for munitions. Aluminium saucepans were handed in to make Spitfires. And beaches were out of bounds, though gradually we got to know where the dunes had been mined against a German landing, and where they hadn't – apart from which there were never any mines on the shore itself, where the tide came up, so that was safe enough. With this uncertain knowledge I made my way over the barbed wire, my boy-friend holding it down with his foot while I climbed over, but still getting my dress caught in the spikes. And some old man always on the look-out would shout: 'You're out of order, crossing that fence. I shall report you to the police if you go on that beach.' We ignored him. For beyond was absolute and wonderful privacy and more than a touch of danger.

The municipal air-raid shelters in Rockingham Terrace below our street were never used in an air-raid – only by us for games of Dare, Truth, Promise or Opinion. They were dark and we went inside to be kissed – sometimes Continental kisses when the boy bent you over his arm. That is until the shelters were used too often as lavatories and then the stench was beyond belief. Dark or no dark it was more than any amount of passion could take.

Flags were put up in our street if any soldier came home on leave. And we all felt shy of him, even when we had known him well, since he was now a hero, though not in hero's clothes. We thought the uniform of our soldiers was 'pathetic', not a patch on the American soldiers' uniform. We all ran down to the railway lines at the bottom of our street when we heard that an American troop train was coming past. The Yanks would lean out of the windows and we'd wave, standing up on the wire boundary fence, shouting, 'Any gum, chum?' They nearly always threw us some, and we'd scramble over the fence after it. I was hopeless at the scramble and never got any.

Sometimes they threw us coins. If they were ha'pennies we would put them back on one of the lines and wait for a goods train to run over them and flatten them out. Then we would try to pass them off in shops as pennies. My father was livid when he found out what I'd been doing. The trains were going fast and if they hit us they would kill us instantly. He'd seen a boy once . . . I'd never let him finish, for he'd always seen something horrific when he was trying to stop me doing something.

My mother could not imagine how I could stoop so low as to beg like that. 'It's demeaning,' they both said.

The longer the war went on, the less likely it seemed that we were going to die. And the blackout, which at first was affecting and scarey, seemed to slacken off and become commonplace. We couldn't remember much of life before clothes and food rationing. And bananas were skins that people used to slip on only in comics.

And of course there was still the cinema, which bore a closer relationship to our lives than did the war. The old Kin, to which we gratefully returned for a spell, was so late getting films that I saw 1930s' Jean Harlow and Jeanette Macdonald and Nelson Eddy films for the first time in the early forties. And double-bill horrors, *Cry of the Werewolf* coupled with *The Soul of a Monster*. *The Uninvited* and *The Old Dark House* with Boris Karloff, whom everyone admired because of his marvellous make-up. We thought in those days that he did it himself.

Often, if the films were X certificate, we could only hear them. We heard them because the old chapel in which the Kin was housed had no sound-proofing. We'd sit on the iron stairs of the fire escape and listen to every word of the film which reached us as clearly as if we had been inside. We'd make ourselves comfortable, often with a bag of chips, and imagine what we couldn't see, helped by a careful study of the stills outside.

We bought the chips from Lily White's. They were lovely chips in Lily White's if you liked them pale and soggy. The owner was famous. There was a chapel in the Ferry called Elim where Revival and Divine Healing Services were held. One week, displayed in the little glass case outside this simple building (it was just a hut of corrugated iron sheeting) was the title of that Sunday's sermon. It read: 'Ezekiel's Dry Bones'. So we went to the service as we thought the bones would be there. We liked it. People were chorusing, 'Yeah, yeah', to everything the minister said and beating tambourines as they sang their rousing, catchy hymns. These were new to us but after a couple of verses we could pick up the tune and join in with the loudest of them.

When they announced that next Sunday they would meet in the Public Hall because a Faith Healer was coming from London – and their chapel would be too small to hold the expected multitudes – we became very excited, and joined in the halleluiahs and promised to be there.

We were. The hall was packed. The man who spoke had a compelling voice which rose and died and when he beckoned, holding out his arms for the faithful to come and feel his healing hands through Jesus, I wanted to go. People were going up on the stage, a long line of them. Some were crying, but the only one we recognised was Lily White the Chip Shop, who was deaf. She witnessed that whereas once she had been unable to hear, now that the minister had placed his hands on her, and God had entered her being, she was no longer deaf.

'Bless you, our dear sister,' said the Faith Healer, 'for your true witness. God be with you for now and evermore.'

We were very pleased for Lily. Monday night as soon as her shop opened we were there to ask her how she felt after her experience. 'Wonderful, darlings. I can hear at last. So don't you be calling me any more nasty names when the chips aren't ready. What's your order love, chips and scraps?' Scraps were bits off the fish batter.

'Just chips, please, Lily,' we said with new respect.

'Sorry, love, what did you say?' asked Lily.

Although we were sorry in one way, we were a bit relieved that this disturbing, inexplicable Faith Healing hadn't seemed to work after all.

We tried out the spiritualists' church up in Neath next. A girl had died in our street. Rita. And we wondered if we could contact her. All we had heard was that a medium had come to Neath, a woman who spoke in foreign tongues and brought messages from the dead.

It didn't convince me. The medium was interesting for a while. A lot of rolling of the head and eyes, body swayings and the odd wailing. And one of us said she felt faint. That something had passed through her. Wind, I said, and Gwyneth Ward and I started our usual giggles. They were soon brought to an abrupt halt when the medium called out, 'Is there anyone here called Margaret?'

A woman in the front put up her hand and so did Margaret from our gang.

'A grey-haired man is calling, calling. Do either of you know a grey-haired man who might be trying to contact you. Someone who has recently passed over to the other side?' Our Margaret did. So did the other Margaret.

'His name begins with – J. Is it John?'

The other Margaret said could J be his second initial as her father was David John. The medium thought it could. She went on: 'He says he is smiling at you. Will you smile back at him? Don't be sad any more. It is very nice where he is.'

The medium asked our Margaret to stand up. 'My grey-haired man mentions you. He wants you to know he is very happy too. And to tell your mother to take good care of you.' I started to slink down in the chair in case she asked me to stand up. I didn't like any of it. I did not believe any of it, but it was affecting me. People were white and strained, hoping for a message. A lot of them looked sad. Some were quietly crying.

I wanted them to have a message. But a good one. A personal one so that they would really know it was their own loved one talking. Our Margaret, however, seemed really pleased with her communication from her grandfather. So I didn't say anything on the way home in the bus as she described the feelings on being given the message. She had gone all cold and then hot. And then she had distinctly heard her grandfather speaking the words that the medium had uttered.

My father was having his supper when I got in. My mother asked me if I wanted anything. Fried tomatoes and bread please. I was starving after Margaret's visitation. While my mother took the tomatoes out to the glasshouse to fry my supper I asked my father what he thought about contacting the dead.

'Leave them in peace, I say. If you can't have some privacy in your grave, where can you have it? I think there's something in it though – don't you Ol?' he asked my mother who was back in our room.

'I don't,' she said. 'I don't believe there is another life. When you're dead, that's it.'

'There you are then,' he said to me. 'The oracle has spoken.'

'I'm answering your question. I'm giving you my opinion. It's only mine. You're entitled to yours.'

'I can't believe there isn't more to life than the steelworks,' he replied.

'This life's enough for me without wishing for another one,' was my mother's answer.

'What does that mean?' he asked her.

'It means what I said. By the time I'm buried or rather cremated – I'd hate to be buried – I'll have had enough.'

To change the subject I asked Dad if he'd ever been to a séance in somebody's house. He had, but nothing had happened, not like Mrs Donovan in Regent Street who had experienced not just the glass moving but the whole blasted table rising. Even though he wanted to believe it had happened, this didn't stop him making fun of it. Just to give me a fright, he pressed his knees up under the table and lifted it off the floor.

22

Going to the County

O NCE YOU HAD PASSED the scholarship to the Neath County
School you went on two important missions. The first was to
go and buy your fountain pen, which was the reward from your
parents for getting through. You went to Whittington's printers and
gift shop in Wind Street, Neath, an old-fashioned shop sparsely
displaying its wares and smelling of paper and pencils. At the top of
two stone steps it had a double door with a latch and a bell which
tinkled as you opened it.

My father and I were waited on by a slightly stooping man in a
suit with sleeves that seemed too short and showed his reddish blue
hands. He was so servile, that I wanted to tell him he made me feel
sad. There was somebody like him in the gents' outfitters, too, who
made me think that he was my paid servant. A badly paid servant
judging by the rough edge of his collars and cuffs and the shine on
his suit.

But here this man was serving us with as much excitement, it seemed, as I was feeling. From the way he handled them, it was obvious he loved fountain pens. Patiently he brought out tray after different tray to show us more. Gently he picked up each pen from its satin-ridged bed and carefully unscrewed its top to show me the 14 carat rolled-gold nib. At this stage I was not allowed to touch one in case I let it fall on its fragile point.

'Before you choose,' he said, 'I need to know a bit about your writing. Is it bold and firm? Or fine and more spidery? Does it slope or is it upright?'

I answered that mine was, I thought, bold and firm and upright and wondered if that was the correct answer for this exact man. Did he approve more of fine slanting writing? I couldn't tell for he just said, 'Then I expect you are going to need a wide nib rather than a thin or even a medium.' There might have been a choice of make, but in those days, in this shop, Waterman meant fountain pen.

Then he fetched another case and a bottle of ink and a blotting pad. He unscrewed a wide-nibbed Waterman pen and placed it delicately so that only the nib was immersed in the ink pot. He raised the lever on the side of its bulging body until it was at a right angle, then slowly brought it back against the pen. We watched this operation with the respect with which people now watch a rocket launch. He wiped the nib clean with a soft cloth. A small pad made from remnants of printed paper was moved in my direction. He handed me the fountain pen and suggested that perhaps I'd like to try writing my name with it. That I did with a big 'M' for Mavis and a big 'M' for Mainwaring, and a sweeping loop for the 'g'. I had been practising my signature for just this moment, which I knew from older scholarship girls, would be coming.

'It's wonderful,' I said to my father and to the gentleman.

'Well don't be too hasty. Try this one.' But that one was mottled black and green. I wanted the mottled black and blue. I tried it, though, for our gentleman. If he had time to turn this into a proper occasion, so did I. For this signature I varied the capital 'M'. No loops. And I said I preferred the first pen.

'Well if you're sure, for it is only you will use it,' said my father, and turning to the man he asked him if it was true that a fountain pen should only have one writer.

'It's quite right that you ruin a fountain pen if too many different writers use it. I would never lend mine to anyone, and I would know if anyone had used mine without my knowing.'

'So,' said Dad, 'there we are then. You have made your choice.' (Would there be as much consultation when I chose my partner for life?)

I said I had.

The man nodded and said he thought it was a wise choice. He found its little box with the guarantee form, which he offered to fill in there and then, if we liked, and he'd post it for just the extra cost of a stamp.

My father said he would like him to send off the guarantee, and he paid him. The pen in its box was put into a plain brown envelope which he handed to me with a small flourish. 'You will mind you don't drop it, I'm sure. Best of luck with it.'

Our second mission was to get the new school uniform. A smart shop in Neath sold it, but my mother said she was going to make mine. The same shop she said sold the material – the navy blue serge for the gym slip and the white cotton for the blouse. I did not care. I was not going to go to school unless I had a ready-made uniform.

My mother said she couldn't afford it. In that case, I said, I would be too ashamed to go, and that was that. I'll make it really carefully, she assured me. I would die of shame in a rotten old home-made uniform, was my reply. Well, don't go then, my mother said, and end up like me.

I tried my sob story on my grandmother. But she said she had no money to spare. She was going to pay part of the cost of the material as it was. And that went against the grain, for if she had her way she wouldn't waste money on educating a girl.

That did it. Now my dilemma was how to say that I *did* want the home-made uniform after all. My father was back from work when I went into our front room looking black and sulky for I was going to have to eat humble pie.

'I hear you've hurt your mother. Your mother works hard to give you things, and does without a lot of things herself,' he began.

'Such as?' I mumbled.

'Get out of this room. Such as her own clothes. Such as eggs. Such as every bloody thing. How dare you ask such as. Get out and go down to your ally in the kitchen.' Livid and practically crying he leapt up as if to wallop me. My mother came in from seeing the twins to bed.

'Have you started on your father now?' she asked me. 'He's worn out doing extra shifts for you. Don't you dare start on him. Perhaps you're right not to go to that school. Go out and earn money as soon as you're fifteen and have children of your own and find out what life is really like.'

My grandmother came in and said she'd never heard any child talked to like that. One of them told her to stay out of it. By this time I was howling, 'I'm sorry, I'm really sorry I've hurt you.' We hugged. But I cried until I was actually sick. I could not stop. They tried to comfort me. Dry your tears, they said, and tomorrow we'd go out and get some of the things for school.

What did they mean some? I'd have to get everything, wouldn't I?

Everything eventually. Some tomorrow and some in future weeks when there was more money, they explained. And I howled some more about how poor that meant we were. How could I have been so beastly to such wonderful parents who sacrificed so much for me?

And yet I was still crying for myself because I knew now for certain that I would not have a ready-made uniform for school. Furthermore – and a new wail escaped me – I realised that my shoes would come from the Co-op, Wheatsheaf shoes, and not Clarks as recommended.

We bought the navy velour hat with the school band on it from the smart shop straightaway. I'd wanted to make sure of that as I had begun to dread that one of my Gran's would be renovated for me. And we got my satchel which my father had ordered from Jack, the cobbler. Officially he had stopped making satchels for customers. But this one was just as a favour for my father.

Jack worked in a bare-board shed which smelt of the Valor oil heater, leather and shoe dye. And candle grease. He ran a lighted candle along the edge of the sole and the side of the shoe where they joined each other before he returned the shoes to you.

He worked with his mouth full of small sprigs, which he seemed to have the knack of spitting out in ones. He'd catch one so quickly that you couldn't decide whether it had really happened. Then with a few sharp taps from his smooth-headed hammer it had disappeared into the sole of the shabby shoe he was repairing.

He had made my satchel, pale leather with big seams.

'A one-off, an unrepeated masterpiece,' said Jack.

My father said it was a masterpiece all right, and it would get nicer and nicer as it got older. Jack explained to me that this leather soap he was selling would give it a beautiful protection. Would it deepen the colour, I asked him.

'Well, yes,' he said. And to cheer me up, or so he thought, he said it would be ages before it really got darker, so not to worry. But he had missed the point – I wanted it dark.

Nowadays I would probably prefer to buy that hand-made satchel. But then I wanted a slim, smooth, dark leather machine-stitched shop satchel, the run-of-the-mill, the indistinguishable one. I was Miss Conventional with no ideas or taste beyond everyone else's.

In our street no one was well off, which made it practically classless. Some people had a bit more to spend if there were fewer children in the family, that was all. But now I was beginning to see that there was class distinction in everything concerning the County School for Girls. The name tabs that had to be sewn on our school clothes, for instance. You had Cash's labels printed for you in red, if you could afford them. Bits of white tape with your name handwritten in indelible pencil or black ink, if you couldn't. I could hardly bear not to have those Cash's tapes. They obsessed me.

I was hardly ever free of this shame of being poor now that I was going into a richer world. I was miserable about feeling it but, to give myself a little bit of credit, I was not so much envious of people who were better off as furious that we weren't too. And furious that my father worked his arse off, as he put it, for so little money.

'You won't want to know us once you've gone to County School,' said the girls in the street who had not passed scholarship.

'Why should it change me?' I protested passionately not wanting anything to change. I did, though, have a sense that it was a watershed. Possibly a parting of the ways.

The scholarship was a big event down our way, and everyone was so keyed up about it that I now wonder how those who failed it managed to survive. There were two clever advertisements in our local paper, one aimed at children who had passed and the other at those who hadn't. Each showed a photograph of a man in a check jacket with collar and tie and wearing specs, with not a hair out of place and an expression of great sincerity. A bit of a gent he looked to be sure, and he'd written these two alternate messages which appeared in the paper on successive Fridays. The first read:

May I again tender my sincere congratulations to the boys and girls who have passed the recent Scholarship Examination. Of course I know that your Dad's promise of a new bike has helped to put that little 'Extra' something into your work and so pulled it off. Now all you have to do is bring Dad round to choose your cycle and I will see that you get a good one.

And this was what he said the following week:

My sympathies go out to all those young folk who did not quite succeed in winning a scholarship. I am sure you all did your best (I have never won a scholarship in my life, so I am just as bad as you). Never mind better luck next time.

Now go and put your arms round your Dad's and Ma's necks and I feel with a bit of coaxing they will be coming to see me about that new bike they promised you should have.

Passing the scholarship for me was a mixed blessing. It meant leaving the nursery slopes of Primary and Junior school for the harder going you knew it would be at County School. I was excited but I felt I was about to take on something that might be beyond me. Much later, but in exactly the same way, I felt this when I was leaving Wales for London.

I had loved that small world of school, just around the corner from home. I felt well protected when Mr Griffiths, our teacher, would ask us to close our eyes while he said the prayer, which was

both comforting and oddly exciting delivered by this man on whom
I had a crush: 'Lighten our darkness we beseech thee, Oh Lord. And
by Thy great mercy, defend us from all perils and dangers of this
night. For the love of Thy Holy Son, Our Saviour Jesus Christ.'

'Amen,' we all chorused.

Here was no anxiety about work and no apparent sense of
competition, though this was something of an illusion. Watkin
Griffiths or I were always top of our class, which was fine for me,
and for Watkin Griffiths.

And we all played games together, with no champions. Everyone's drawings went up on the wall. If there was a specially good
one, we all admired it. We sang folk songs together in the hall and if
someone had a good singing voice, it was only a bonus to swell the
music. If you were tone deaf, that's what you were, and you
mouthed to the music. School plays had a part for anyone who
wanted one.

Some people, nevertheless, had a harder time of it even in this
mildest of worlds. Dai Richards had a runny nose and dirtier, more
ragged clothes than any of us. He also had a thoughtful, humorous
look in his eyes as if he were standing back from what was
happening around him. He used to wink at me for no obvious
reason from across the room. And I'd wink back.

Something about him enraged our teacher. Dai regularly got a
piece of chalk chucked at his head. One day he caught it and threw it
back, hitting our teacher on his bald patch. Enraged, he dragged Dai
out from his desk by his ear and hurled him along to the Head for a
caning. He didn't get one because – so Dai told me in the playground afterwards – he had argued with the headmaster. 'Sir' had
thrown chalk several times at him. He had only retaliated once.
'Anyway, they'd be afraid of my old man coming up. Or worse my
mother. She's been up once threatening them with a poker.'

I wanted to know why didn't it bother him that he was disliked in
school. He shrugged. I don't want to be teacher's pet, he told me. I
asked him if he thought I tried to be teacher's pet. He grinned:
'Don't look so worried. It's not your fault. You might grow out of
it.'

That moment I wanted to be in the same camp as Dai and have

chalk thrown at my head for being an outsider – which is what I was about to become in the County School.

I feared that passing the scholarship meant goodbye to endless play. Goodbye to the gangs who came home together, loitering, pinching apples, sharing each other's gob-stoppers, knocking people's doors and running away. My tea would be waiting for me at home so that I could gulp it down and dash out in the street to play for hours before bed. Or we went to the pictures together. What was homework?

There had been bad moments of course. The day the nurse looked for nits in my hair. And found them. I felt I might as well jump in the Docks after that discovery. 'Don't be silly, we'll get rid of them straightaway,' my mother reassured me. 'You'll find everyone will have them in your class, once one of you has them. They're catching.'

Was it because we were dirty? Of course not. They're a fact of life, my mother said, while she washed my hair with burning shampoo, and then ran a fine-toothed comb through it over a sheet of newspaper. I could hear the dead creatures fall onto it.

Dental inspections hadn't so far frightened me as I had never had toothache. So I walked unafraid into this one at school, sat down, opened my mouth and grinned with my eyes at the nice man. What did he say to my mother? What did this leering monster say? Nine teeth out to make way for my second teeth?

So it was gas from that hideous mask which looked just like a football, smelt foul and felt suffocating over my face. Not a pang of pain in any of my little white ivory castles and yet they were yanked out? I was gummy, completely gummy, and the traitorous dentist was saying they would soon come through, my second teeth. How could I go out looking like this? What if the others never turned up? I'd have to have a set of teeth like Martha Jane's in a glass beside my bed for the rest of my life.

But those had been bad moments in an otherwise uncomplicated and sheltered life. Now I knew that the centre of my world was about to shift threateningly four miles west from Briton Ferry to Neath. I vaguely felt excitement, but even more keenly I felt apprehension.

23
First Day in Decima's Den

Decima's Den (Morfydd, 1st row 2nd from left, me, 3rd row, 3rd from left)

I RECALL the first day at County School For Girls as suffocating. My Burberry coat was so big that two of me could get into it. The sleeves went down to the floor and I couldn't hold anything in my hands because they were well out of reach, suspended where my elbows should have been. My mother had told me I would soon grow into it. My hat was down over my eyes. I couldn't see where I was going unless I put my head right back. I was carrying not only my satchel but my house-shoes bag which had strings so long that it trailed behind me. At least, I did not stand out in my Burberry as there were dozens of other hidden people inside dozens of gigantic macks.

It was a great relief when we were all given a hook in the cloakroom to shed our outdoor clothes. At last, relieved of my hat, I could count how many girls were wearing home-made gymslips. Not many.

Was I going to grow as big as those girls who were called prefects? I could not stop looking at their legs in their gymslips. Tree trunks. And their busts? I wondered if they were backward in learning since they were still at school at their incredible age.

When we trooped into the hall I was suitably impressed because it was wood-panelled and had a large shield on the wall, like the roll of honour on a war memorial, which listed all the past head-mistresses and head girls.

Decima Jones the present headmistress walked up to the plat-form. Short, with a cube-shaped body supported, amazingly, on legs as thin as matchsticks. Bobbed grey hair. I already knew she was the tenth child in her family, hence her Christian name. And I assumed she came from a well-off family since they obviously understood enough Latin to have given her such a name. She began by welcoming '*my* town girls; and the rest of you from the valleys and towns outside Neath.' I detected the first of many such distinc-tions.

Almost without exception the girls from outside Neath were from poorer backgrounds. The well-off invariably lived in Neath or Cimla, an outskirt of Neath, where the bigger houses had been put up for the professional classes. And usually – since it was a small town – Decima knew the Neath girl's fathers.

Much later when Mali Williams took me into her home – to her semi-detached house in an avenue in Cimla – I could not believe it. Marble tiles on the floor in the hall. A cloakroom downstairs. A panelled breakfast room off the kitchen and a lounge. Mali had a bedroom, so did her parents, and there was a spare one and a bathroom. I stayed there once and was so scared that I daren't drop off in case I spoke in my sleep and her mother would hear me say I slept in the same bed as my grandmother. Or that our lavatory was out the back. And that it had torn-up newspaper and not a toilet roll like theirs.

I remember it was a cold house or I was cold from nerves. I was hungry all the time. I refused things to eat in case I made a *faux pas*. Mrs Williams commented on this and said what a dainty appetite I had.

They were out to make me feel at home. Any friend of Mali's was more than welcome. But I was too scared to enjoy it. The only people I could liken them to – they were completely different from any other parents I had met – were the parents of girls in the boarding schools I read about in stories.

And Mali called them Mummy and Daddy: the first person I had known, outside a book, to use these names. I picked this up as a tip for covering up my traces. I used it as soon as I could when Mrs Williams asked me about my mother.

'Has your mummy always lived in Briton Ferry?'

'Yes, my mummy was born there,' I said, and it didn't sound quite right to me. Later, going over everything about my stay, I stopped dead in my tracks and realised I should have said 'Yes, Mummy was born there.' Posh was 'Mummy.' 'My mummy' was babyish. I went back to Mam.

The aim of our school was to make ladies of us. Ladies did not eat buns walking along the street. Ladies did not wear their gymslips short. Ladies had good deportment – the school awarded badges for good posture. Ladies always wore a school hat without a tuck in it and without hat pins – and with an elastic to hold it on under your chin. When you were in the fifth and sixth forms, that rule was relaxed. Then you could wear the elastic round the back of your hair. The school could not insist on it, but they preferred you to wear your hair simply, and not artificially curled.

The Briton Ferry mob as we were known – a group of us who travelled in to Neath on our own special school bus – started to break all those rules. Our hair was so ornately curled that we used to pin it up high on top of our heads, and every morning our form teacher would ask us kindly to let our hair down. We would. Slowly taking out the clips that held it up. And placing a huge pile of them on our desks. Our teacher used to say we carried a steel works around in our hair, and why did we want to ruin such lovely hair as ours?

I was voted form prefect at the end of the first year, and then every year afterwards through the school. I don't really know why it continued to happen. Perhaps once the class had chosen me, they didn't like to vote me out of office next time round. I pretended I wouldn't mind if I were dropped as form prefect one year, but I died inside at the very possibility. The job was a source of terrific pride. It was scarcely a job. My duties were practically non-existent. I was supposed to keep order in between lessons. For that I would be out in front sitting at the teacher's desk and making them laugh. Loving them. And loving even more their attention and laughter.

I was supposed to set a good example in class, but in gym lessons, I didn't even try. I hated them because of the showers. The rule was strip, file shivering into the shower, twirl once, run out, dry yourself. This was all done under the suspicious eye of our gym teacher. What carnal sin was she out to detect? What, in our blue naked bodies, was she searching for? She stood looking far too interested, just like a prison warder.

The experience was humiliating. And puzzling. What was the point in all the palaver of showering when you couldn't soap yourself or even enjoy staying under the spray? There were shower curtains, but we were forbidden to draw them. And what was more, another class was usually waiting to use the gym and was able to see us clearly through the open door. The younger ones in particular used to watch brazenly to see what we'd got, making the whole business even smuttier. If they were still there when we left, we'd hiss as we passed them, 'Stare a bit longer and you'll know us.'

There was no encouragement at all to enjoy what we'd got. For the other silly rule was that we couldn't wear our brassieres in the gym. So the bigger our breasts, the more they flopped up and down and hurt, adding to our self-consciousness.

I tried forgetting my towel to dodge showering. That didn't work for long. I was made to shower without one. Dripping wet in the middle of the changing room, I announced, 'Girls I'm now on the horns of a diploma.' Everyone laughed and someone threw me her towel. If not the first, it was the most public, of the malapropisms which friends began to expect from me.

School had begun to give me ideas above my station. Some of my rough edges were getting a bit smoother. So I was out to smooth the edges of anyone else who needed treatment, like Richard John Mainwaring, for example. I decided to point out to my father when he was making mistakes in his grammar – 'Not *was*, it's *were*. Plural after a plural noun or pronoun.' I also picked him up on his pronunciation of words. If he dropped an 'h' I grimaced. That phase didn't last too long – not because I saw for myself how foul I was being, but because my mother put me right about it.

I had made some cheese sandwiches for my father's box, and he had just gone off to work on his night shift uttering his well-known, 'Bloody unnatural, this is,' as he closed the door. Or in this case, since he was feeling particularly bad, as he slammed the door. He loathed working nights.

Only my mother and I were still up, for by now it was nearly midnight. She had been helping me with my maths homework. Without warning, she said:

'I'm surprised you're still cutting Dad his sandwiches and making up his box for him to go to work.' What did she mean? I had been doing it off and on for ages. 'Yes, I know,' she said, 'but that was before you decided you were superior to him. Before you took it on yourself to correct the way he speaks.'

I was taken aback but didn't show it. I was arrogant enough to say that I was only pointing it out for his own good. She didn't lose her temper, even at that.

'No,' she went on, 'you're doing it because you've got a swollen head.' Hadn't I grasped, she said, that education did not make me better than the next person, just luckier. And that Dad, unluckily, had not had any of my chances. 'Stop it, anyway,' she warned, 'for whatever reason you thought you were doing it. Dad is far too hurt to say anything himself, and he would be very angry if he knew I had told you. I needed to warn you before you go too far.'

It hit home. What should I do to make it up to him? I wanted to do something immediately. I wanted to wipe the slate there and then. 'Nothing,' she advised. 'Just stop doing it and Dad will start to be himself with you again.' Hadn't I noticed he had been very distant lately? Not really – I had been so full of myself.

It took a while to woo him back. I began to notice for myself that he was not his usual self. He had stopped asking me about school, and stopped encouraging me over everything I did. I found this out after a concert in the Gwyn Hall in Neath to which he had come. I was performing in our display of free-expression dancing. This was

taught us by a Miss Diggle, who was unembarrassed about express-
ing herself through 'dawnse', as she put it, and I loved it.

We wore green Grecian tunics slit right up to the waist with
matching knickers and our legs were darkened with gravy brown-
ing. To the music we became trees and wind and streams, and in my
case a snowdrop emerging from the cold earth as the Sun Goddess
touched me.

I asked my father what he thought when I got home. And he said
he didn't quite know how to put it. Except he would never go again
to one of Miss Fiddle's (I didn't correct him) concerts. He was also
wondering whether as a rate-payer he ought to refuse to pay his
rates if that was the kind of rubbish being taught in schools. It was a
complete and utter waste of public money.

'You were the worst. A black-headed girl pretending to be a
snowdrop. That really took some beating.'

I took it without a murmur. Heap more on me, Dad, I thought,
and hoped that this was him getting his own back. Perhaps now we
could get back to being proper friends again.

24
Market Day

Mr Betts beside his stall

ON WEDNESDAYS, after I came out of school, I didn't go home
on our special school bus to Briton Ferry, for my grandmother
came up to meet me in Neath. And we went straight to the market. It
was a covered market. High glass roof. Big flagstones, worn smooth
but very uneven underfoot. All through the year the stalls were decked
as if for Christmas. Toys and highly-coloured hard-boiled sweets.
Welsh tapestry blankets hanging all round the stall that sold Welsh
flannel working-men's shirts. To get the attention of the owner you
had to pull a blanket aside as if you were opening a tent-flap.

My favourite stall consisted of a small square table with a white
tablecloth. On it was a bowl of fresh eggs and jam jars of mint and
parsley.

The smell that first hit you when you entered the market was of
faggots and peas. There were three rooms – open-fronted, more like
alcoves, but with coal fires inside – where they served this by the

plateful, piping hot. Each had an oil-clothed trestle table and wooden benches. On the counter were fruit tarts with one triangle already cut out to show you the filling. It was the frustration of my life that Martha Jane most emphatically would not eat at these counters.

'They're spotless, I know, but I would rather know exactly what goes into what I'm eating.'

Ikey Jones's was my grandmother's favourite stall. He made toffee. Normally a quiet man, he would greet her with, 'Here's my old faithful.' He'd had a soft spot for her since they were at school together. Gran would stop there to buy a bag of plain toffee, a bag of toffee with brazil nuts and, for my mother who specially liked it, a bag of Palm toffee, very dark brown with a white line through it. Ikey would break it up into pieces with his various-sized silver hammers. He used a different one according to whether you wanted it in big, medium, or small pieces.

Afterwards we'd go to the stall that sold needles and pins in rows on pieces of pink paper, fasteners, safety pins, hooks and eyes, elastic, embroidery silks and transfers, reels of cotton, hair nets (very fine for day wear, thick for bed to hold your dinkie curlers) and pipe cleaners, which were more often used to curl hair than for cleaning pipes. My grandmother would spend ages there. Did she need the narrowest ribbon or the next size up for her vest? And the stall holder would be just as engrossed in this momentous decision, worth at most three pennies to her.

'If you want my honest opinion, Mrs Davies, the narrow one will bite into your skin once you have washed it a few times.'

'You're right. A yard and a quarter of the wider. No, make it a yard and a half.'

After that she would pore over the transfers and ask if I thought she ought to buy the crinolined lady or the cottage on its own. If I wanted us to get on round the other stalls, I'd choose the simplest one, because next there would be the long, serious perusing of the skeins of silks. There would be at least ten shades of each of the many colours for her to pick from, and she encouraged me to help her with the choice. I liked matching up these silky tails, but not for hours and hours.

On to the crockery stall with its odd cups and saucers and goldfish bowls and chipped teapots at half price. These would still be dear at half the price, according to my grandmother who could give the stall a few for nothing if they wanted them. Damn cheek. I loved the ornaments: the boy sitting on a boulder, arm aloft, head tilted, mouth open forever waiting for the tempting cherry which dangled from his hand; and a woman with two alsatian dogs straining at the leash. I liked the folds in her skirt – how could they make the pottery look so lifelike?

Whichever stall we passed, I wanted to stop and touch things, except the laverbread (*gudge-y-fi*) – the sticky black seaweed in a shallow wooden pail that got sold out as soon as the stall opened. Martha had a regular weekly order for hers, so it was always waiting in its greaseproof paper. But she provided the brown paper bag for it to go in. With half-a-pound of oatmeal on it, it would be fried for Pop's breakfast. I ought to eat it, I was told, as it was full of iodine. You don't, I told her. That's because I don't need it, she'd retort. I'm not growing any more, well not upwards anyway.

And then she'd say, 'Cha cha cha,' stamping her feet in time and holding her hands either side of her waist. She always did this if she referred to her appearance when she was dressed up. I suppose she was good-looking and striking. Her dark hair had hardly a trace of grey, even in her seventies. Perhaps she fancied herself as Spanish or South American like Carmen Miranda. I don't know where would she have got that idea from – she never went to the pictures.

There was an atmosphere about the market that suited her (and me). She was chuffed with all the backchat that went on. There was something cheeky, brassy, risqué about the place. People were confident about the positions they held and they were familiar with each other. Lots of the women who worked there wore floral overalls as if they were at home, which added to the air of domesticity. Mugs of tea would be handed to the stall-holder over our heads while we waited to be served.

'Oh, come off it. You bought me one yesterday,' she'd say.

'I'm not doing it for nothing, luscious lips,' the bearer of the tea would answer.

'Well, if it's like that I'll have a sandwich and a slab of cake then,' she'd reply. And to us, 'He's not joking, if I know him.'

'He'll be lucky, won't he, with chops like his,' my grandmother would add, and he would slap her on the bottom and say, 'Chance would be a fine thing, eh Martha?'

'Watch out, boyo. There's life in the old girl yet.'

'Don't doubt it at all, girl *fach*. I remember you . . .'

'And you remember who is standing next to me, all ears. My granddaughter.'

'Pull the other. Go on, she must be your love child.'

'True if I die on this spot. Take a guess as to how old I am?' My eyes would now do a squint and I'd be off to another stall so that I didn't hear the next bit of familiar patter. I was getting fed up: Please let's go . . . concert's over, Martha Jane, count to ten . . . eleven, twelve, come on *now* or I'll scream . . .

I'd tug her coat. And she'd turn and ask if I wanted to do a piddle. When she first said this, I wanted the floor to open up. I denied it and looked down with a black scowl and a vigorous shake of the head. But I twigged quite soon that it was much the best plan to admit to that unmentionable activity in mixed company, for it did get her moving. I'd have admitted to diarrhoea to get her away by this time.

So eventually we left to 'wend our weary way', as Martha Jane Davies put it, having her own dogged style of repeating favourite phrases at every given opportunity. And now it was 'on to our next port of call', which was to Mrs Betts' shop in Queen's Street.

On our way out we had to pass a man without arms, begging at the door of the market with a coin box on a belt round his neck. Sometimes my grandmother would give me something, a ha'penny or a penny, to put in. But it had to be her idea. If I asked her for some money for him, she'd pull me up and say I could save my sweet money if I really cared about him. 'Don't be too sorry for him. He's got plenty stashed away.'

There were many beggars in Neath on market days and Saturdays, and a lot of them hovered outside Woolworth's. Some played accordions. Or concertinas. Martha Jane was more patient with them. At least they were doing something for their money. The drunks she brushed aside, telling them to go and have a good wash and do an honest day's work for their living. 'You stink,' she told them as they came up close to us, holding out a hand and pleading that they hadn't eaten for a week, darling.

'Don't darling me,' she'd tell them.

'Oh, you're a hard one, missus,' they'd go on.

'And you're a daft one, mister,' she'd answer back, giving them a sizeable push away from her.

'Keep your hands off me or you'll feel the back of this hand across your face, even though you're a woman,' they'd threaten.

She would take the upraised hand and shake it back – by this time my heart would be thumping with fright and delight – and she would say, 'And it would be the last action the back of that hand would ever do.'

Mrs Betts at the shop was my grandmother's oldest friend. They had sat next to each other in school. She and her husband owned a nursery on the outskirts of the town, and they ran a shop as well as a market stall. Mrs Betts served in the shop, a small, dark room with bare wooden floor and wooden drawers up the wall. I can smell it now. Mrs Betts sold seeds and fertilisers and home-grown tomatoes. And chicken feed. She looked just like a Rembrandt portrait, all browns, and she merged into the background of her shop, with her earth-coloured overalls and her nut brown face.

There was a tall chair by the side of the counter which Martha Jane sat on. Mrs Betts leaned on her counter. I sat on a sack of seed. My grandmother always had some paper bags for Mrs Betts, and Mrs Betts always made a bigger fuss of thanking her for them than I thought used paper bags warranted. 'You never forget Martha – very, very greatly appreciated as per usual. You're a pal of the first order.'

I would be kept quiet with a bag of Ikey Jones's toffee, while the two of them asked after people they knew, and remembered the old days, and my grandmother would make her sly allusions to men. 'Men think they are *it*, and we're fool enough to pretend to them that they are. I suppose you get more peace quicker that way . . .'

My grandmother rarely bought anything from Mrs Betts. A few bulbs which she planted in her maroon and her bottle-green bowls.

And some fresh tomatoes in the summer, though only occasionally, explaining that a neighbour of hers often kindly dropped her in a few from his glasshouse for nothing. It was as though Mrs Betts ought to follow suit, a broad hint which used to make we want to sink into the sack of seeds with embarrassment.

At last my grandmother would say, 'Home, James, and don't spare the horses,' and we'd say goodbye to Mrs Betts and either go home or along to her youngest brother, Willie, and his wife, Olive, the mildest, kindest woman I knew. I could never fathom out what made Olive want to please so many people so much of the time. Particularly since she seemed to have such a hard time of it since Uncle Willie had been gassed in the war and had a large part of his arm blown off by a hand grenade and was out of work a lot. Their daughter Alma, my second cousin, a happy-go-lucky girl, asked him if he would show me where they had built his arm up again. It looked odd to me. There was quite a big hard lump. I never let on I thought this, for he was very proud of the operation. He said he owed his arm to the miracle of medicine.

He and Alma always walked us down to catch the last bus. The lights were on in the houses we passed, and I tried to guess from these what stage the occupants had reached in going to bed. Front room light on still, up talking. Bathroom light, getting ready for bed. Bedroom light with curtains open, not quite ready to undress for bed. Hall light on and no others meant either a small child who was frightened of the dark or someone still out and yet to return. In the summer, through the open doors and windows you'd hear the rattle of supper dishes. Here and there a man would be outside smoking his last pipe, checking his garden and giving the sweet peas their last watering.

I loved this last bus as much as the one from Llandarcy. Having few customers to look after, the conductor would come to sit beside us with his cap tilted back and his knee up on the seat in front of him, not taking our fare. If an inspector didn't board the bus, he would let us off the fare altogether. There might be a tired, nodding drunk talking to himself just to keep my grandmother on her mettle. And, pressing my face up against the glass of the bus window, I had all the houses to look into and the rare sight of two people leaning up against a wall kissing. I noticed that the girl always looked more demonstrative than the boy – or less embarrassed.

On the short walk home from the bus-stop we usually met Mr Harris. He wore an open-necked shirt whatever the weather, and walked at an incredible speed, eyes on some distant horizon, a stout walking stick thrown forward in march time to his hectic pace, singing at the top of his voice. A man, my father said, who was wiser, saner than the rest of us. He never caught cold because he was up on the mountain top in the middle of the night opening up his lungs. And he was happier than the rest of us poor mortals put together. My grandmother maintained that the man was an idiot and should be locked up.

25
Yours Sincerely

Muriel and me

FOR A TIME all of us in our class at school were mad about autograph books. Mine was tan mock leather with the word *Autographs* embossed in gold script on the front. The pages inside were coloured in autumn tints of yellows, fawns, greens, and oranges. It went everywhere with me just in case, since I never knew whom I might meet . . . Ray Milland (who was born in Neath) showing Claudette Colbert around Victoria Gardens, maybe. It would be a pity to miss them.

Instead, I met only friends and family – and they were forced to sign up. Our autograph books weren't filled with the signatures of celebrities, who were in short supply in Neath and Briton Ferry. They were testaments to kinship and friendship.

Mine included only one famous name, Sybil Thorndyke's. She came to Neath and played in the Greek tragedy, *Medea*, on the stage at the Gwyn Hall. The whole school went to the matinée, and some of us left our autograph books for her at the stage door. I didn't actually meet her face to face, but it was the first time someone on a stage had made me cry. After this experience, I decided it was more likely now that I would become a great stage actress than be discovered by a film director and become a famous film star. 'Famous' was what I wanted to be, though for what, I wasn't sure.

I asked my mother for the first signature in my book, and dictated to her my favourite verse, the one I thought most apt for her – and the lines I would definitely write, I decided, in the autograph book of any child of mine:

> Your Future Lies before You
> Like a Path of Untrodden Snow
> Be careful how You tread it
> For Every Mark will show.

My father simply wrote:

> Yours as Ever, Daddy.
> (R. J. Mainwaring)
> 19.10.1942.

Grandma said she would never put anything down on paper for it was too final. I asked Pop when I bumped into him one day along the main road. He said he couldn't see with those glasses. He had the wrong ones on for writing. I was to ask him another time.

I went to see my Aunty Gladys Devereux – I liked going down there for she was going to have a baby. I knew because she had told me: the first person to admit it before the event. She wore a pretty smock and you could see the bulge underneath. Without prompting, she put in a perfect verse, that absolutely suited her:

> Roses are red, Violets are blue,
> Carnations are sweet, And so are you.

And it suited her spanking clean house. Her curtains, which she made herself, were in bright flowered material with a matching pelmet which we did not have. And what thrilled me was that she had matching covers for everything in the room – her easy chairs, and her uneasy dining chairs. The odd stool. She'd even used up a last scrap and made a tea cosy and a kettle holder.

I felt part of this embroidered scene that she had created, as I settled at her feet on the flower-covered pouffe while she sat with her knitting clicking away. Aunty Gladys always had some knitting on the go – dinky clothes for this third baby, lacey flowery jumpers for herself, polo necks for Ken, cardigans for Ruth, Fair Isle pullovers for Uncle Cyril. There was always a kettle on the boil, too. And delicious-smelling food in the oven ready for my Uncle Cyril when he came home from the steelworks. His entry in my book was like my Dad's:

Your loving Uncle Cyril
(Evan, Willy, Cyril Rees Davies to put it in full!)

I got my best friend Morfydd to write another of my most treasured verses which I thought was right for her since her father was a Minister of the church:

When Life's battles here are ended
And Earth's paths no more are trod
May Your Name in Gold be written
In the Autograph of God.

But I had been torn over whether to ask her to copy a piece from *Eōthen* by Kinglake – one of our set books in English at school – describing a ceremony in which two friends prick their fingers, and then press them together, joining themselves through their blood; they then eat some plain bread and salt, thus pledging eternal friendship. Morfydd and I had performed this ritual in our back kitchen one night when no one was about. I remembered we both took ages to pluck up the courage to prick our finger with a needle.

Muriel, my best friend in Mansel Street, wrote without any prompting:

My heart is like a cabbage
'Tis sometimes split in two
The leaves I give to others
But the heart I give to you.

174

There were two pages for the teachers at the County School to write their names: B. A. Williams, Pat Hughes, K. Goskar, V. Tyler, Enid Morgan, Dr W. M. Davies, Miss Blackledge, Mrs Charmion, Doris Hart. It should have been our chance to find out all their Christian names, but some still foiled us by using their initials. Instead we discussed what Christian name suited them. Miss K. Goskar (Geography) . . . what would the K stand for? Katherine? Kitty? (never) Kay? (nearer) Kate?

We hung around outside the staff room hoping to hear them use their first names to each other, and so fill another gap in our collection. Our form teacher at the time, Betty Smith, was very conscientious and wrote in all our autograph books nice long verses which were greatly appreciated, even though she took up a whole valuable page. Her handwriting was pleasing and so was the Thomas Hardy poem.

> This is the weather the cuckoo likes,
> And so do I . . .

All the same we preferred it when an entry was utterly appropriate to the writer. Since Latin was Miss Smith's subject, a poem by Virgil might have been more apt. Eva Jones (English) hit it spot-on as she always did, and just as she always sat with one profile to us in class because that was her best side.

> The quality of mercy is not strain'd,
> It droppeth as the gentle rain from heaven
> Upon the place beneath.

Freda Poley, the best artist in our class, drew a painted head of an old-fashioned young woman who had Titian hair and wore a flowered straw hat. But I also wanted her to write a poem she had made up:

> *Autumn*
> Swift couriers with gale-blown hair
> And streaming cloaks of royal red,
> Fleet huntsmen on an open plain
> Pleased to have left the woods behind;

Sunbeams which rush like music
From the frosty harp of heaven;
Such is the glorious death-flight
Of gaily-dying leaves.

Gwyneth Ward wrote:

Some albums are red, some albums are blue
In Africa, albums are black

She would!

Jean used the trick of turning down the corner of a page, and over the triangular little flap drawing a heart. She also wrote a message:

Do not open.

When I did open it all the same, underneath was written:

Now you have broken my heart, boo hoo, love Jeanette Philips.

I wanted Ann Griffiths to write this verse in my book because she had a pretty garden:

The kiss of the sun for pardon
The song of the birds for mirth
One is nearer God's heart in a garden
Than anywhere else on earth.

On the last page of my book, as in almost everyone else's, Norma W. had written:

By hook or by crook
I'm the last in this book.

But Jill Tonner had added underneath in very tiny letters:

By powder and paint,
I'll see that you ain't.

When I was asked to put something in a friend's book, I would draw either Mae West with an hour-glass figure, dangling earrings and a slit up the front of her dress, or Carmen Miranda with an hour-glass figure, dangling earrings, a turban of fruit salad and a split up the front of her dress. They became my trademarks because they were also the two stand-up imitations I could do – along with Vera Lynn, though I couldn't draw her.

Our autograph books were a part of our Romantic notions of Friendship. We sought out quotations about Friendship:

> Grow old along with me,
> The best is yet to be.

We were forever trying to define it:

> Friendship is to know all about someone and to love them just the same.

Friendship meant dressing alike. Liking the same film stars, eating the same food. Doing everything together. Parting only at the very last possible moment, even if it meant courting a row at home for coming in late. My mum would say she couldn't think what we found to say to each other all this time.

Before we separated we would decide on a time – say, 11.00 at night – when we would be on our own in our bed, and we would arrange to think hard about that other person. To see if we could pick up what she was thinking.

Lying alongside my grandmother, I found it difficult to stop her talking to me. I did not want to tell her about our telepathy experiment or she'd have mocked it. I used to say that I needed to memorise something so would she be silent, for, say, twenty minutes.

Then I thought hard: one night it was to be a quotation that we arranged to think about. Mine was: 'Be good, sweet maid, and let who can be clever'. And I had dropped enough hints to Morfydd for her to get my thought-transference clearly enough. She did. We were convinced we had telepathic powers – especially since I guessed what she had been thinking. Be good sweet maid etc.

But these all-enveloping Friendships had not yet enabled me to tell a single soul that I slept in the same bed as my grandmother. At this age I would simply have lied if anyone had asked me, but nobody did so I never had to. Instead, I lived in dread of one of my friends finding out by chance. I felt silly about it. Undignified.

Ashamed. And even though I started to realise that we all harboured the same secret longings and hopes, I knew for a fact that none of my friends was in the same stupid fix as me. It had become a guilty secret which I didn't want anyone to discover.

26

Bikes – Our First Wings

On my first bike

WHEN I WAS about twelve my mother and father said they could manage to buy me the two-wheeler bike which I had been nagging them about for ages. But I had better learn to ride one first.

My father took me into the lane behind our house and told me to swing my leg over the bar on his bike and I'd soon be off. I was. Off and onto the floor, only grazing the leg a bit but making a huge fuss up to amputation level. Meanwhile my father said that if I didn't get straight back on I would never learn to ride a bike at all.

I got back on. It was not easy. His bike, a BSA racer, was a drop handlebars job with a high seat even after it had been adjusted to its lowest point. It was also the longest, hardest ridge of leather that you could imagine. We had heard you could lose your virginity on a bike. Exactly how, we didn't know. But I had a rough idea after these lessons.

I got there in the end with him holding the seat and running with me; then letting go a little, and me wobbling and telling him not to let go since I wasn't balancing. Then he let go for longer, and finally he let go completely and I was off, making it up and down the street on my own. I wasn't too keen on the picture of myself bent earnestly over the handlebars as though racing a mile. All I was prepared to do was tootle around a bit each day after school. Not risking the main road.

I had felt there was something rude about racing bikes ever since a man on one exposed himself to us. He was sitting on his racer and leaning against a lamppost eating sweets from a bag as we passed.

'Like a sweetie?' he called out.

We must have been about nine or ten at the time and had been warned at school never to take sweets from a stranger in case they were doped. There had been something in the papers about it, a case of men taking advantage of children. It was all a bit vague. But when he offered, we hesitated. Why not? He seemed a nice chap in his plus-four trousers and Fair Isle jumper. We moved nearer and then saw what we saw. And ran away until we were out of sight. Then immediately we wanted to go back to see if we had really seen what we thought we had seen.

He was still there but now he was smiling and beckoning to us.

Rita said, 'You dirty old man, showing us your old thing.'

'Come closer and you'll see things better,' he invited.

We were off, except for Rita who was still calling him a dirty old man. She was indignant. The rest of us were scared.

But we couldn't quite leave it alone and went back giggling for another peep at this phenomenon. He had gone, and we wondered why he had done it, and also whether we should tell our mothers? What could we say he had done? Taken out his willy? We couldn't say that. What could we say, then? Rita told her mother while we were still debating because she said dirty old men had to be reported.

So we all had to troop down to the police station to give our descriptions of him. We got the clothes right, but we argued about the colour of his hair. And when one girl said he looked like a dad and was on a racing bike, I died at the thought, which I could have killed myself for having . . . what if my dad ever went on his bike to another town and did what this man had done? And what had this man done? According to the police, 'He was a dangerous customer. We'll find him. Can't have gone far.' He never seemed a dangerous customer to me. Just unfathomable.

As did the next chap up in the woods who behaved in the same way as the cyclist. We were ready for such men by this time so we behaved more boldly. We all chanted, '*Ych-a-fi*, you ought to be ashamed of yourself, you dirty old pig.'

'Put it away. We're not interested. Boring, boring, old man snoring,' we jeered. We really went to town with this one. 'If you don't watch out, we'll report you to the police.' He got up, buttoning his flies, and fled from the scene of the crime.

My own two-wheeler bike transformed my life. My mother and father sent away to a firm called Graves for it, paying off the cost by Postal Order. I loved it, even though it was a utility model painted black all over. No shining chrome. That was because of the war effort and not because we were unable to afford a shiny one. So I accepted it with no more than a sigh for the chrome.

I loved it most of all because it gave me independence. Where before I could only break out of my home ground by going on the bus (if I had the money), now, as a free-wheeling bicycle owner, I could ride as far as my strength and the hours of daylight would let me. It was an instant release.

My constant friend Morfydd lived some way away but in future I would be able to meet her outside school hours. Nearly all our gang had new Graves bikes. Except for Morfydd with her second-hand Raleigh. And Gwyneth Turner who had a bone-shaker inherited from her cousin. It was harder work than ours but looked classier.

The day we set off together for the seaside, bathers strapped on the back, sandwiches in the basket on the front, on our tod, no train, no parents, was like growing up overnight. We didn't make it to the seaside that time as we found we had taken on too many miles. Anyway we faced a strong wind going and had to keep getting off. Our legs ached and Jeanette's cardigan fell from her waist where she had tied it and got trapped in the back wheel. It took ages to extricate, and we and the cardigan got covered in oil.

Soon we could manage those miles easily enough, and when we

rounded the last bend and saw the sea, we felt it must have been as good for us as it had been for Christopher Columbus to spy land.

The heady sense of freedom, of innocent joy we felt was what H. G. Wells had written about in *The Wheels of Chance* as long ago as 1896, though it was many years later that I discovered the book and it took me back to those seaside rides. His hero was setting out on his first holiday . . .

> At the crest of the hill he put his feet upon the footrests, and now riding moderately straight, went, with palpitating brake, down that excellent descent. A new delight was in his eyes, quite over and above the pleasure of rushing through the keen, sweet morning air. He reached out his thumb and twanged his bell out of sheer happiness.

Whenever we went down a long hill we would laugh and shout to each other, and as we grew more daring on our machines we'd half turn in our saddle and wave to make sure the rest were feeling as exhilarated as we were. With so few cars on the road we could line up two or three abreast and chatter as we rode along one-handed. In those days, we loved the wolf whistles when our skirts blew up. We felt so free we hardly knew that we weren't as liberated as we imagined. We'd be singing the latest Deanna Durbin song: 'I'd love to climb an apple tree'.

Now that my bike took me up to Morfydd's, I could call on her after homework to continue the endless talks which previously had been restricted to the school yard. We were partners in tennis, which became our great pash. We'd whizz up to the Town Field's courts and challenge Sheila, Gwyneth, Marjorie Rees and Margaret Williams who was nicknamed Maggie Boots because her mother kept a shoe shop. All in skimpy, white, tennis dresses, monogrammed with our initials on the breast pocket if we could be bothered to embroider them.

Marjorie and Maggie were only a bit older than the rest of us, but they seemed much older. They went to dances on a Saturday night; we were still too young to be admitted. I don't think they were old enough either but they got in because they dressed as if they were older.

We were only allowed to buy a spectactor's ticket and sit upstairs in the gallery around the hall. Enviously, chin in hands, leaning on the rail, I ached to be down there in somebody's arms for the last waltz. I'd given up trying to sneak in because if you were seen, the chap on the door would come right up to you when you were dancing and poke you in the back with his finger and say 'Out. Now. I mean, now. I'll report you to the police if I catch you again.'

Sometimes Maggie and Marjorie's latest flames, whom I had seen dancing with them would come up to the courts to walk them home after tennis. The boys teased the rest of us as if we were their kid sisters.

'I can see your knickers.' But if Maggie Boots bent down there would be a low wolf whistle.

They were up to far more than we were, you could tell for sure by the way they walked off with the boys back home through the woods. Or were they? We never knew.

We kept up our teasing of the boys until they were out of sight, pathetically trying to get their attention: 'Don't do anything we wouldn't do.' And they, good-humouredly, shouted back, 'Bet that gives us plenty of scope, then.'

I longed for the sophistication of Marjorie and Maggie. I wanted their fellows to see me as they saw them. But, unable to join them, we called them flirty. They were a bit fast for our liking, we said, as if we disapproved.

My earnest tennis ended, though I went on playing for fun, after I competed in a tournament at Llandarcy against my cousin Eileen. I didn't see her out of school now that we both went to the County. And since she was a year younger than me, we didn't really meet at school either. So, to make up for missing out on each other's company, I went up to stay for a few days.

Her village held a tournament while I was there and my uncle asked if I, as a visitor, could be allowed to play. They called me Mavis Davies, which was no name to dignify a serious tennis player. In fact, I believed it was insisted upon as a handicap for me as a non-club member. Why else should I have to take Eileen's surname to enter their tournament?

Perhaps the dotty name put defiance in me but I got to the semifinals against Eileen who was a very good player. I was erratic. But because they cheered all her shots and were silent over mine (except for my loyal Uncle Crad and he, I knew, must have been secretly willing Eileen to win) it egged me on. I beat her.

That did not go down well at the Llandarcy Tennis Club. Here was I, outsider Mavis Davies, in the Grand Final. It must have cheered them up a bit that I was now up against a girl three or four years older than I was. She must have been fifteen to my eleven. And more than a foot taller.

The cheers, the urgings on for her, the 'Oh, bad luck' when she missed a shot were enough for me. I stuck out my chin, I gritted my teeth, I turned my eyes to steel, seeing nothing but the ball, and I set out to show them.

It was a close match. They announced me as the winner to applause that kept time to the Dead March. The first prize was £3 in Savings Certificates, £2 for second, £1 for third. But owing to the fact that I was a visitor, they announced, and not a paid-up member, they thought it only fair that I should get half the prize. I don't know who got the other half. And I didn't care. I wished I'd had the nerve to refuse that prize. If only I'd had the wit then to walk off, head held aloof, as girls in school stories did so that no one should see the scalding tears that threatened to run down their cheeks.

At that moment of victory I felt isolated. No one there was pleased. Eileen came up and hugged me but I knew the gesture was half-hearted – she was terribly disappointed at losing and thought my victory a bit of a fluke. My uncle offered to make the money up to me. No – I was very agitated at this suggestion.

I had never felt so home-sick as that night. We all felt bruised and impatient. They wanted me to go, I thought. I couldn't wait to get back and tell my father, who I knew would get his hair off.

And when I told him later, he did: 'Those Llandarcy snobs should be reported for doing what they did to you. It was daylight robbery. I have a good mind to go and demand your rightful prize from that gang of – who the hell do they think they are? I'm not letting this go forgotten.' But when he had calmed down, and we had decided it was too late to do anything, he asked with a chuckle:

'But bloody hell, Mave, you'll go far one day if you can keep this up. I would never have backed you against our Eileen. What got into you?'

Whatever 'got into me' as I played that day never 'got into me' again. Victory had not been worth having. I had ended up feeling that no one liked me. And that I could not take. I'd rather have lost. Anyway, I chose to become a clown at sport after that, rather than be seen as someone who was set on victory. Eileen went on to be captain of the school sports.

27
Fantasies

We dreamt we were princesses

THE YEARS from eleven upwards were filled with fantasies. They were more real than what was going on in my life. I had become a great fantasist even before I knew the word or what it meant. When very young, but old enough to be trusted with a candle by which to read in my bedroom, I would see in its flame a pretty butterfly which would take me like Thumbelina on its back and carry me off and away over the roofs of our smoky little industrial town to the green meadows and mountains beyond. And a turreted castle. Easy to see where that one came from. I was simply reliving fairy-book illustrations.

Later I had a fantasy that I was a princess. On the Births, Deaths and Marriages page in our Holy Bible (the big one with two clasps to lock it up), I noticed from the dates that I had been born before my mother and father were married. And since the stork and the Queen would deliver babies only to married couples, it must mean that I was not their child. I looked at their faces and then, in a mirror, at mine. No resemblance whatsoever.

It wasn't easy to convince myself that I was a princess because princesses always had golden tresses. Then I remembered Snow White, and for a while based my fantasies on her. I didn't know what to make of the dwarfs. So I just left them out.

Eventually I read an even more rewarding version of my fantasy in Angela Brazil:

I've always thought I'd like to be a foundling. It is so delightfully mysterious to be picked up from a wreck on the sea shore . . . and nobody knows who you are, or anything about you. They always keep your beautiful baby clothes and the gold locket round your neck with the portrait inside, and then, when you are grown up, you turn out to be the only daughter of a Duke, who has been mourning you ever since you were lost.

I was relieved to find that other people had the same daydreams as I did and revelled in mine all the more once I knew they were shared. I started to look for new plots in books and films which I could adapt for myself. A gipsy queen had left me in a basket on my mother's front door. And now she – my real mother – was wandering the world barefoot with a sad, mysterious look in her eyes. Never staying anywhere very long, singing love songs and dancing wild dances which entranced men. Yet all the while her heart was breaking over her dark-eyed baby girl.

I'd make myself cry over this one. I'd be silently weeping in bed (with my grandmother fast asleep beside me) because by this point I was the gipsy mother, since her part was meatier than mine.

I had enough of a hold on reality, though, to worry that I might not belong to my mother and father. Finally I showed my mother the entries in the Bible. Oh, that was just a slip of the pen. She and Dad were married in December 1929, and I was born in October 1930. This unromantic truth, confirmed years later by seeing the marriage certificate, put paid to this piece of make-believe.

I was both glad and sad to relinquish it, for I had looked forward to embroidering the details each night. But there were more where that came from.

When I liked a book I wanted my friends to read it quickly so that we could compare ideas about who was like whom in it. We flattered ourselves by telling each other the characteristics we shared with the heroine.

Little Women gave us the most scope, for between them the four girls possessed all the qualities needed to find a match for each of us. Mostly we wanted to be Jo, I certainly did; but I willingly renounced that role once I had been unanimously voted most like Cathy in *Wuthering Heights*. This vote sent me into a frenzy of imagining. I had been given a major part. A perfect one. A tragic figure, someone dying of consumption, was just up the street of someone who loved making herself cry.

I had a field day once I had seen Merle Oberon play her in the film. I stood in front of the dressing table mirror pulling the sides of my eyes so that they looked Oriental like hers. And I made my hair look wild.

The Mills and Boon books fired my imagination with clichés. I tried to be a cut above them. I wanted to meet a classier kind of person in my fantasy, not their old run-of-the-mill Counts, doctors and horse-riding squires.

I was a lone lady traveller who'd meet a sheik in his harem or a wild gipsy bandit by the fire in his mountain cave. My pillow was often in my arms as I was swept up by these hot-blooded heroes. But I always had to be careful that Martha never caught on. I didn't want her barging in.

My fantasy only ever ventured a little ahead of reality so that my lover's lithe bare body – in a silk-walled tent on mounds of satin cushions – would draw near to mine, his strong bronzed arms would hold me down and then, as in romantic novels, there would be a row of dots. I would call it a night and go to sleep legs crossed.

It was difficult exploring these worlds with Grandma beside me. I didn't even start to do so until she had gone to sleep. I was finding it harder to talk to her these days. Her huffing and puffing over my father, and pulling faces behind his back, had become ludicrous. She had grown careless about it and didn't seem to mind who saw her. I was embarrassed both for my father and for her – and for myself. But I couldn't say anything about it because nothing was ever openly admitted.

We couldn't fall back on talking about the story of her life. I knew a little about it, but she quickly lost interest when I asked for more details. Among the fragments I picked up was that her father had been a miner, and had once been trapped underground by a collapsing roof. He'd been lucky to escape with his life but had lain, she told me, next to his dead mates for hours.

He had been a man with a wonderful head of raven-black hair, my great-grandad. But after this disaster he woke up to find all his hair on the pillow. And when it grew again it was white as the driven snow.

She said they owned a horse. I wanted to imagine her as Lorna Doone riding wildly over the hills but no she said she had been too scared to get on its back. Otherwise they were poor. Her parents had to work harder than anyone ought. 'Drab lives,' she said, 'perhaps not so drab as mine.'

I tried to change the tone of this conversation by asking her where had she met Pop? She said she couldn't remember and she wished she had never set eyes on him: 'He has wasted my life.' She stated this so emphatically that I should have dropped the subject. Like an idiot I didn't.

'But you're a mother with three children,' I said. I was a great believer that we children were godsends.

'They're not all happiness, I can tell you,' she answered. 'I had two more, as you know.' Her voice made me feel sad for her. A baby had died at birth and then a little girl of at least eight.

'Alma was the most darling little girl you could ever have met. Your mother was only very young when her sister died but I don't think she ever really got over her death. Your mother loved Alma, more than anyone else in the world.' Did you, Gran, I wanted to know. 'I loved her more than anyone else once she'd died. You do because you miss the dead such a lot. I seemed to mourn her so much, I forgot the living.'

Had she forgotten Pop?

My grandmother sounded bitter again: 'Fat lot of good your children are to you once they marry.' I argued with her that she still had my mother with her. She's good to you, I said.

She asked me how did I arrive at that conclusion. 'She's company,' I said.

'Since when?' she asked.

'She helps you with the house, and she pays the rent.'

'The rent!' she said, to my utter astonishment. 'They don't pay rent. Well, hardly any. Mind, not that I want that repeated. I'm glad I can help out. It means they can buy all the more for you and you are the whole world to me.'

'Gran, I don't understand you. Don't you like anyone but me? Mam, Dad, you don't seem to. In fact I sometimes think you hate Dad.' This came out before I could stop myself. I hadn't meant to go as far as this.

She gave a false laugh. 'You are a funny little thing, you are. What an imagination. Too much imagination, my girl, is not healthy.'

'You haven't denied it,' I told her.

'I'm too shocked. Now I don't have to say I love him to satisfy you, do I?'

'So what is there to hate about him, I ask you?'

'He's just a man.'

I suggested she might not like men at all. Anyway, whatever she said, I knew she didn't like my father.

'It's mutual then,' she said 'he definitely doesn't like me.'

I wanted to know who started it. I told her I thought she was hardly even civil to him. And she got very angry at this and told me there was nothing wrong with her manners. She didn't pass wind in public. She didn't blow her nose in a bowl of cold water.

I immediately sprang to my father's defence. He had a bad stomach from the war. And he cleared his nose from all the dust of the works. So would she if she worked in the steelworks.

'You're very ready with excuses for your father. I wonder if you defend me when he runs me down.'

'He never does,' I said.

'Pull the other one. It's got bells on it.'

'You can't stand him because he doesn't drink like Pop and he's good to Mam, and Pop wasn't good to you.' I was practically in tears.

She turned on her side away from me and went silent, and I lay there immediately sorry for what I had said. Oh, lord, help me. Her shoulders were shaking. She must be crying. I turned towards her back and put my arm over her and snuggled up to her.

'Gran, I'm sorry.' Still no answer and her shoulders shook some more. 'Gran, I love you.'

'Sure?' she said with a sniff.

'Positive.'

She swung round and she was laughing, as she had been all the time. I was furious with her. She had such an ability to wriggle out of anything I wanted to discuss.

'Look, what I have got here,' she said. 'Smuggled it up for you.' There was no need at all for her to smuggle food, but she enjoyed the conspiracy of it. 'A nice juicy blood orange – half for you, and half for me.'

And up she sat, her hair in a plait down one shoulder, peeling the orange. 'Now tell me, what do you think you are going to be when you grow up. Something imaginative.'

Maybe an actress I'd say – like you, Gran, I registered silently.

28
Trouble in the Vestry

Kissing Derek

I WAS JUST into my teens when Mary, a friend at school who lived in the valleys, asked me to her chapel social because Peter, one of the boys in her gang, wanted to meet me. I would have to stay the night with her, which was exciting. Not so good, however, was the fact that we had rehearsals for a play after school, and so we would be turning up for the social late and still wearing our school uniforms.

On the way there in the train we moaned that no one would pick our number in Postman's Knock. 'You'll definitely be all right,' I assured her. 'You know boys think you're attractive whatever you're wearing. They queue up for you.'

'What about you, then? You know Peter's got a big crush on you already.'

'Not after seeing me like this.'

We got there as they were playing Catch the Plate. A tin plate was spun in the middle of the circle, a number was called out, and whoever's number it was had to dash and catch the plate before it stopped spinning. Mary's number was called and as she bent to pick up the plate, it occurred to me that our short gymslips showed our knickers and the top of our suspenders and stockings. Something that did not seem significant in school with only girls around.

I had just registered this when the game changed to Postman's Knock. After a while my number was called. I went out to see what boy had called it. No boy there, but one of the chapel deacons. He caught hold of me – this ancient twenty-eight-year-old man smelling and tasting of tobacco – and he kissed me as I had not been kissed before, with his tongue in my mouth. It flashed through my mind that this was the way, wasn't it, that you could have a baby? Certainly it could make you unconscious. I couldn't breathe as it was. Released, I patted my hair straight and tried to pull down my very short gymslip, and avoided his eye as though I were the guilty party.

'Lovely,' he said. Was this a reference to that kiss? 'Call your number now. Try lucky 13,' he suggested.

Like a fool I called out 'thirteen', and there was the other deacon – this one even older. He was in charge of the club and was just like one of those uncles who are always cracking corny jokes you'd heard before. He came outside and closed the door, chuckling and rubbing his hands together and saying this was his lucky day. I was flabbergasted. But I had no time to be, for here was the big grab again, and a similar, but clumsier kiss and my pushing him away with an embarrassed laugh. Then he called out his number! Mary's, of course. And I couldn't warn her except with frantic signals of the eyes.

We walked back to her house afterwards, she with her boyfriend and me with Peter. Nothing happened. We loitered under the lamppost and arranged to meet inside the Empire Cinema in Neath the following Saturday. First one there was to keep seats for the others.

Once inside Mary's house we couldn't wait to get up to her bedroom to talk. But her mother had made us cocoa and wanted to know about school and the social. Was Mr Thomas there? We kicked each other under the table. 'He's so good with you young people.' We kicked harder. As soon as she could Mary yawned and suggested that we turn in. Yes, said her mother; there was school in the morning.

No sooner had we shouted down our goodnights and closed the bedroom door than we flung ourselves face down on the bed to stifle our giggles. Lying there on our stomachs we told each other everything that had happened in minute detail, and then said it over again at least once more.

Mary admitted she had actually enjoyed the kissing. She thought I would have, too, if I had relaxed about it.

'They were nearly the nicest kisses I've had,' she said.

'Nearly the nicest?' I jerked up for a better look at her. I wanted to know if any boys nearer her own age had kissed her like that. Maybe, she said. Maybe meant yes. Who? I wanted to know, but it took a long time getting it out of her. Then she told me that her older brother's friend, who played rugby for the town, had kissed her. And he went even further.

I was now sitting bolt upright holding a pillow tightly in front of me. I demanded more details.

'Well, he touched my breasts,' she paused. I was not breathing. 'Not only outside . . .'

'Inside your brassiere?' I could hardly ask it. 'You're joking, Mary.'

'I'm serious, Mavis,' and she giggled. 'I would have let him do anything after those long kisses. You know the ones that go right through you, so it pains you in between your legs.'

I was lying on my stomach again, my head reeling. I turned to peer covertly at Mary through my hair, which was partly concealing my face. I tried to fathom her, size her up. What was the difference between us? She looked more placid, at first glance. If you didn't like her, you might have called her mousey. You'd say if you saw her on the street that she was a bit old-fashioned. She never wore colourful clothes. And never any lipstick. I wore some, at the pictures, where no one could see. So why hadn't I enjoyed my first dangerous kiss?

Mary, with surprising primness, then went on to say that she didn't think it right for the two deacons, who were married men after all, to make passes at us. It was fine just this once as a bit of a lark, but she'd not let it happen again.

And there was I hoping it would happen again as I felt I had missed out on something.

Mary was now wondering if the reason our deacons had been all shaky and worked-up when they kissed us was that they didn't do it much at home. I didn't blurt out that as far as I was concerned it was inconceivable that mothers and fathers ever did anything along 'those lines' at home or anywhere else.

We were in our two beds by now. And Mary asked had I ever heard my mother and father making love? She had, she said, and more or less seen them once. One night she had felt ill and had gone to her mother's bedroom. 'I opened the door without knocking. My father was on top of my mother.'

It was now clear to me why Mary had enjoyed those kisses. She had inherited a passionate nature from her parents. I was pretty sure my parents didn't do anything – crowded as our bedrooms were. And suddenly I felt sorry for them. Was that why my father flared up so often? I was quite pleased with these thoughts. It meant I was more mature than I had been just two minutes before – when I hadn't believed married people ever did 'it'.

I could not get to sleep for ages. I wanted to relish being in a bed of my own for the first time ever. And I was thinking about 'going further', as Mary had.

I was just dropping off when Mary said, 'And something else I forgot to tell you. I found something in my father's drawer that he wears so that my mother won't have a baby.'

That remark put paid to sleep completely. What on earth was it like, I wanted to know? Let's creep in and have a look, Mary said. With my heart in my mouth (and nibbling at the corner of it) we stole in. The bedroom was frilly. It smelt of lily of the valley talcum powder. When she opened the top right dressing table drawer there were a pair of her father's suspenders with his socks and a small square envelope which, she whispered, contained French letters. I nearly asked who they were from before I remembered . . . I'd heard a joke along those lines about them once.

She started to open the packet but my nerve failed me. Let's go, I urged. I was sure I could hear her parents moving around downstairs getting ready for bed.

Safely back in her room, I asked again what a French letter looked like?

'A balloon shaped like a test-tube . . . Night, night,' she called out. 'Sweet dreams.' No chance.

When we got to school the next day we couldn't wait to tell the gang. We asked them to meet us at the garden bench over by the tennis courts in the lunch break. But when we told the girls what had happened, they did not at first believe us. We had to swear on our mother's death that every word was gospel. And Sheila said: 'But Mr Thomas' – he was the second of the kissing deacons – 'has got a daughter in the first year.'

We'd die if he were one of our fathers, we swore. Then Rita went quiet and we noticed she was quivering, as though holding back tears. When we asked her if she was all right, she said her father had once kissed her. Don't be daft Rita, we interrupted. We aren't talking about the way fathers kiss daughters. These kisses were something quite different. Rita didn't answer.

Shortly after staying at Mary's, on one of the now frequent wakeful nights when I would be pretending to be asleep, I heard my grandmother leave our bed. I was just going to ask her if she was all right when I realised she was not heading downstairs. She had gone into my grandfather's room. What for? It was bewildering. None of my business, I thought for a second. Then I was sitting bolt upright in bed, leaning my head against the wall to hear all the better.

The bed springs creaked. There were quiet huffs and moans and a conclusive sound. A bit like a sigh. This didn't really mean anything to me but I knew it was something to do with what must be going on: making love. I felt frightened, and excited. And then I was suddenly furious. If she could sleep in there once, why could she not sleep there always and leave me to a bed of my own.

I'd move into Pop's room, the smaller room, and leave them to this great big feather mattress. And its horrible companions which I was sure were even now hatching in armies ready for their defiant march up the wall.

In order to concentrate I stayed sitting up, with my back against the cold rails of the bed. I was half glad about this episode, since I wanted my grandmother to be happy with my grandfather. But I couldn't make sense of it. I was not at all convinced that my mother and father had a sexual life – well, at the very most, not much of a one. So it was utterly breathtaking that my even more ancient grandmother and grandfather had one.

I thought about it some more. Why just this once? Or could it mean that they would now be reunited forever. And why do it secretly? What did she say when she entered his room? How did he greet her? It must have been a surprise, unless I had been asleep all these years while it had been a regular occurrence. If so why not stay there?

Oh bloody hell, bugger and damn, I said almost out loud. This was a mystery and I wasn't going to be able to talk about it to anyone in the world. And I'd burst if I couldn't tell someone.

Perhaps the answer was to wait for Martha Jane Davies to come back to bed, and confront her. But when she did come creeping silently into the room I was so deep in thought I didn't hear her. Not until she was climbing into bed, when I started with fright and felt unaccountably guilty.

So I just asked her if she was all right, and she said, 'Yes, thanks for asking.' She had not been able to sleep so she had been sitting downstairs so as not to disturb me. And for a moment, because it really would have been a relief from all this bewildering, inconclusive thinking, I wanted to believe her.

But that would have meant I had a dirty mind. Not blooming likely. So, I had to accept this for what it was. But what was it? My mind went around in circles. And afterwards I kept several tiring vigils to check whether it happened again.

No quiet tap through the wall from Pop. And only genuine snoring from Martha Jane which kept me awake long after I had decided to pack in my night watch. It made that one night of love even more mysterious. My father had the record of a song with that title, sung by Grace Moore, which I listened to for more clues. But in the end it went no deeper than 'One night of love, when two hearts were one.'

29
Totally Immersed

Aged fourteen, in the white dress

I WAS FOURTEEN when I was baptised, totally immersed in the pool in our chapel. It was at the age when hymn singing, organ playing in the darkened chapel, or listening to a record of Beethoven's *Moonlight Sonata* moved me to tears. I also attributed all beauty to God, and I wanted to give myself to him and especially to his son, Jesus Christ.

There were eight of us at the time who were going to take the plunge together. We met once a week for a month in the Minister's house. He had the only study I knew. It was a bit like my friend Morfydd's front room. Chintzy chairs, and books on every wall. But this was a room for him alone. There was a lounge besides. I coveted a study like that. I'd think deep thoughts if I had one, I decided. Also I longed to wear specs as he did to peer over at people who would then know I was brainy without my having to prove it.

We understood that the more books you read, the sooner you would have to wear glasses.

The Reverend Trevor Evans, BA, BD, BLit, always carried an umbrella, rolled immaculately. His shoes shone on his tiny feet which trod the pavement daintily, as if they didn't quite want to.

He was an introspective man, very well read and more capable of making an intellectual appeal than an emotional appeal in his sermons. But when he talked to us in his room about the teachings of Christ and the meaning of baptism he put a lot more feeling into it. So we reacted with fervour to his questions of faith. He asked us if we believed in God? Yes. Would we study His Word? Yes, yes. Would we be willing to serve Him for the rest of our lives? Yes, yes, yes. Lay down our lives for Our Lord if need be? A pause, and then maybe it was Alan who said he hoped he would. And I said solemnly, to join Alan, for whom I had a soft spot at the time, that I would want to but being a bit of a coward I couldn't be sure.

I think Mr Evans had hoped not to have to go into that too closely. Most people usually said yes, because they did not think for one moment they would ever have to put their lives to the test.

But we had all become great debaters of every sentence said to us, and in this we were encouraged by our chapel youth club leaders. They had never known such a large and formidable group of young people to be as active in the chapel before. They were so proud of this 'body of youth rising to bring fresh life to this our mother church', so keen to keep us interested, that they gave us platforms to express our views. We were often up in the pulpit leading the church in prayer or spouting our views on the Brotherhood of Man. And when not doing so, we were pouring scorn on mature attempts to preach to us. We soon became rather too fond of the sound of our own voices.

Our Reverend – whom we knew irreverently as the Rev Trev – was one of the adults who much preferred the sound of his own voice. And we had to do hard battle with him to be allowed to prattle on. He moved on to tell us the indisputable meaning of the baptism, our total immersion. We were like Christ. We would die as we descended into the pool. We would be buried, symbolically, as the water went over our body and head. Then we would rise again, and like Christ be resurrected. We would then be purified and cleansed of all our sins.

On the chosen Sunday morning we sat through the service, which was a bit shorter than usual, waiting for our great moment to come. Below the altar, the pool which was normally covered over and empty of water, now lay glinting, greeny-blue.

Like the other girls I had changed into a white tennis dress with a band of elastic round the hem of the skirt so that it would not ride up in the water. No shoes just white socks. The boys wore cricket togs, white trousers and a white shirt and also white socks with no shoes. Our Minister, in thigh-high waders and black flowing robes waited solemnly (and warmly) in the pool for us to enter shyly, one by one.

For us the water was icy. I stepped down the stairs, the water rose to my waist, and I could hear myself making great gulping noises as the cold took my breath away. I, who had wanted to step in like a saint with an unearthly beauty lighting up my countenance. Our Minister took my hands clasped in front of me and caught hold of the scruff of my neck and prayed to God to accept this maiden who was declaring herself in his name. Then he pulled me down into the water so that I was completely under it, and as I emerged to the congregation singing 'Hosanna, Hosanna', I felt there was no more important moment in my life. I loved Jesus and I would be His for evermore. I would become a missionary, and a preacher of His word.

Meanwhile, a deacon waiting at the edge of the pool threw a cloak around my body to which the tennis dress was clinging. And I was hurried down into the vestry to the splash of another body being totally immersed and hosannas bursting out.

In the vestry we were handed towels in front of a gas fire which was on full, and, as soon as we were changed, a steaming cup of tea and a biscuit were put into our hands. The loving fussiness of the women waiting to help made us feel as though we had performed a feat of physical endurance like swimming the Channel. And their friendly smiles of welcome into the new sisterhood of the chapel made us glad we had taken the plunge.

I felt so pure that I thought when I got home and saw myself in the mirror I would find that all my spots had been erased. I also remembered wishing I had sinned in some big way to make this a really dramatic moment of purging. Pinching apples, disobeying my parents, bullying my brother and sister, kissing boys, wearing lipstick as soon as I got round the corner out of sight of home – this didn't seem an impressive catalogue of sins. I felt that there would never be a better chance of forgiveness, so while I was at it I might as well have had a lot to be forgiven for.

That night after chapel the girls who had been baptised decided that we would go off on our own – not meet the boys. We felt they would lower the tone of our lofty spirituality, which turned out to be brief but intense that night.

Norma W (there was another Norma in our chapel clique and she was known as Norma D) said we could go to her front room and sing some sacred songs round the piano and read some poems that inspired us. Our favourite was:

> Though poor be the chamber
> Come here, come and adore
> For the Lord of Hea-hea-ven
> Hath to mortals gi-iv-en
> Li-ife for evermore
> Life for evermore
> Li-ife for evermore

We were passionate about our new faith, and wanted to share it with each other. Some of us read poems, and I chose one by the mystic Welsh poet, Henry Vaughan:

> I saw Eternity the other night
> Like a great ring of pure and endless light,
> All calm, as it was bright;
> And round beneath it, Time in hours, days, years,
> Driv'n by the spheres
> Like a vast shadow mov'd; in which the world
> And all her train were hurl'd.

But I liked reading this better when we were up in the woods high above the town with the street lights and the orange glow of the steelworks and the estuary of the river merging into the sea all spread out below us.

We talked about Jesus, familiarly, as a desirable man. In the vestry there were pictures of him which I would stare at during the lesson and think how fresh it must be to wear flowing raiments and how free to walk barefoot with him into the wilderness. It was almost like being in love. And he was unattainable which made this love nice and safe as my earthly feelings were not.

My heart went out to Jesus, I worshipped him as I had my father once. I sang to him through hymns:

> My song is love unknown,
> My saviour's love to me,
> Love to the loveless shown
> That they may lovelier be.

At night in the dark I prayed to him. I tried to write him poems. He spoke through music which I listened to with tears flowing down my face. He was the wind in the trees. The moonlight. The stars. All those things that I felt I had discovered. Everything was piercingly clear and pure. I half believed I was on the way to becoming his saint.

30
Teens

As a teenager

I HATED the fashion when I was fourteen and fifteen for curly hair. It meant going to bed in Dinkies – metal curlers which were very uncomfortable to sleep in. Throughout the night I'd be sitting up in bed, trying not to wake up completely, with arms of lead lifted to tighten a loose curler. Invariably one would have escaped in the darkness so that by morning a single strand of hair would be hanging down like a rat's tail amid a bush of tight curls.

We were soon influenced by advertisements for Permanent Waves which would do away with our sleepless nights – 10/6d, 12/6d, 15/6d. Eugene at 21/-. Full head, unlimited curlers. Your Hair's your Climax. The Keystone to your Complete Toilet.

But though perms were the order of the day it took me a bit longer to be persuaded to have one. My reluctance dated back to when I was very young and I had gone to take a message to my grand-mother. She was in Madame Winnie Owen's hair salon at the top of our street. I opened the door, a bell tinkled, and the smell of ammonia nearly knocked me over. Martha Jane was sitting with streaming eyes, wires sticking out of her hair, under a ferocious hair drier. She looked like the Bride of Frankenstein. I stopped dead in my tracks in front of this instrument of torture.

My grandmother shouted from under the drier not to worry – it was all for the sake of beauty. But I fled from this roomful of puce-faced ladies imprisoned under their domes, and vowed never to be one of them.

Now, however, at the age of fourteen I was torn between wanting to look like a siren with sultry eyes and long dark locks, and a tomboy.

I found the model of the girl I wanted to be in Angela Brazil's Peggy in *The Terrible Tomboy*

> . . . she was so eager, so active, so full of overflowing and impetuous life, with such restless daring and abounding energy, that in the excitement of the moment her wild spirits were apt to carry her away, simply because she never stopped to think of the consequences.

That was the girl I wanted to be, especially when I read:

> Such natures as Peggy's taste life to the full; for them it is never a stale or worthless draught. Each moment is so keenly lived that time flies by on eager wings and though there may be stormy troubles sometimes, as a rule the spirit dwells like swallows, in an upper region of joy which is scarcely dreamed of by those who cannot soar so high.

At the time this did not strike me as high flown or purple prose. I thought like that, and it seems to me that all through my teens either I was soaring for no apparent reason, or sinking into dark, troubled, brooding waters, equally for no apparent reason.

Once I started my periods the soarings and the sinkings were riotous. The event itself was so mishandled I almost wished I had been born a boy, though that was about the only time I did so. I didn't seem to suffer from penis-envy. For one thing, I'd had never heard the word 'penis': we referred to them as tobies and they had been comic objects ever since we found an old postcard in Margaret Esmond's grandmother's piano stool. The postcard had been brought back from France by her grandfather, and showed a fountain in the shape of a boy peeing.

Our periods were deadly serious: alarming and mucky, and we compared notes for comfort because we got no solace from anywhere else. I was hoping Morfydd's mother, being a nurse, would shed light on it but all she said was, 'It's a simple fact of a woman's life, a problem that has to be endured.' Mine said she couldn't really tell me what it was all about. Harmless. She knew the blood wasn't the same as coming from a wound, but she didn't know what it actually was. Something to do with the lining of the womb coming away.

Jeanette's mother told her, 'It means you're a woman now.' And Sheila's said, 'There, there, poor old girl. You've joined the club. I'll just get you one of these towels you have to wear. I'll warm it by the fire before you put it on. Don't worry it's the cross you have to bear for being born a girl. It isn't serious, lovey. But it's the bane of our lives.'

As clear as mud, what it was really all about. Was it dangerous? Was I ill? It hurt terribly. Could I have a baby now? How? Sitting on a warm seat just vacated by a man? Going as far as Number 10 – which meant kissing with your mouth open? Easier to believe babies came from the queen than to believe they were somehow connected with this flow of blood. It wasn't as if our mothers knew more, to tell us more. They had made do with the sort of vague explanations that they now handed on to us.

Even sanitary towels were not common round our way. A lot of us, including me, were given either an old towel cut up and folded, or a piece of old sheet which you handed over to be washed. It rubbed the side of my legs raw. It smelt. It leaked and marked the back of my dresses.

It took a bout of hysterics from me, before I had proper STs. And then I didn't have the courage to go and ask for them myself in the chemist's. The owner of our chemist's was a man, and if he came forward to serve me, I just asked for a packet of hair grips and left. I got my mother to go instead.

It was better when 'Elsie's' started to sell them. Elsie was a milliner and her shop had big deep mahogany drawers in which she stored her hats wrapped in tissue paper. In a corner of one of these, hidden under extra layers of tissue paper, she kept 'you-know-whats'.

She always took the name off the packet before she put them in a bag in case they fell out or the bag broke and opened on the road. 'Awful messy business isn't it? But never mind, love, think of your three weeks off afterwards. Can you take grandmother's hat with you? See if she likes the new trimmings I've put on it. Veiling and a gardenia.'

Elsie was viewing herself in the long oval mirror with the hat at a saucy tilt – as Martha would not be wearing it at Whitsun. 'I've made the veil long enough for it to peep down over her eyes if she wants an alternative' – again as Martha would not be wanting, I could tell her now. And I wasn't even sure that the gardenia would stay. Martha would be out looking for a bunch of cherries and a plain band of ribbon, was my guess.

I was wrong. She tried it on and fell for the veiling and the gardenia. 'Ring in the changes. Why not? For tomorrow we die.'

My grandma noticed my packet of STs and reminded me for the umpteenth time not to wash my hair while I had my 'flow'. Nor should I go round the house without my shoes on at this time of the month. That's why I was suffering from such pain. And I definitely should not bath either, as this would make the bleeding stop and all the blood would stay inside me.

However, even though having my periods meant I was now a woman, I was still intent on being a tomboy. And the other tomboy influence in my life was Sally Warner, head of The Merrymakers, the main character in a serial in *Girls' Crystal*, a weekly magazine which I lived for. I was Sally Warner and Morfydd was Sally's best friend, pretty Fay Manners, who had a becoming stammer.

Sally with a merry laugh and twinkling eyes said things like, 'You're all being chumps,' to the seething Merrymakers, or 'Steady on, playmates,' and 'Follow me, kidlets.'

I was so influenced that I decided to form a club called The

Merrymakers – for girls only. About ten of us. I suggested we asked Miss Sims to be our club's nominal leader. She was the Head of our Senior Sunday School in Chapel, and had a lot of quiet influence there. I suppose I was first drawn to her because she was a leader without any bossiness. She organised groups to go up to Cimla Hospital and read to the patients. And I joined these.

Then we happened to sit next to each other in a prayer meeting. It was being led by one of our deacons, Mr Harding, who always put aitches where there weren't any and left them out where there were. ''Eavenly Father, 'ear hus, your 'umble servants in hour prayers.' At the end I whispered, 'Hamen, Mr 'Arding'. And Miss Sims stifled a laugh and nudged me.

We asked her and she accepted as long as she didn't have to be present for every meeting. In fact, we just needed to use her name so that we would be allowed to rent the Old Aged Pensioners' Hall in Mansel Street as our clubhouse. We were to meet once a week and decided our serious intention should be to raise money for a good cause: we chose the NSPCC.

We brought out a small magazine to sell – mostly to our parents. We made things which we sold – mostly to our parents. And when Miss Sims turned up she organised play readings and encouraged us to write our own play for public performance. We put it on in the hall in front of an audience – mostly of our parents.

I wrote the play. A murder featuring identical twins. They depicted the good and the evil side of the same person. I had my eye on this part, and got it. It meant I was never off the stage and I went through the gamut of all emotions known to woman. I'd written a star part for myself.

The small proceeds of this went to the NSPCC, and by the time we got a receipt thanking The Merrymakers for their donation, we were already at an end of our enthusiasm for Merrymaking.

It was around this time at Fellowship of Youth – the chapel club for over-11s which met every Wednesday in the vestry – that the Rev Trev informed us that the District Health visitor was coming to explain to us the Facts of Life. We received this with giggles. Blushes from some. Nudges. Deliberately keeping a straight face from others. And one boy blew a wolf whistle. 'We think,' said Mr Evans, 'that you are all old enough to take this properly without any silliness.' He glared at the boy whistler. 'And I hope you will take advantage of time at the end of his talk to ask him some worthwhile questions.'

Before the next week, conferences took place about how we were going to keep from laughing and dying of shame or going beetroot red. We couldn't possibly sit in the front row. And we could not, absolutely could not, sit next to Alan or any of the boys.

The Wednesday night came round and we called for each other. 'You go in first. No you. Don't push.' Not one of us wanted to be the first to walk in. 'Oh, do let's just go in. This is silly.' And with a push from someone behind her Gwyneth Turner, red-head held high, led us in, the rest of us squashing up fast behind her wedging ourselves in the doorway, tripping over each other's feet. Now the terror was of being last one in.

Once inside the lighted vestry we jostled our way along the benches so that we were practically sitting on each other's laps in our haste to slink down and out of sight.

When the health visitor arrived with our minister we kept our heads lowered. What was he like, we whispered? Had anyone had the nerve to look at him?

He began by telling us that the art of living was the appreciation of the qualities of others. That to give succour (we thought that word sounded rude) enriched the giver as well as the receiver. That man did not live by bread alone. (When was he going to reveal all?) Day by day our bodies were becoming more like a man's or a woman's (nudge from a neighbour). Breasts were developing (Oh, my lord. And your nipples sprang up to prove it.) Body hair would start to grow (Had he said body hair? We hardly dared mention it even to each other for fear we were the only one in the world growing it). In the fullness of time we would meet someone of the opposite sex with whom we would fall in love and share the appreciation of art and music and poetry, with whom we would enter into marriage and start a family. Now wait for it. Now all would be revealed.

When two people made love their bodies fused. And he went on to talk about sperm and eggs ovulating. No mention of how the sperm and the eggs came to get together. Nine months later the baby was born. That was that.

We were as wise after the talk as we had been when we went in, except for one new word, 'sperm'. Where that came from was a complete mystery.

I had plenty of food for thought that night. One part of the talk stuck in my head: 'When two people make love their bodies fuse.' At home recently my grandmother had been arguing with my father over our gas light. He wanted, at his own expense, to change to electricity. 'Over my dead body,' she said. 'What if it fuses?' Which made sex sound a trifle dangerous. So I took nothing away from the lecture except a feeling of alarm. Though at a time when contraception was in its infancy, so to speak, maybe alarm was all we could afford to feel.

Anyway I went home and told my parents that I knew the Facts of Life. They said they were pleased that I knew and that they trusted me. Be friendly with boys, they said, but best to keep it strictly on friendship lines.

'How old were you two when you met?' I asked them.

'Not till your mother was twenty-two or twenty-three, and I must have been − twenty-eight or nine,' my father said. They looked about that in a sepia photo I'd found of them having a picnic. Time enough to start being serious with anyone, he said. Too soon, my mother added. Don't saddle yourself to marriage before you see the world a bit.

My father was fiddling with his false teeth. The top set was hanging down a bit. Some food had got stuck. I decided I could never fall in love with someone who did that.

'Where did you meet?' I asked my mother.

'At a dance,' she answered, 'and it ended very late, I remember, so Dad rode me home on the bar of his bike.'

'Fancy remembering that, Ol',' my father said obviously pleased.

Under the stars, I visualised that little scene. So they had once been young and romantic. I wanted to ask them more but the gas went out and there was a search for pennies for the meter. And I missed my chance.

I got into bed with grandmother and woke her to tell her that I

Olive, Dick and Aunt Flo picknicking

knew the Facts of Life and she said, 'Well, if you do, you are a better man than I am, Gunga Din.' And no, she didn't want to hear them. She would hear them some other time.

Sex went on being shrouded in deep mystery. And it was given no opportunity to emerge from under its thick cloud of guilt. It was certainly not to be enjoyed until you were married, and I couldn't make out if it was meant to be enjoyable even then. We had hints of illicit pleasure. One woman we knew, who smoked openly, out on the road, was said to 'go' with men. We reckoned that had to be something to do with a bit of fun.

Films didn't help us. All you ever saw anyone do was kiss and that was pretty tame on the whole (unless it involved wicked ladies like Margaret Lockwood and you could see their cleavage). Even then the picture dissolved before something untoward was bound to happen.

But kissing was what we did.

Wonderful long kisses full of yearning. I put all I had into them, for it was all I was going to get, or something untoward was bound to happen.

I knew there was more to it than kissing from the feelings I was getting 'down there' as I stood up against the stone wall in our back lane away from the lamp lights. Emerging into the lighted street with a bruise on my neck that I would have to hide when I got into our house, I longed for the next time.

The next few times were more adventurous. Ken, handsome, tall, green-eyed Ken, would meet me from chapel and once the weather was fine we'd take a walk up to the woods. He'd spread his mac on the grass and we'd sit on it, still pretending we were just resting here in this deserted bower!

Then, locked in each other's arms, we'd slowly lie down. The grass was long and rustly and felt bouncy under the mac, and we couldn't see anything but green blades all round, so we knew we couldn't be seen either. And we would kiss as no one else has ever done. Indignantly, disappointedly, untidily, crossly, I'd disentangle myself when things were going too far.

Then we'd quarrel. I'd feel fed up with myself for not letting him go further, and with him for wanting to go further.

We'd make it up under a tree, walk with arms around each other, stopping at another tree for a longer kiss, and then start running. We were late and the park gates were locked at nine in the summer.

They would invariably be locked. Ken would climb over the railings, and then I'd jump down into his arms and wonder what it would be like to spend the night together in the woods.

All the boys I fell for at this time, the ones with whom I even began vaguely to imagine a future, were only there with half a chance. I had to move on. So much of the time was spent quarrelling out of frustration that it was safer and more agreeable to break off and start afresh with someone else. Then it would take that much longer before the kissing once more failed to be enough for this restless girl racked with guilt and caution.

31
An Explosion

At St Madoc – me in the centre

THE SUMMER BEFORE I went into the fifth form, I came under
the unlikely influence of chapel-goers from the small Oxfordshire market town of Bicester. And also of a writer, the author
of more than a hundred books (the list filled the top quarter of his
personal notepaper), Sid G. Hedges. A name scarcely remembered
now but very familiar then, especially to Methodist Sunday School
and youth club leaders.

In 1945 a group of ten of us from Jerusalem English Baptist
chapel went to the St Madoc Christian Youth Camp. Miss Sims had
been there, I think for a weekend conference, and said, 'I thought it
had something very special about it which I'd like you to experience.' That was enough for us. She explained that its land and
buildings had been bought by a man called John Dennithorne, a
Quaker. He wanted young people to live together there in a single

communal way, and to work out their religion by example rather than from preaching.

I was terribly excited about it. And to enter into the spirit of the pioneering life I bought my first pair of jeans – which in those days didn't mean denim, but simply tight trousers which ended half way down the calf.

They were not a great success at home. When I showed them off to my father all he said was: 'What the hell have you got on?'

'They're jeans, Dad.'

'I'd give them back to her. They're too short for you.'

Most of us covered the thirty miles to the camp at Llanmadoc in a hired coach. And although I found exactly what Miss Sims expected me to find there, the whole experience was a curious mixture of the sacred and profane.

A few of the chaps decided to cycle down, among them Alan and Malcolm. Alan was now my boyfriend; Malcolm, his best friend, was of the belief that I was a very bad influence on him. Anyway Malcolm didn't want to lose Alan as a companion, certainly not to a girl; he went red if any girl so much as looked at him. Though bashful, he was also defiant and boasted of being a misogynist.

My being a bad influence on Alan was a view even more strongly held by Alan's mother and by his only and older brother, Steele, who was also to be at camp with us. I'm not saying that Steele was an officially appointed guard, but both he and Malcolm, I felt, were under unspoken orders. I was more flattered than alarmed at this and liked to play on it, presenting myself as a bit of a Carmen to put them even more on the alert.

On the night of our arrival, the Briton Ferryites, as we nicknamed ourselves, walked to the headland, and there were glow worms to light the way. I was hand in hand with Alan, (Malcolm and/or Steele not more than a foot behind), yet even with all that extra company breathing down our necks, I felt we were among the stars.

This was the first time most of us had ever been away from home. And the first time many had been in the middle of proper country-side. Real, wild, remote countryside. We were outside Llanmadoc, a village on the Gower coast, with a beautiful headland which took your breath away however many times you stood there looking out

Inside the barn

to sea. Its beach was long and golden and clean. Empty for miles. You could easily believe that you were the first to see or set foot on it.

The camp was a couple of farm buildings converted into dormitories with iron bunk beds. One for girls, one for boys. Another building was the kitchen and the bare dining room.

The barn was our meeting room and chapel. And – perhaps this was at the heart of what Miss Sims was getting at – it was the first building I had ever entered which seemed to me holy without even trying to be. It was a square, stone, whitewashed room with colossally thick walls and small windows that let in the light sparingly; and at night it was candle-lit as there was no electricity, which inspired further delirium in me.

At St Madoc's, for the first time in our lives, we willingly performed the kind of chores – spud-bashing, cleaning out the dorms, washing-up – that would have seemed the depth of domestic drudgery at home. But then at home we never worked in groups, singing part songs or being entertained by Alan's and Malcolm's version of 'He was only a farmer's boy and she was a Jersey cow'. Nor was there that moment of stardom when it came round to your turn to say grace before the meal: 'For every cup and plateful, Lord make us truly grateful.'

We weren't the only group at camp. There were people not only from other Glamorgan churches but from distant parts of the country. Forty of us in all, and about six came from Bicester, a town I had never heard of. Between their broad Oxfordshire and our strong South Wales accents, at first we found it almost as difficult as foreigners would to communicate with each other. What made them even more exotic to us was that one of them had come down here on a giant Sunbeam motorbike. Although I have forgotten all the other strangers in the camp, Dorcas Leach, Norman Coward, Les Blackman, Derek West, those four at least of the Bicesterites became as close to us over the next couple of years of pen-friendship, meetings and exchange visits as any of our Ferry friends. And none of this would have happened but for the eccentric personality of the Bicester leader, Sid G. Hedges.

Sid Hedges

He was a tall, thin, bony-featured and bespectacled man, a one-time draper's assistant who had determinedly made his mark in his home town by becoming a writer and sage on a dozen subjects. He contributed a regular column called 'Super's Diary' to the *Sunday School Chronicle* and had edited anthologies of popular prayers (*Down to Earth and Up to Heaven*) and biblical quizzes. Starting with *How to Play the Violin*, he had progressed to the *Universal*

Book of Hobbies and the *Home Entertainer*. He wrote books on swimming which he called swim books, and youth club song books which he called sing books. Fun for the Not-so-Young. Children's fiction. Detective yarns.

In fact he practised many of the things he wrote about. He was an excellent swimmer and keen to get others started on this 'great and clean and good-fun sport'. One day he persuaded us all (including the older ones like Simsie – as Miss Sims was known – and Mr and Mrs Martin – whom I now called Mr and Mrs M – to lie on our stomachs on the seat of a chair and practise the basic strokes. He was our camp leader for this week and talked to God as if he really knew him, quite casually – far more so than our minister, the Rev Trev, ever prayed.

He had formed a mouth-organ band – 'I never want to hear the words mouth organ again,' spluttered S.G. with a roguish twinkle in his eye. 'They're harmonicas'. His band was called the Red Rhythmics and, starting from scratch, he had taught young and not-so-youngs to play together. They were famous in Methodist circles and toured round Oxfordshire, and beyond, giving concerts in their white shirts, red ties and red berets to raise money for their Sunday School. They were the first to play harmonicas in the Albert Hall, beating Larry Adler to it by six weeks.

One of them, Les Blackman, was easily as good as Adler to our ear, especially when we listened to him up on the headland playing 'Clair de Lune' in the actual moonlight on our last night at camp. And then round a huge bonfire we sang our hearts out, vowed eternal friendship, and exchanged addresses so that we could write, until we'd meet again in St Madoc the following summer.

We were determined that we would meet this Bicester lot again. S.G. for all his corniness – and he used to pride himself on his all-purpose collection of corny jokes – had a Pied Piper's magnetism for someone like me. And he also had undeniable style.

He would not let a year pass without setting foot on French soil, even if it was only for a day trip, on which he would wear a black beret. He changed into bowler, black jacket and striped trousers for his church committee meetings near St Paul's. A couple of years later when I went to stay with him and his family in Bicester he took me in a punt on the Isis. He had already started referring to me as Zuleika Dobson. And to complete the Edwardian fiction he dressed up for the occasion in a striped blazer, white trousers and a straw boater. I felt embarrassingly under-dressed but, although I was uneasy about the outing, I was grateful that he taught me how to punt along the river as though I had as much right to be there as any Oxford undergraduate.

So, from this remote camp on the Gower coast, my world had begun to open up. And my first visit ended memorably enough as it was. After our week there – with no shops, no cars, no papers, no radio – we stopped our coach to call on Jack Maddox in the village of Penllergaer on the way home. Maddox, a Briton Ferry man, had settled here on his retirement. In his excitement at greeting us, and wanting to tell us a piece of momentous news, he got up from his chair and stepped firmly into the cat's full saucer of milk, as he said: 'They have dropped the Atom Bomb.'

32
After Llanmadoc

Hiking trip

I REMEMBER believing that the 'Unutterable Beauty' (a favourite phrase of mine borrowed from the title of a book of poems by Studdart Kennedy which Les had sent me from Bicester) of life at the camp had transformed me into a better person. I vowed I'd help beggars – and no longer merely because they might turn out to be millionaires in disguise. And I'd do more at home (back to this again) to help my mother. That resolution never came to anything. She used to tell me I was getting in her way. And, thanks, but it was easier if she did it herself. Why didn't I go away and enjoy myself while I was young? Plenty of time after I got married to become a drudge.

I used to try to argue with her. If I did more to help her, then *she* would have more time to do nice things she wanted to do. What nice things was I referring to? I'd say, well, didn't she want to go out more? Where was there to go, she'd ask.

I always ended by asking her whether she'd really wanted to get married. Whether she'd really wanted to have us?

And she'd say, 'Now, don't start on that, because you'll start taking it personally. And it's nothing to do with not wanting you and not loving you and not being glad I had you.

'The best thing you can do, my girl, is not think about helping me but get back to your books and make sure you have something to your life before you even contemplate getting married.'

I'd pick up a book, sit in the corner, and I'd end up not reading but talking, while my mother ironed. And we'd often end up singing songs together – our favourites being from Ginger Rogers and Fred Astaire films. Or 'Linden Lea', since we knew all the words to all its verses.

On Sundays after chapel, to keep the camp spirit intact, the whole gang of us would go to one or other of our houses to talk. And at Alan's house, we'd sit round the table solemnly listening to classical music on their wind-up gramophone.

Though he and I were much keener now to be on our own, he still had to be in early and his mother wanted to know exactly where he was going and with whom.

My chance came to push the boundary a little further forward when he had his tonsils out. He was back home but still in bed. I told Miss Sims I had to see him. I had missed him like mad. I can't live another day without seeing him, I told her. Did she know how I felt? Couldn't she take me please to his house? Alan's mother couldn't object if she were my chaperone. Miss Sims said she really didn't dare. More than her life was worth. She admitted she was a bit scared of Edith Thomas – a powerful contralto singer at chapel, much admired, and a strong character – though you didn't know quite how strong because she wore thick specs which hid what she was thinking.

I persuaded Miss Sims in the end. My mother gave me some jelly in a basin for the invalid – the best thing to swallow after you'd had your tonsils out. This was a very tactless move. Edith prided herself on being the head cook and bottle-washer in her own house. She had brought up her two boys by her own sheer hard work, going out and cleaning after their father had died young.

She was furious that I had dared turn up at all – and livid that I'd brought something for Alan to eat. But, she told us grimly, we had better go upstairs and see the patient. The patient was given the jelly. And was obviously dying from embarrassment.

He told me afterwards he had admired my nerve. But my nerve, he knew, would only tighten the cordon around him. He was right. It became even more difficult for us to meet. We went on some walks up to the woods but only when his mother thought he was out with Malcolm. We always felt as though we were being followed. And we had to keep a close eye on the time.

Kissing when he was wearing a white shirt, and I was wearing lipstick or powder, became a mad, reckless activity – bound to be detected by his launderer. 'Don't worry, girl,' he'd say, with one of the brilliant smiles for which he was famous. 'She can only kill me . . . And then you.'

The funny thing is that as soon as Alan and I stopped going out with each other I used to go over and have long talks with Mrs Thomas in her back kitchen. We became really pally – but on the understanding that I was no longer a threat and that her son was out of my clutches.

One Sunday night when I got back from the house of one of the gang, I asked my mother if half a dozen of us could come back to ours for supper next week after chapel. Oh, for heaven's sake, my mother protested, we haven't got the room.

Couldn't we ask Gran to borrow her middle room? My mother said she certainly wasn't going to ask. If I asked then, I wanted to know, would she make the supper? She would, but it would be a miracle if I got yes for an answer from Gran.

It took a lot of persuasion on my part but she eventually agreed. Not with good grace. Martha Jane couldn't see the point of outsiders eating in our house. Why didn't they go home to their own house for food?

'Because I want them to come to my house,' I said as patiently as I could. *My* house she corrected. *Your* house, Gran, trying to sound really pleasant. Why did I want people poking their nose in our business, she asked. 'What business Gran?' 'The way we have to live here,' she said. 'What's wrong with the way we live here?' Well, you can't call your small front room well furnished. It was a really pretty parlour when I had the run of the place. (Count to ten, Mave, I said to myself, if you want to get your own way. 1,2,3,4,5,6,7 . . .) I'm only glad your mother keeps a net curtain over the windows so that people can't see in.'

'Oh, Gran, don't say that. Our room is clean.' (8, 9, 9 and a half, 9 and three-quarters. Could I keep my temper?) 'Anyway, you've got really nice furniture in your middle room, Gran.' (I was nearly there). 'And that's all they'll see.'

'Well, perhaps being that it's you,' she said doubtfully.

'Thanks a million, you're a pal. And can I borow your best plates off the dresser?' (Gone too far?) 'They would look nice on your polished top table.' (And with arms round her now for the final effort.) 'Come on, Grandma-of-my heart, please say yes.'

'Wonders never cease,' my mother said when I told her. 'How did you bribe her?' I did not say it was by biting my tongue, swallowing my pride, not rushing at her in wild fury.

On the night my mother had laid the table with a really nice white cloth which she said she had borrowed – 'off my aunty' with a wink. My mother used to say she had to pay a visit to her aunty when she wanted to go outside to the lav. She must have 'borrowed' the table cloth out of Gran's chest upstairs. That was living dangerously.

Six of us then, after chapel, decked in our Sunday-best clothes, were just sitting down to eat when my grandfather walked through the room from the back kitchen. He had to do this to get upstairs to bed. His bedroom in those days was just above the middle room. In that moment, the world turned red for me as I realised he was carrying his bucket. His pee bucket. As my mother was serving out the chips, and as my grandmother – who wasn't going to be left out of the action – was offering a plate lined with a doily (orders from me) of thin pieces of bread and butter cut in triangles (my orders again), Pop began to pee over our heads. Thunderously. I definitely wanted to die.

My life was saved by Alan Morgan winking at me and saying, 'Let's pretend we're in a restaurant by a waterfall.' And everyone laughed.

But I was seriously thinking of murdering Pop. I mean, why

hadn't he gone outside to the lavatory? Why go upstairs and pee straightaway? This baffled me. Waking up in the middle of the night and not wanting to go out in the cold, I could just about understand. Though I was getting less and less patient with that too. Martha Jane's 'widdles', as she called them, were getting on my nerves. Recently, she didn't seem able to squat down to the chamber pot on the floor any more. She was now having to hold the white china pot up under herself, carefully rolling her long nightie up and holding it bunched under her arm so that I could see her bottom if I so wished, which I didn't – not after the first look.

Okay, okay she was old. Weak bladder. But Pop doing it before he got into bed at nine o'clock at night made me wild. It went bashing around in my head so that I only half-attended to the jolly supper they were all having, while Martha Jane teased the boys, who seemed to find her amusing, for a while anyway. Ken Donovan, who had an attractive speaking voice, thanked her formally for her very nice hospitality, which bowled her over. 'Come again, especially you,' she beamed.

But it was the one and only supper I asked for in Mansel Street. My nerves couldn't take another.

I'd much rather go home to Norma D's. We were complete opposites, and because of that we could tell each other everything. She was younger, taller, quieter than me with curly hair which she tried to straighten, while mine was straight and I tried to curl it. Her mother – Mrs Donovan – was outrageous. She had a mop of vivid red hair, swore like a trooper, told jokes that made even my hair curl, and was an angel. Her husband had died young of TB, leaving her with three young children, whom she supported with a full-time cleaning job up at the hospital. She made me laugh and Norma blush.

I was able to get her laughing, too, when eventually I told her the story about Pop and his bucket. She roared and said the story would be better if I called a piss pail a piss pail. Oh Mum, protested Norma.

'Look at your faces. They're like two smacked bums. We all do it, don't we?'

'No,' said Norma, 'we don't use that particular word.'

'What word – pail?' she said with her dirty laugh. 'Who's for a nice strong cup of tea? None of your cricket's piss.' Once she'd succeeded in shocking us, she'd be sure to use that word again.

Up until then I'd always had best friends – a series of them – but in the gang it was almost a matter of honour not to favour one girl over another. So we confided in everyone in turn.

I remember confiding in Jeanette Philips, the wise old owl amongst us, my religious doubts. Ken Donovan and I were walking her to the bus stop one rainy Sunday night. I went on to say that I felt awful having doubts, because of our leader – Miss Sims, whom I increasingly admired and wanted to be like.

'You'll have to accept you aren't like her. To be frank, I don't think religion will win with you in the long run.' And turning to Ken, Jeanette said she thought *he* was like Miss Sims. Apart from the obvious similarity that he was going to study Latin – which was Simsie's subject – she thought he'd remain religious. Wise old owl was proved correct.

The gang was extended after we met the Bicesterites at camp. One of them Dorcas, an overgrown tomboy, as she described herself, kept me down to earth. She'd call me soppy if I went on too much about feelings. She had plenty herself but she'd rather keep mum about them.

For a while, Bicester and Briton Ferry were like twinned towns forever exchanging visits and letters and love and kisses. In two years Norman Coward and I exchanged a total of one hundred and forty-two letters.

33
Purple Pages

Relaxing at camp

AFTER ST MADOC CAMP, we got to know Miss Sims, Miss F. Eileen Sims, much better, and took to calling her Simsie. I was told she had a brilliant degree, a double first, and had gone on to take an MA. But she taught in a Primary School and I asked her if all teachers were MAs. No, not in primary schools. She was there because she couldn't get a job teaching her subjects – Latin and Greek – at a County School. There simply wasn't a post locally and she couldn't leave her mother to go away to work.

She was a short woman with jet black hair, huge, kind, humorous dark eyes, a gypsy-coloured skin and a big nose that she made fun of before anyone else could. And she was the first and only woman deacon appointed in our chapel's history.

She helped run Fellowship of Youth – the young people's club held in the chapel vestry every Wednesday night. She was our great ally – backing up our ideas and encouraging us to speak out about what we believed. She was quick to recognise, as she put it, that we were a bunch of rather special kids. Other adults thought we were too big for our boots.

I began to develop a deep devotion for her. It was more than a crush. I'd go and call on her so that I could walk with her to chapel and, before I decided what my opinions were, find out what she thought about topics which had cropped up during the week.

Whenever I went to her house, she was always ready to leave. In fact I began to suspect that she must have been waiting at the door, so quickly did she come out, ready to go at once. Sometimes her

Simsie

mother, if she wasn't going to chapel, appeared on the doorstep to see us off. She was more gypsy-looking than Simsie with eyes that begged you to feel sorry for some great tragedy in her life, a misfortune you didn't know the half of. I'd seen photos of old-time film star vamps with those same mournful, turned-up-to-heaven eyes.

As far as I knew, I had never seen Simsie's Irish step-father, Mr Thompson – her mother's second husband. He was a bit of a mystery. Someone said he had a hell of a temper and was a bully, and that was why Simsie couldn't ask people into her home.

I went there one night unexpectedly to ask her something. He answered the door. A mop of brilliant white hair, a red face and twice as tall and broad as I had ever expected him to be. A big man for round Briton Ferry where most Welshmen were on the short side. A giant with a club foot in a mighty, heavy black boot.

I had been wishing I could meet him for some time. Imagining that I would so charm him that for ever after he would be sweetness and light to Simsie and her mother. Now I wasn't so sure. He was smiling at me and frowning at the same time, and his voice was insinuating: 'So, you've come to call on Miss Sims, you say. Our Eileen, you mean? Come in.'

Simsie was just behind him.

'I'm ready. Shall we go?' She had on her coat – she who was not expecting me.

'You'll not be wanting to go before I talk with this young lady?' he insisted. 'Sit yourself down. No, over there by the fire.' He pointed to a stool and gave me a slight push towards it. I knew Miss Sims' mother always sat on that seat.

I sat down abruptly, too dumbfounded to do anything else. There seemed an air of menace about the way he insisted. Or was I simply being affected by Simsie's twitchiness? Obviously she did not want me to stay.

Her mother came in from the scullery plaiting her long wet hair which she must have been washing. I got up to let her have the stool. I could smell my coat singeing from the heat of the fire.

'You'll stay where I put you,' he said.

I dared to say that it was, pardon me, very nice of him I'm sure, and thank you very much, but I was too hot sitting there. The nervousness of Mrs Thompson and Simsie was definitely catching.

Simsie said, well, then, why didn't we go now.

'Come and visit us any time,' he called after me.

Once outside, I said I was sorry that I had embarrassed her, calling as I had without warning.

She told me her step-father was a difficult man. He had always been. Terrorising the house with his violence. He was so unpredict-able that they could never ask people to visit, much as she and her mother would have liked to.

I said it wouldn't ever matter to me how he behaved. Pop at home was often drunk. Well, it wasn't so much the drink as his violent temper, she said. Had he ever hit her? No, but she had often had to intervene on behalf of her mother. Is that why she didn't want to go away to work? It was. A bit like my mother, I said, who had stayed put for much the same reason. Not that Pop was ever violent towards people, I wanted to make that clear. Just things in the house. Oh, my stepfather is like that too she said.

I was chuffed that Simsie had confided in me. And doubly so when she told me that I was easy and comforting to confide in. I went home on air. And I quite forgot to mention what I'd wanted to talk to her about.

I took the next chance to tell her I was worried about my Latin exam. I had to pass in this subject or I would not get Matric. If I didn't pass Matric, I wouldn't get to the sixth form. And that in turn meant not going to college. I wanted to know if she could lend me some books to swot up on my Latin.

She said that she would give me extra lessons – for nothing – on Saturday mornings when her step-father was out at work. And if he turned up, I would understand if she cut the lesson short.

Simsie was my Miss Moffat, the teacher in Emlyn Williams's *The Corn is Green* who turns a working-class lad into an Oxford scholar. I had seen it as a play on stage in Briton Ferry and as a film with Bette Davis. And to heighten my conviction that Simsie was exactly like Miss Moffat, with faith in an equally pathetic waif, she told me one Saturday that she thought I'd be notable in some way.

Our lesson had been going badly. I was being stupid about the translation, which I hadn't really prepared; I had just sneezed and, instead of asking for a handkerchief, I held the sneeze from my nose in my hand. Too gauche to do something about it, I sat there miserable and inattentive.

Simsie told me I must buck up and get my exams because she believed that one day I would make a hit of something, though she didn't suggest what this would be. 'You won't be content with the Ferry.'

How could she say this? It was my whole world. I loved it and everyone in it. Simsie and chapel, the gang, my family – what did she mean? 'I'm not saying that you'll despise the town. Perhaps you'll stay on here, but I can't really imagine it. I know you say you want to be a teacher. But you're not going to be content with what I've been content with. And what else is there for you here? You're going to fly off.'

I couldn't bear to hear this when good old Briton Ferry provided the safe, though sometimes inconvenient, borders of my life. Yet what she said thrilled me, and because I admired her so much I believed in what she was saying. It was a simple act of faith, and I never lost the feeling that somehow I must fulfil her prophesy.

But it was only when I was in close contact with her that this bigger idea of myself existed. So I clung on to her for a while. She, too, needed me, I discovered: she said I made her feel good about herself.

I admired the smarter clothes she began to buy. Her Hebe Sports tweed suit with white polo neck sweater had us both thinking she was 'it' – and why not? 'You're a good-looking woman,' I said. 'My mother thinks so too, by the way.'

She worried that enjoying such clothes was vain and wordly – now wasn't it, she asked. No, it was just a matter of respecting herself, I argued. Otherwise she'd be in sackcloth and ashes. 'Part of me thinks I should be,' she said. I knew she did, and I was trying to steer her away from that idea. In some ways I felt more adult with her, and than her.

Simsie was a naturally religious woman. Her life was guided by her beliefs as a nun's would be. Devoted was the term people used about her. When I was sixteen and seventeen I went through a period of precocious piety which I don't regret, though the way I expressed it in letters and conversation makes me cringe with embarrassment now.

I did have a real zeal for religion – I was up in pulpits preaching the brotherhood of man and praying with heart and soul for it – without losing my equally strong devotion to clothes and make-up, the cinema and boys.

Had she ever been in love, I asked Simsie on one of our slow walks to chapel. 'Once. Don't ask me any more. It's a hopeless case. I have never told anyone and never will, because it is out of the question.' Does he know, I wanted to know?

'Heavens, girl, absolutely not and never, ever will. That's why,

Miss M, you must not ask me anything more and please don't try to guess.'

Having become friendly with Miss Knight, another teacher at her school, for the first time Simsie had a friend with whom to go off on holidays abroad. I thought it was marvellous to know a real traveller at first-hand. The rest of us couldn't even imagine how you set about arranging that sort of thing.

Simsie's friendship with me was by no means exclusive. All the gang had a great regard for her and she for them. So on these short trips of hers we kept in touch by post. She kept the letters and her sister, Elsie, sent them to me when Eileen Sims died in 1974.

My first was written when she went off on her first trip to France in 1946. To read it reminds me of the rawness of my teens: I can hardly bear its unguarded exposure.

> I don't really have to say polite things like – I hope your crossing was good; I hope you find everything going well, and I hope you are loving every minute of being in France – you know I mean all those things but don't want to list them off, for they always sound forced.

> Pont Nedd Fechan is a place out of this world. The beauty is almost too good to be true, and the purity of it all makes oneself seem so insignificant and impure. I wouldn't have missed the outing for worlds – the gaiety, the loveliness, the togetherness and the water made everything complete – almost; it would have been if you were there, but we remembered you, and as Alan informed you we threw sticks downstream after pausing to think very hard, as we held our stick, of a message to our beloved. I don't quite remember how mine ran. Something like: keep safe and have the happiness you deserve and gosh I love you. Sounded better when I said it to myself looking down to where the river shone, the fall cascaded, its music echoing all the time – then it seemed like a moment complete, apart and very lovely.

Our devotion to Miss Sims and the feeling of a tremendous debt we owed her is clear from this joint letter written by the gang. Alan kicks off:

My Dear Miss Sims, (cat calls and all such appropriate noises)

I have taken it upon my shoulders, the shoulders of a lock-forward, to begin the gang's omnibus letter to its darling leader (tumultous cheering from all present. I'm on my own in the front room of No 4).

Our expedition to Pont Nedd Fechan was a huge success. It was a perfect example of organised travel (à la gang). We started out to catch the 10.15 bus from Neath and triumphantly caught the 11.15.

In your honour, at 4.20p.m. Friday we performed the ancient ritual in which all present held a stick. Then for one minute thought of you, and cast his or her rod to the waters. Mine sank.

Well that is enough of a kick-off. I'll hand over.

It went on:

This is Norma D. carrying on the epistle from the Gang to our most illustrious, wonderful, magnificent etc Miss F. E. Sims. We parked camp for tea and dear old Nobby, trying to act as if he'd paddled across rivers all his life proceeded to give us an illustration. Do you know how to lie down in a river? Ask Norman. We hung his clothes up over trees while he ran round looking like a Greek god dressed in a flowing mac. Must close.

Norma W. calling now. If my writing is a bit peculiar please be kind and put it down to the fact that my eyes are now very weak after having had a staring out session with Malcolm.

The thing that is uppermost in my mind is how different S.S. [Sunday School] was without you and how much we miss you. Must stop now dear.

To our dearest heart-throb, These are your dearest admirers Kenneth and Bobbie calling to our luscious lump of loveliness P.S. Ian says if this is an omnibus letter, this is where he jumps off. Space for laughter.
P.P.S. Don't forget the spying glasses for the Folies Bergère.

The letter ended with a row of kisses.

When Simsie was in hospital some time later, after a thyroid operation, I wrote to her. By then, though, I was seeing less of her. Latin lessons had stopped when I passed my exams; I had a boyfriend unconnected with chapel and the gang, and I was drifting away from the fold.

Dear Eileen,
Dinnertime we had an honour. We're heads of table (Morfydd, Jean, Gwyneth and I) and who should plonk herself at the head of our table but the Hon. Decima Jones!!! [our headmistress] One thing I thought extremely funny that she said.
'Going to be a teacher Mavis?' asked she.
'Maybe' answered me.
'Well here is a hint on how to keep discipline. If you make a rule, press it down hard right from the start.'
    Even Plato couldn't have been wiser than that. Miaow. See you next letter. Cheerio. Chin Up. Keep smiling. Gang send their wishes that you will soon be well again and back with us. From dad, mum, gramma, Sylv and Gray love and all the best. And from me my love as always
    Yours Mavis
    P.S.
                        I'm saying Simsie brave is
                        To read all this letter from Mave-is.

With that letter I enclosed an advertisement – obviously I was impressed by its purple prose. It had a drawing of men and women in smart clothes looking at pictures in an art gallery, and read:

THIS WE FIGHT FOR

In that New World for which we struggle, Art shall enter the lives of people, serving to express them and raising a standard in Labour as in Life. The temples of leisure to house our noble art heritage shall be the treasuries of fancy, invention and imagination, to help, to encourage, to inspire.

Issued by CO-OPERATIVE WHOLESALE SOCIETY

Besides sending this to Simsie, I read it aloud to my mother and later to my father, so that they would know what I believed in, too.

And my father said he thought he saw what it was about and that I had a fine chance to see to carrying it out with the education I was getting.

I'll bet my father thought the advertisement was 'high faluting'. He hinted at this when he cautioned me that some people liked to show off their education by the way they talked. He didn't mean simply by having an affected voice, putting on a twang, but by making their thoughts sound deep and difficult to follow. In his view, a truly educated person should want to and be able to express him or herself so that everyone could understand what he was trying to say.

Whatever I did, he said, I was never to become a snob. A really educated man is never a snob, he maintained. It was only ignorant people who thought they were a cut above the ordinary man, just because they had more education or money. They were the stinkers. Snobs were the ones to watch.

34
Confidences

Aged 15, with Sylvia, aged 8

SOME DAYS my father would take a sack and a shovel and go up to the woods to collect leaf mould for the garden. I'd ask to go with him if I thought the real reason for the outing was that he'd had enough, and wanted to get out of the house.

'That woman never says anything outright. You can't have a flaming row with her and then forget it. She just tuts under her breath. Have you heard her? Or she smirks. And she mocks everyone behind their back. I know, because I've caught her at it. She's evil. I damn well believe she's evil. She is poison. There are times when life is not worth living in that house.'

He was so wound up I couldn't think how to calm him down except by keeping up with him as he walked very fast to the top of the woods – away from the park attendant's eye. As we struck out through the thick drifts of fallen leaves they'd rustle and some would lift up with the speed and the power of his tread. Then he'd stop, both of us by now a bit breathless, to dig up his leaf mould. I'd sit on a fallen tree trunk and hold the sack open for him.

He was still livid and went ranting on: why was he bothering to enrich her garden? Why was he working every hour of the day, for what?

I blurted out, why didn't we move?

'You tell me. I wanted to move ages ago. We could have put our name down for a council house. But your mother wouldn't budge. She says she couldn't leave her mother. Don't ask me why not. She doesn't owe her mother anything.'

He unwrapped a Rennie. 'I wouldn't need to eat these by the packet if we'd only got ourselves out of that hell on earth,' he'd rage.

'You eat those because you got gassed in the First World War,' I said matter-of-factly. I was frightened by his fury. I didn't want him to think 5 Mansel Street was hell on earth. I didn't want to hear what would come next: Why haven't I jumped in the docks/put my head in the gas stove/ended it all?

Instead, he said, 'You'd rather believe that. You don't really want to hear the truth about that grandmother of yours.'

I told him very emphatically that I couldn't fail to know the truth about that grandmother of mine. I didn't miss one single expression of that grandmother of mine. And I loathed the atmosphere that grandmother of mine created in the house as much as he did.

'Do you think I want to be in the same bed as that grandmother of mine?' And as soon as I'd said this, I felt guilty. I didn't want to disown Martha Jane and I didn't want him to feel that I thought all of this reflected some failure on his part.

I couldn't express it – and suddenly I felt very angry over my lot. But I did not seem to have anyone to lash out at. It was a stay-put affair. I understood that we didn't have the means to move. And if we had, perhaps the emotional energy was lacking? My mother said she wanted to stay in the house where she was born. Was she scared of more financial insecurity? Did she want to protect my grandmother from my grandfather? Or herself, in some way, from my father's attentions? My father had never insisted enough on moving and I have no idea why not. Supposedly, it was because he felt my mother didn't want to move and he couldn't persuade her.

Meanwhile, my grandmother in her queenly way declined to sleep in the same room as my grandfather, without worrying that this added further to the complications of the household. My grandfather was by then in a permanent semi-stupor and didn't seem to care about anything but his beer. In the end, they were all simply people with very little money. They thought they had no alternatives, and they didn't dare have bigger aspirations.

I couldn't see what change to ask for – let alone insist on – without hurting someone or other. Except that, specifically, I had begun to think that Sylvia and Graham should not be in the same room as my parents. On that November day in the bronze and bare woods, it became crystal clear to me that they shouldn't be.

My father was now feeling better for his outburst.

'You're my girl,' he told me, 'putting up with things as you do. But damn it, I'm not sure if we ought to, any of us.'

It had turned cold and we were not walking so fast. 'Have a Nip-it,' he offered. These were very strong cough sweets. Tiny black squares – often still joined together – which you had to split off with your finger nail. You could only eat one at a time, so a packet lasted for ages. These and Rennies were always in the top pocket of whichever coat my father was wearing.

'I'm a great believer in Nip-its. A Nip-it warms you up when you turn blue, and cheers you up when you *are* blue,' he joked.

I was both. Something was nagging me: 'Dad, just in case I've run down Gran a bit too much . . . you know I love her, don't you?'

'Yes, I do and I don't want to influence you against her on my behalf, you know that. We can fight our own battles, Mave. I think it's damn right that you treat people as you find them. And she's been good to you, by some fluke, the old . . . Leave it, Dick,' he said, as I said warningly. 'Dad, stop.'

He was back to his usual self again and saying that he'd go right off his blooming head if it wasn't for going Old Time Dancing with my mother. 'You'd have to lock me up. I love my old dancing. Your mother's not so keen. She's a bit stiff – she'd be good if she'd only relax on the floor. You ought to come some night. I'll give you a dance. As long as you don't mind being part of a long queue.'

His offer to 'give me a dance' struck the wrong chord with me, as did the idea of having to wait for a boy to ask me to dance. Quite a number of women told me that my dad was a good dancer. He had a bronze medal from Sydney Thompson, and he had gone to Cardiff for a competition finals once, when his 'king' was playing: the great Victor Sylvester.

He laughed when I called him Briton Ferry's answer to Fred Astaire, but I knew he didn't consider it much of an exaggeration. He thought he was pretty damn good at dancing. I didn't tell him I'd have died of embarrassment if I had to take the floor with him. My cousin Thelma often accepted a dance. I'd seen them dance a tango once while I was up in the gallery. I just couldn't imagine doing it with my own father.

When we got home from the woods, I told my mother I had been reading a book on the Psychology of Sex and that it could do harm for children to sleep in the same room as their parents. I was wound up and upset. This must have struck home, for she said she would change things straightaway. She'd been worrying about it herself.

First of all, Sylvia would have to come in with Gran and me. And Graham would go in with Pop. I knew it. The accepted fact of life was that Grandma would not be shifting.

Sylvia moved in with us. She slept in a single bed in the small alcove over by the window, and I learnt directly from her, what I had already suspected, that she hated Grandmother. I had noticed Sylvia staring frostily at Gran, those strange, sphinx-like eyes of hers not missing a blink.

She wanted to know why on earth I liked Martha Jane. I said that when I was younger, Gran was really nice. She'd grown slowly more impossible over the years. And I loved her because she had always loved me when I was a kid.

Sylvia said she could never forgive her for hating Dad. My defence was that I had been close to Gran before I caught on to her game. It's not a game – it's hate, said my little sister, clearer-eyed at eleven than her older sister had ever been.

I liked having Sylvia there and wished I'd suggested it long before. And I felt we were allies. When she had her first period, it was I who talked to her about it – sitting on her bed. Since I had been told nothing clearly, I wanted to give her the facts that I had learnt by then. My more scientific explanation did not seem to comfort her much either.

I'd always felt unappealing when I started my periods. So I tried rather clumsily to boost her confidence. I told her she had a pretty name that suited her, and that I knew two lovely songs about a girl called Sylvia. Schubert's 'Who is Sylvia?' did she know it? 'What is she? That all our swains commend her?' And how about this in the other song: 'Sylvia's hair is like the night, Touched with dancing starry beams.' I don't think she knew how to react to all this. She said nothing. I couldn't see her expression in the dark. I called over to her, 'Goodnight Sylv,' but got no reply. She might have nodded off.

She was not at the age for waxing lyrical as I was. Everything, anything, that impressed me I read out loud in the bedroom, where I went supposedly to do my homework, beside the Valor Oil lamp that 'stifled', and by the gas light that flickered. I spouted poetry to the mirror to see what beautiful expressions would be reflected on my face. I made up fulsome prayers to God who I was pretty sure was listening.

I played with the thought of what it would be like to catch TB. I could be pale and poetic. I'd want to catch it only seriously enough to warrant a tiny room in a sanatorium, with the window wide open, and to be on my own for a couple of months. Just in case I were to be struck blind, I used to try to find my way around the house with my eyes closed; or I'd put my arm in a sling made of one of grandma's silk scarves, in case another tragedy befell me. All to the bafflement of my sister. And the indifference of my mother. I once lay on the floor pretending to be in a dead faint, but she stepped over me and told me to get up or I'd dirty my clothes.

Although Sylvia and I were at very different stages from one other, this was the time when our friendship began. The difference in our age was still marked but it was just starting to seem less important. And we definitely had each other in mind for future reference.

My brother, Graham, I knew less well than I knew my sister. We were chummy enough but had little time to spare for each other. Though, when he was ten, I did his homework for him until the teacher grew suspicious, (since he got bad marks in the class tests). He owned up, started working and passed his scholarship to County School; while Sylvia chose not to take the exam.

In his off-hand way Graham was pleased that the boys I went round with made a fuss of him at school. They told me he was jolly and popular – and, more important to them, would be really good at cricket if he kept at it.

But he turned out to be quite as self-willed about leaving County School as Sylvia had been in refusing to go there. At fourteen he decided to stay on as an errand boy in the Co-op shop, where he had been working in the summer holidays. My mother asked me to talk to him. I was to try to persuade him to stay on at school.

I did the big sister act and copied my father's pet phrases. 'No man can ever take your education away from you.' 'Get your exams and then decide.' 'You're too young to know what you'll want to do later on. Passing exams first isn't going to stop you working in the Co-op later on.' 'Put off working for as long as you can. Work is more of a prison than you realise.' 'Plenty of time ahead of you . . .'

But I didn't have my father's powers of persuasion. Graham was singularly unimpressed. I was too airy-fairy for him. So I left it at that.

What's more he made fun of me for wanting to become an actress, and that put him beyond the pale as far as I was concerned. I could take jokes about other things, but not about that.

And not at this time. I had been given a part as a nun. Not a walk-on part; I had one line to say in a production with the travelling rep that was lodging in Briton Ferry and performing in the Public Hall. One of their cast, Emrys Leyshon, was a film star. He'd had a part in the film, *The Last Days of Dolwyn*, which was doing the rounds. I was sick with excitement.

I spent a long time in front of the mirror with a black scarf round my head practising my one line: 'I too have come a long way.' I don't remember the title of the play. There was another nun who was played by one of their regular cast. She had a lot to say. I wasn't jealous. I knew my one line could make my reputation, as long as I put all I had into it.

The play was only on for one night. I was made up, and thought I looked holy. Almost as beautiful as Jennifer Jones, say. Not quite as beatific as Ingrid Bergman, perhaps. Along those lines, though – I mean, not far off.

The actor who was meant to give me the cue for my line muffed it on the night. Muffed it so that the other nun went on to her next speech – the one that was supposed to come after my line – 'I too have come a long way' – and I never got to say one word. Mute. Opportunity had not knocked.

I stood for the rest of the scene in a state of high dudgeon. When we finished and took our curtain I went up to the actor who had betrayed me, ready to spit in his face. He took my two hands in his, pulled away from me, and looking deep into my eyes said, 'You were magnificent.'

When I got home my mother was quivering with rage. We had read the play – taking all the parts between us. She knew where I appeared and she knew without asking me what had gone wrong. That hopeless actor should be reported, she said. 'He has the nerve, as it is, not only to dye his hair but to paint the bald patch on the top of his head black too. As if we can't see. I hope it gives him blood poisoning.'

I could not stop thinking about it. I had imagined them offering me a job in their company. I had been planning how to break the news to my mother that I would be off, starting on the road to stardom. Instead, she said very gently after her outburst, that she did not think I was right for acting. I asked her why not and she said, 'You wouldn't want to start from the bottom.'

I would have to do that in whatever I did; it was silly to say that, I told her. But she persisted. She wasn't saying I couldn't act but that acting was different. I wasn't cut out for that kind of life; well, not yet. Perhaps later, but she didn't think so even later. 'I may be wrong, we'll see.'

In bed that night I told Grandma about my disappointment and she said that surely I wasn't put out by that. I had known, hadn't I, that no one would notice if I had said that little line or not. Not to worry: no one would have missed it.

I should have known. I should have known not to say anything when it mattered to me. Don't ask for sympathy from Martha Jane.

35
Leaving Home

Going to college

A FEW DAYS before I went to college, I saw my grandfather walking towards me on the main road. Head down, shuffling along, humming a tune, lost to the world. 'Pop,' I said loudly, for he was a bit deaf, 'Hi.' He jumped out of his reverie and on seeing me clicked his heels and saluted.

'I'm going to live in college, Pop.'

I nearly added, so I won't be seeing so much of you, and realised I hardly ever saw anything of him as it was, even though we lived under the same small roof. He still worked nights as watchman and was in bed all day or out in the pub.

'You're going to live in college? Since when have you sat your exams? No one tells me anything. *Merch*, I wish you'd keep me informed.'

I felt sad hearing him say that but I also wanted to tell him that he was pretty unapproachable himself, which made me feel just as

240

bleak. It was hard to work out what mattered to him. And yet it struck me as peculiar that my grandfather, living in our small house, was an unknown quantity to me.

This had come home to me when Norman from Bicester was having lunch in our house one day and Pop walked through the middle room. Norman got up and said, 'Good morning, sir,' and Pop murmured, 'And the same to you, sir.'

Norman asked me who he was, this nice gentleman, and I said, 'Pop.' As if to say, who else could he be? Where did he live, Norman wanted to know. With us, I told him, and he looked surprised. But for me that was the end of the subject. I hadn't resolved the question of Pop sufficiently to give him a better explanation.

The night before I went to college, my father asked me to go up to his bedroom for a quick word. 'I shan't be here when you go tomorrow. I'm working. Let me take down your new address.'

He unlocked the drawer where he kept his papers and took out his diary which I always gave him at Christmas. He used it to fill in his shifts at work and his dances and to ring our birthdays. He'd scribble in the name of a wintergreen someone recommended for his chest. Or the name of a rose. And now here was my hostel address: Beck Hall, Sketty, Swansea, and the telephone number.

We were sitting on the side of his bed and he handed me a Nip-it.

'I'm going to phone you, Mave.'

'I'd really like that, Dad. I'm going to miss you.'

'I'm not certain of that telephone box, that's the only snag.'

I told him not to worry. If he dialled 100 for the operator and then followed her instructions, it should be plain sailing. Button A and Button B got him confused, he said. Didn't I know it. He tried ringing me once when I was away and lost the line over and over and over again. Both the operator and I were urging him down the line not to press button B, press button A. And he was yelling at the top of his voice when he did eventually get through, believing the further he was away from the other person, the louder he had to speak.

'I'm proud of you, Mave, and you're doing the right thing. It won't be the same without you. You're an ally. I can let off steam with you and know it'll go no further.' He broke off for he was tearful and so was I. We hugged each other and he got a hanky and gave it to me and squeezed two pound notes into my hand.

'That's from my own money. I want you to have it from me. We've arranged, your mother and me, to send you some each week. But this is our secret.' This was a lot of money for him to spare. He handed the entire contents of his wage packet over to my mother every week, and she'd give him back some pocket money, depending on how flush we were. It was going to be the same for me. When my County Education grant came through, my mother would keep it and send me my pocket money.

And then my father noticed, in the drawer, a Victor Sylvester Dance programme signed by the maestro, from the time he went to Cardiff for the finals. And he started looking through his other bits and pieces, while I wandered downstairs to write a letter to Simsie.

The note-pad, lined (Basildon Bond) had matching blue envelopes and was inside a zipped, tan leather writing-case. My mother had given it to me to take away with me, and in it were some stamps, so I had no excuse not to write, she said.

This letter (another painfully fulsome one) to Simsie was in answer to the one I had received from her that day with my going-away present.

Dear Miss S,
I know that God has been good, that He is the one way. I feel there is a real need for Him in my own Life and I feel that without Him I must only write life with a small 'l'. But, Simsie, there's a heap of weakness in my heart, and I need more then heavenly guidance. I need a human prod which is what you are with your letter and the copy of the New Testament, and no, I had no feeling that you were sermonising and being priggish or grinding an axe. I will try and read it every day.

It is 12 o'clock and nearly the beginning of some new chapter. I am scared, and I am regretful that the last chapter has now closed. And wistful that something has ended.

I can't feel confident but I am aware of the pinching and scraping as you put it that has to go on for me by my parents and perhaps this will be a good goad. And please know that whatever

I turn out to be and wherever I end up I shall always be continually grateful and devoted to you.

Yours Miss M.

I looked up. My mother was at the table knitting. Sylvia was in front of the fire undressing for bed. Dad, plus his torch, had gone to hunt for a tiny screw in the shed. Graham was staring bleakly at the innards of his watch spread out on my father's white handkerchief.

I had tried to warn him not to let Dad near it. Once I had taken my watch in for repair after one of Dad's efforts and the jeweller's eye glass practically popped out at the sight of its once-dainty workings. He solemnly told me he'd never seen the like of this destruction before and hoped he'd never live to see the like of it again. He handed the ruins back with a shake of his head.

I licked the envelope addressed to Simsie and stuck it down. I was looking at the two long narrow pictures on the wall in front of me, of a reindeer in snow and of a reindeer in summer landscape. These, like the two swans in my parents' bedroom, had been painted by O. I. Davies, 1920 – my mother in her late teens. My eyes stung. I did not want to be leaving the next day.

I went upstairs with Sylvia and curled up on the end of her bed, sticking my feet through the bottom of the bed-clothes. I suggested that once I was settled in hostel, she should come down to Swansea. It was only a question of catching a bus in Neath. I'd meet her off it at the other end. Her beautiful green eyes gave nothing away. Her face was impassive. It usually was. That's if you'd like to, I added. Would you like to? Um, I think so, she said. I wanted a more definite answer. 'I don't want to persuade you against your will. Don't say yes unless you really want to, Sylv,' I persisted. I so much wanted her to *want* to come and visit me. And I desperately needed her to show me that she wanted to.

No doubt, because I was the one leaving I felt more sentimental than she did. I wanted to know I was loved before I went to stay at this alarming hostel full of people who didn't know me. I longed for her to break down and say she couldn't bear to see me go. But how could I have reasonably expected that when she and I had led such separate lives? I couldn't risk a rebuff, so I briefly hugged her and

said, 'Sleep tight. See you in Swansea, then, sometime, Silver Paper.'
She tutted at my corny nickname for her, and at the same time
laughed and looked me in the eye. 'I'll be there,' she said.

My brother had already gone to bed. I opened his door and
whispered, 'Graham, I won't see you in the morning.'

'Huh, What?' He was trying not to wake up, and snuggled further
into his pillow.

'I'm off tomorrow. See you soon, Gray.' I bent and kissed his
forehead and he said, 'See you, sis,' without opening his eyes. 'Not if
I see you first,' I said.

The next day when I left home for college was – though I didn't
know it at the time – the day I left home for good. I had a strong
notion that it might be, but it was far too big a notion for me to add
to the sickening terror I felt at the prospect of sharing a room with a
girl called Mary Davies, a *doctor's* daughter.

I was wearing a fitted emerald green coat with a big stand-up fur
collar. Brand new. Too hot for early October. And my new gloves
were iron tight on my hands, so that my fingers had to stay straight
in them. If I tried to bend them my circulation stopped. So whatever
emotion I was feeling was muffled by my physical discomfort.

My grandmother gave me a pound, which I folded into a small
square and put in my purse. She gave me a hard hug, as close as she
could through my voluminous coat and said, 'Don't forget me.' And
I could have wept for her and for me. I had already forgotten what
she wanted me to remember. Our early closeness which she had
suffocated with her possessiveness. Her bitterness towards my
father. But for old time's sake I had to remember, and I wanted to
tell her something marvellous.

'Grandma, you were like a mother to me when I was little. I'll
never forget that.'

'Oh I couldn't have been like a mother to you. Your own mother
was your mother to you. I couldn't have been that.'

I knew I had to persist and flatter. I owed it to her.

'But you were. Like a second mother to me.' That didn't do.

'Second best,' she said, as though she had won.

'Not second best. The same.' I couldn't leave it like that. 'Except
mam was my mother and you were my grandmother, but you were

more like a mother.' And all the while there was a mounting rage in me. She was daring me to let her down, and at the same time urging me to say something really loving which would now be a lie.

She was digging her fingers in my arm as she held on to me. I could feel them even through my thick coat. It was making me feel hot and bothered.

I didn't go to my grandmother's funeral. I can hardly bear to write that down. But I grabbed at excuses not to go, like not wanting to travel down from London with a small baby. At the time, my grandmother having drifted out of my mind for years, it seemed a good enough reason to me. And then my mother helped. She urged me not to come. It was silly to go to the expense and all that upheaval. 'And it will only upset you,' she told me.

'You know what you felt about Grandma when she was alive. And you know you meant the world to her. They were the best years of her life when you were little. Life has got to go on and people change and other people take our place. You've left me now as you should. And she has left you.'

I suppose Martha Jane had died for me ages before. Maybe I, too, had died for her when she had made it a test of loyalty: to choose between her or my father. I couldn't do that when she wanted me to. And as I got older, our relationship cooled fairly naturally, without sides having to be taken. She'd be asleep when I crawled late into bed; and I'd be up and away before she had finished her morning cup of tea.

But Martha Jane, at this moment, lives clearly. Fox fur astraddle her shoulder. Thin black elastic band cutting into the back of her neck, holding on the shiny basket-weave hat with the artificial white gardenia in the band. A white-gloved hand dipping into her hand-bag for the money to pay the bus conductor. The whiff of Evening in Paris from the open satin-lined bag. A gleam of shiny, gold-wrapped Radiance toffees nestling in the bottom; toffees which she would pass to me once we had gone a little distance, then complain that they were buggers for sticking to her chinas. Teasing me that she would have to take her teeth out in the bus in front of all the passengers. Then indeed loosening her false teeth and lowering them so that I would be helpless with laughter and begging her not to, please, NO . . . and her doing it right until the conductor came up to our seat . . . and, with spot-on timing and great dignity, asking him if he would like a Radiance . . . and him saying they were hopeless as he had dentures . . . and her looking so sorry for him as if she had no such trouble whatsoever.

She'd wink at me. I'd tuck my arm through hers, she'd squeeze it to her bosom, and we'd stare out of the window as the bus moved on to Llandarcy. It was at least three-quarters of an hour away and the longest journey my grandmother ever took anywhere in her life.

'I've forgotten my gloves, Gram.'

'Like to borrow one of mine? Borrow the right one. Your left hand is warm under my arm.'

So I'd slide my hand into her glove. The white mid-length we had chosen for today before we came out. She had long ones, short ones, mid ones. Black gloves. White. Brown and cream gloves. Lace and kid gloves and gauntlets edged in real fur. I held my hand out in front of me to see what her glove looked like. Just so that I would know for when I was grown up and wearing a white mid-length glove of my own.

Then my grandmother would say, 'Ouch, my shoe is pinching me,' and slip it off. And I would slip my foot in and lift it up more secrectly now to see what it looked like. Too old. Gloves were any age. These shoes were for grans. Low-heeled and broad. I knew I would be into the highest heels I could find before I resorted to these.

'You'll be wanting the fur off my neck before long. Have a Radiance,' said Martha Jane.

We'd unroll the toffee from its paper. And we would see who could smooth her piece of silver wrapper the smoothest. And she would give me a penny to turn into a half-crown by wrapping it up in the silver paper and pressing it until all the letters and the date and Britannia stood out. And the king's head the other side.

She told me that a lot of people said she looked like the old Queen Mary. I told her she did not. She insisted that there was a likeness.

'Gram, I don't think so. She has white hair. Yours is dark. And she has thousands of lines on her face and you haven't got thousands.'

'Hundreds do you mean?' with a false laugh.

''Course not. All the girls at school say that you look so young they think you're my mother.'

The Radiances came thick and fast after that. Goodbye, Martha Jane.

And here I am in our front room ready for my first goodbye, and as it turned out, my last one, too, from home. I'm now sweltering in my over-warm green coat with the collar that made me hold my head stiffly so as not to ruffle my hair-do and which I had put on much too early.

Dave Evans, a porter from the station, came up with a hand trolley to take my trunk. My mother and I walked down with him to the train. He was the handsomest chap I knew off the silver screen. But too old, and engaged to be married to Beryl Gethin, an assistant librarian who wore glasses. We had mixed feelings about her. We took it that any girl who wore glasses was therefore plain. But because we believed Dave could get any girl he fancied, we also assumed that when he took Beryl's glasses off she became trans-formed, as film stars were, into a beauty. And anyway some of us had an inkling that there might be more to girls than good looks because Beryl was vivacious and clever and could make men laugh.

My mother and Dave talked about how wonderful it was to be going to university. How no one, not even the Tories, could take that away from you once you had education. And I was worrying about what mistakes I'd make with my new room-mate. Would she ever find out we didn't have a bathroom?

We bought my ticket and asked for the times of trains back from Swansea so we could feel reassured that I wasn't going off into the wilds. I put the cardboard ticket inside my glove which made it tighter still. We stood on the platform discussing arrangements. My mother would send me down my STs every month to save me having to buy them from a strange chemist, and also some Welsh cakes. And then I noticed my mother's eyes were filled with tears.

'I'm not going forever, Mam. Swansea's not very far away,' I said as I hugged her.

'I'm not crying, love, because you're going to college. I wouldn't want to stop you doing that for the world.'

'Well, why then?'

'I suppose it was you telling Gramma that she'd been like a mother to you.' I tried to interrupt her, but she wanted to go on. 'No. I'm being daft about this. She *was* like a mother to you. And I'm glad you realised that about her. But I still regret having to hand you over to her.'

'Oh, Mum, it wasn't like that, come off it.'

She ignored this. 'I honestly thought it was the best thing I could do for you, once the twins were born. I wanted you to have so much.'

'Mam, I did.'

'The way I saw it was that you had my undivided love for five and a half years before the babies were born. And I thought it was better, if you couldn't have mine, to have hers. It nearly killed me.'

Half of me had always known this without being told. But, when I heard those words, I realised that another part of me had needed to hear them for a long time. Now the train was pulling into the station, and I was so scared I'd miss it that I hadn't time to tell my mother what I felt.

I climbed into the carriage and took a seat by the window with my big bag on my lap. A man asked if he could put it up on the rack for me. I couldn't let go of it. I had been on very few train journeys and I was afraid of missing the stop if I had to take it down from the rack.

My mother stood on the platform. She threw me a quick kiss and her tears glistened, and my throat hurt so much I thought I was going to be sick.

I got up awkwardly and said through the little opening, 'I'll write straightaway, Mam. And I'll explain about Grandma.'

I threw her back a kiss with the taut hand that had the hard ticket biting into it. The train hissed and started to move, and my mother's figure grew smaller and smaller. And although I was moving further away, she was now nearer than she had been for ages.